Contents

Acknowledgements   iv

Section I   Analysis and Production

Chapter 1   Introducing Analysis   1

Chapter 2   Introducing Production   7

Chapter 3   Analysing Prose Fiction   25

Chapter 4   Analysing Drama   57

Chapter 5   Analysing Speech and Speech Representation   97

Section II   Comparative Analysis, Poetry and Non-fiction

Chapter 6   Studying Poetry   147

Chapter 7   Producing a Comparative Literary Study   181

Chapter 8   Extending Comparative Analysis   197

Chapter 9   Re-casting Non-fiction Texts   217

Section III Preparing for Assessment

Chapter 10   Revising Set Texts and Handling Unseen Texts   237

Chapter 11   Handling Coursework   241

Chapter 12   The Chief Examiner's Perspective: Helping You to Succeed 245

Literary and Linguistic Toolkit   **249**

Index   **261**

Acknowledgements

The authors and publisher are grateful for permission to reprint the following copyright material:

Extract from BBC Tees (formerly BBC Radio Cleveland) transcripts from live football commentaries by Ray Simpson and Kevin Smith; and extract from interview between Mark Turnbull and Ian Garrett, reprinted by permission of the BBC.

Extract from BBC Television transcript of an interview with two elderly ladies, *Century Road*, BBC2, 1999, reprinted by permission of the BBC.

Extract from BBC Television transcript of an extract from interview between Michael Parkinson and Billy Connolly, *Parkinson*, BBC Television, December 1999, reprinted by permission of Michael Parkinson, Tickety-boo Ltd. for Billy Connolly, and the BBC.

Extract from 'Roger the Dodger', *The Beano Book 2001* (D.C. Thomson, 2001), reprinted by permission of the publishers, D.C. Thomson & Co. Ltd.

Extract from NHS Direct article on www.nhsdirect.nhs.uk, is Crown copyright material and is reproduced under the terms of the Click-Use Licence Number C2007001380 with the permission of the Controller of Her Majesty's Stationery Office and the Queen's Printer for Scotland.

Extract from 'The Low Down... Paul Ga Ga Gascoigne' from *The Onion Bag*, Issue 12; copyright holder not traced.

Extract from PGL Travel advertisement leaflet 'Never a Dull Moment', reprinted by permission of PGL Travel Ltd.

Extract from interview between Louise Candlish and three authors, *Books Quarterly*, Waterstones, Issue 27, 2007, copyright holder not traced.

Chinua Achebe: extract from *Things Fall Apart* (Heinemann, 1958), reprinted by permission of David Higham Associates Ltd.

Gail Anderson-Dargatz: extract from *The Cure for Death by Lightning* (Virago, 1997), copyright © Gail Anderson-Dargatz 1997, reprinted by permission of the publisher, Little, Brown Book Group.

Simon Armitage: 'I Say, I Say, I Say', 'On an Owd Piktcha' and 'The Anaesthetist', from *The Dead Sea Poems* (Faber, 1995), reprinted by permission of the publisher, Faber & Faber Ltd.

J.D. Atkinson: review of *Hamlet* from BTG website 2005, www.britishtheatreguide, reprinted by permission of the British Theatre Guide.

Iain Banks: extract from *The Business* (Abacus, 2006), copyright © Iain Banks 2006, reprinted by permission of the publisher, Little, Brown Book Group.

Louis de Bernieres: extract from *Captain Corelli's Mandolin* (Secker & Warburg, 1994), reprinted by permission of The Random House Group Ltd.

Joanna Briscoe: extract from *Skin* (Phoenix, 1997), reprinted by permission of Curtis Brown Group Ltd.

Christopher Brookmyre: extract from *Quite Ugly One Morning* (Abacus, 1996), copyright © Christopher Brookmyre 1996, reprinted by permission of the publisher, Little, Brown Book Group.

Bill Bryson: extract from *Notes from a Small Island* (Transworld, 1998), reprinted by permission of The Random House Group Ltd.

Wendy Cope: 'Strugnell in Liverpool' from *Making Cocoa for Kingsley Amis* (Faber, 1986), reprinted by permission of the publisher, Faber & Faber Ltd.

E.E. Cummings: 'anyone lived in a pretty how town' from *Complete Poems 1904–1962* edited by George J. Firmage, (W.W. Norton, 1991), copyright © 1991 by the Trustees for the E.E. Cummings Trust and George J. Firmage, reprinted by permission of the publisher.

Carol Ann Duffy: 'Havisham' and 'Welltread' from *Mean Time* (Anvil, 1993), reprinted by permission of the publisher.

Brian Friel: extract from *Translations* (Faber, 1981), reprinted by permission of the publisher, Faber & Faber Ltd.

Jane Gardam: extract from 'Stone Trees' from *The Pangs of Love* (Hamish Hamilton, 1983) and extract from *The Iron Coast* (Sinclair Stevenson, 1994), reprinted by permission of David Higham Associates Ltd.

Ricky Gervais and Stephen Merchant: extract from *The Office: The Scripts* (BBC Books, 2007), Series 1, copyright © Ricky Gervais and Stephen Merchant 2002, reprinted by permission of the publishers, The Random House Group Ltd.

Tom Hanks: extract from speech broadcast on US television September 2001; copyright holder not traced.

David Hare: extracts from *Murmuring Judges* (Faber, 1991), reprinted by permission of the publisher, Faber & Faber Ltd.

Seamus Heaney: 'At a Potato Digging' from *Selected Poems of Seamus Heaney* (Faber, 1980), reprinted by permission of the publisher, Faber & Faber Ltd.

Susan Hill: extract from 'In the Conservatory' from *A Bit of Singing and Dancing* (Long Barn Books), copyright © Susan Hill 1973, reprinted by permission of Sheil Land Associates.

Barry Hines: extract from *The Heart of It* (Michael Joseph, 1994), copyright

© Barry Hines 1994, reprinted by permission of Penguin Books Ltd.

Michael Hodges: 'No Reward for Gallant Gazza' from *Sunday Times* Sports section; copyright holder not traced.

Alistair Horne: extract from *Death of a Generation – From Neuve Chapelle to Verdun and the Somme* (Macdonald, 1972), reprinted by permission of the author.

Khaled Hosseini: extract from *The Kite Runner* (Bloomsbury, 2004), reprinted by permission of the publisher.

Ted Hughes: 'Football at Slack' from *The Remains of Elmet* (Faber, 1984), reprinted by permission of the publisher, Faber & Faber Ltd.

John Irving: extract from *A Prayer for Owen Meany* (Bloomsbury, 1989, 1994), reprinted by permission of the publisher.

Rory Johnson: extract from 'Storylines', *The Guardian*, 9.9.1991, copyright © Guardian News and Media Ltd. 1991, reprinted by permission of Guardian News and Media Ltd.

Sebastian Junger: extract from *The Perfect Storm* (Fourth Estate, 1997), copyright © Sebastian Junger 1997, reprinted by permission of HarperCollins Publishers Ltd.

Marcel Junod: 'Visiting Hiroshima' from *Warrior Without Weapons* translated by Edward Fitzgerald (Jonathan Cape 1951), reprinted by permission of The Random House Group Ltd.

Philip Larkin: 'First Sight' from *The Whitsun Weddings* (Faber, 1964), reprinted by permission of the publisher, Faber & Faber Ltd.

Valerie Martin: extract from *Property* (Abacus, 2003), copyright © Valerie Martin 2003, reprinted by permission of the publisher, Little, Brown Book Group.

Toni Morrison: extract from *Beloved* (Chatto & Windus, 1987), copyright © Toni Morrison 1987, reprinted by permission of International Creative Management, Inc.

Grace Nichols: 'Hey There Now' from *The Fat Black Woman's Poems* (Virago Press, 1984), copyright © Grace Nichols 1984, reprinted by permission of Curtis Brown Group Ltd.

Jane Oddy: extract from 'Asher: People think I'm dead!', *The Mirror*, 2.11.2007, copyright holder not traced.

Redmond O'Hanlon: extract from *Into the Heart of Borneo* (Vintage, 1987), copyright © Redmond O'Hanlon 1984, reprinted by permission of PFD on behalf of Redmond O'Hanlon.

Ned Overend: 'Five Minutes of Your Time' interview in *What Mountain Bike* No 74, September 2007, reprinted by permission of Future Publishing.

Dorothy Parker: 'Resume' from *The Collected Dorothy Parker* (Duckworth, 1973), reprinted by permission of Gerald Duckworth & Co. Ltd.

Harold Pinter: extract from *The Caretaker* (Methuen, 1960/Faber 1991), reprinted by permission of the publisher. Faber & Faber Ltd.

Sylvia Plath: 'Morning Song' from *Ariel* (Faber, 1965), reprinted by permission of the publisher, Faber & Faber Ltd.

Philip Pullman: extract from *Clockwork* (Corgi/Transworld 1997), reprinted by permission of The Random House Group Ltd.

Anthony Quinn: 'Oh What a Lonely War!', review of William Boyd's *The Trench*, *The Independent*, 17.9.1999, copyright © The Independent 1999, reprinted by permission of *The Independent*.

Jean Rhys: extract from *Wide Sargasso Sea* (Penguin, 1966), copyright © Jean Rhys 1966, reprinted by permission of Sheil Land Associates on behalf of Jean Rhys Ltd.

Anita Shreve: extract from *Eden Close* (Macdonald, 1990/Abacus, 1994), copyright © Anita Shreve 1990, reprinted by permission of the publisher, Little, Brown Book Group.

Graham Swift: extract from *Waterland* (Picador, 1992), copyright © Graham Swift 1992, reprinted by permission of the publisher, Pan Macmillan, London.

Dylan Thomas: 'Do not go gentle into that good night' from *The Poems of Dylan Thomas* (J.M. Dent, 1952), reprinted by permission of David Higham Associates.

Alice Walker: extract from *The Color Purple* (The Women's Press, 1983), reprinted by permission of David Higham Associates Ltd.

Tennessee Williams: extract from *A Streetcar Named Desire* (New Directions, 1947), copyright © 1947, 1953 by Tennessee Williams, renewed 1975, 1981 by The University of the South, reprinted by permission of Methuen Publishing Ltd. on behalf of The University of the South, Sewanee, Tennessee.

Although we have made every effort to trace and contact all copyright holders before publication this has not been possible in all cases. If notified, the publisher will rectify any errors or omissions at the earliest opportunity.

Analysis and Production

1 Introducing Analysis

This course is exactly what its name implies: it is the study of both English Language and Literature, and the specification has been designed with the total integration of these two aspects of the subject in mind. Consequently, you will be asked to study a range of writing representing a variety of genres, including the main literary types of prose, poetry and drama, from both literary and linguistic viewpoints.

You will also be expected to study a selection of non-literary texts, especially those that could feature as part of the unseen analytical comparison in Section A of Unit 3 and those that will appear as part of your adaptation of language in Section B of the same paper.

You will furthermore be required to study features of speech and be expected to analyse a range of speech situations, including transcripts of spontaneous speech; coupled with this, there will also be representation of speech in Unit 2 and it may also crop up in the unseen analysis of Unit 3. This topic may well be one that is new to AS students of English Language and Literature, but it is an integral part of the specification and this is reflected in the weighting of the Assessment Objectives at both levels. However, it is likely you will find that this new departure is both interesting and rewarding, as well as enhancing your analytical skills and fostering your critical faculties.

Aims of the course

This course aims to cultivate a deeper understanding of both English Language and English Literature than that gained at GCSE level, by examining **texts** from both literary and linguistic viewpoints.

> **Text**
>
> A text is simply a piece of writing or a piece of speech. Michael Halliday famously outlined the possible range of texts as being 'prose or verse, dialogue or monologue, it may be anything from a single proverb to a whole play, from a momentary cry for help to an all-day discussion on a committee'.

By examining a variety of texts in this way, you should be able to see whether a literary, linguistic or integrated analytical approach helps you to understand a text more fully. You will be encouraged to do this by applying differing analytical **frameworks**.

> **Framework**
>
> A framework is a critical skeleton around which you can build the body of your analysis. Different frameworks may be more suited to different texts and it will be up to you to learn which one best serves your analysis.

Frameworks can be made up of a variety of critical 'bones', and this book will help you learn the most effective ways of constructing your own frameworks for analysis, when to apply them and how to review their effectiveness.

However, it is also necessary for you to be able to apply the detail of the frameworks to different texts; to do this, it is necessary for you to know about the different 'bones' that join together to make different frameworks. You will have learned some of these 'bones' at GCSE level (alliteration, imagery and metaphor, for instance), but there will be many more that you need to become familiar with so as to increase the breadth and effectiveness of your analytical interpretations and responses. The most notable difference from your GCSE studies is that you will need to become familiar with linguistic terms; all aspects of the course require you to understand this terminology.

The advantage of engaging in combined literary and linguistic study is that you will have the best of both worlds: you can seamlessly use terms from both disciplines to inform your analyses, and you will learn which terms and which frameworks help you to deconstruct texts most effectively. It is essential that you do this, as Unit 3 of the specification will test your ability to adopt an individual approach to unseen textual analysis. Similarly, you will have the opportunity to study two texts in Unit 4 and construct your own question, and by definition your own approach to the answer, in the coursework unit.

There are other points that must be taken into account before we begin the study of the content relevant to each part of the course. There are certain underlying principles that you need to be aware of when you are engaged in either AS or A2 study. You will need to study a minimum of six set texts across the course, supplemented by the study of shorter texts to help with your textual analysis. At AS level for AQA Specification A, Unit 1 requires you to study two texts, which could be two drama texts, two prose texts or one from each genre. For Unit 2 you will study a third text, again either prose or drama. The advantage of this is that you can specialize in one genre if you so wish, or if you prefer to study the different genres more widely, you can cover both genres. You will also need to work on unseen texts, particularly examples of writing which contain the representation of speech so as to help with the comparison that you will need to do between the speech texts given in your Unit 2 examination.

At A2 level, your studies will become more penetrating and be solely based on **comparative study**, except for the textual recasting task. You will need to study a poetry text, a genre not included at AS level. This will need to be compared to another text (from a given list) which may be poetry, prose or drama. You will also need to do a detailed study of the non-fiction set text to help prepare you for the textual recasting paper.

We will guide you through these sections which will require you, at all times, to consider the **purpose**, **audience** and **context** of each piece of writing you study, as well taking other points into consideration, such as comparison, textual adaptation and authorial attitudes. These principles will be pointed up at each opportunity in this book and we will show you how they fit into the study and assessment of the course. This book is organized to help you become familiar with the particular genres and topic areas that you will encounter; consequently, it is organized by genre and topic rather than unit by unit. This reflects the integrated nature of the course; however, to help you practise the types of question that might apply to specific genres, you will find appropriate questions at the end of each relevant chapter.

Textual analysis

Because textual analysis is a skill that you need to learn from the outset, we will spend a little time first building a framework for analysis which you can then apply throughout this book, adapting it and refining it as you see fit. Textual analysis lies at the heart of this subject, and the application of it (through whichever framework or method you choose) will enable you to become a more confident, informed and skilful critic of English Language and Literature.

As you will see, all texts whether written or spoken have a **purpose**, **audience** and **context**; these terms are all dealt with in much greater detail in the rest of the book. Essentially, the terms refer to what a text does, who it is written for and where it appears. When you are engaging in textual analysis, it is always a good idea to start with these three areas as they help you to find a route into the text. When you have identified these, you can continue by examining the text at a variety of levels, moving from individual words through phrases, sentence structures and other grammatical and syntactical issues, to how the text is put together, and finally on to what it looks like as a whole.

Use the flow chart below to help you use one method of deconstructing any text you are studying; once you have become accustomed to the methodology, you can adapt it for your purposes.

One method of textual analysis

What? Who? Where?	
1 What is the text trying to do?	➡ Purpose
2 Who is it trying to communicate these ideas to?	➡ Audience
3 Where will the text appear?	➡ Context
4 What does it look like?	➡ Form

⬇

How?	
5 Use of specific words or terms from a certain area	➡ Semantic field/ Field-specific lexis
6 Use of certain types of words and word classes	➡ Grammar
7 Use of other constructions in phrases and sentences	➡ Syntax
8 Use of sound features and style devices	➡ Phonology and stylistic features
9 How the text fits together	➡ Cohesion
10 What the text looks like and how it is laid out	➡ Graphology

⬇

Effect?	Evaluation of...
11 Does the text do what it sets out to?	➡ Purpose
12 Does it hit its target readership?	➡ Audience
13 Does the place where it appears help the text?	➡ Context
14 Does its layout help?	➡ Form

Of course, analysing a text in such a way does not construct an argument for you. A simple and effective way to do this is simply to chain your points together by using a three-point critical sentence. In this you would:

1 identify the point you want to discuss

2 give an example from the text

3 comment on how it works within the text in terms of purpose and audience.

This is a tried and tested method that helps you to focus on each example that you choose to discuss. You may have been taught a variation of this at GCSE level (one such version is PEE: point – evidence – explanation). Use the version you have been taught if it is easier for you and has worked in the past. You will be able to practise textual analysis at many points in this book, which will help you to engage with the unseen textual analysis required in Unit 3.

Activity

Read the following texts; they are all short examples of the different types of written genre you will come across in the course. You will be familiar with each as you will have studied all four of these genres at GCSE level. Choose one of them and then follow the task outlined below to write your first piece of short textual analysis.

1 Identify the range of examples and ideas that you could use in a textual analysis.

2 Tabulate your findings: this will give you a series of points that you can use as the basis for your response.

3 Using the flow chart on page 3, organize your findings into relevant sections.

4 Write out your textual analysis of the piece you have chosen.

Prose non-fiction

The Perfect Storm

A soft fall rain slips down through the trees and the smell of ocean is so strong that it can almost be licked off the air. Trucks rumble along Rogers Street and men in t-shirts stained with fish blood shout to each other from the decks of boats. Beneath them the ocean swells up against the black pilings and sucks back down to the barnacles. Beer cans and old pieces of styrofoam rise and fall and pools of spilled diesel fuel undulate like huge iridescent jellyfish. The boats rock and creak against their ropes and seagulls complain and hunker down and complain some more. Across Rogers Street and around the back of the Crow's Nest Inn, through the door and up the cement stairs, down the carpeted hallway and into one of the doors on the left, stretched out on a double bed in room #27 with a sheet pulled over him, Bobby Shatford lies asleep.

He's got one black eye. There are beer cans and food wrappers scattered around the room and a duffel bag on the floor with t-shirts and flannel shirts and blue jeans spilling out.

Sebastian Junger

Prose fiction

The Cure for Death by Lightning

When it came looking for me I was in the hollow stump by Turtle Creek at the spot where the deep pool was hidden by low hanging bushes, where the fishing was the very best and only my brother and I figured we knew of it. Now, in spring, the stump blossomed purple and yellow violets so profusely that it became something holy and worth pondering. Come fall, the stump was flagrantly, shamefully red in a coat of dying leaves from the surrounding trees. This was my stump, where I stored my few illicit treasures: the lipstick my mother smuggled home for me in a bag of rice; the scrap of red velvet that Bertha Moses tucked in my pocket as she left the house on the day of my fifteenth birthday; the violet perfume I received as my gift at the Christmas pageant the year before; and the bottle of clear nail polish my father threw into the manure pile after he caught me using it behind the house, the bottle I had salvaged, washed, and spirited away.

I was in there, hiding, my knees up to my nose, listening to the sound of it rushing, crashing through the bush, coming for me. A cobweb stretched over my face, an ant roamed over the valleys in my skirt, spiders invaded my hair, and an itch started on my nose and traveled to my arm, but I stayed still.

Gail Anderson-Dargatz

Poetry

A Poison Tree

I was angry with my friend:
I told my wrath, my wrath did end.
I was angry with my foe:
I told it not, my wrath did grow.

And I water'd it in fears,
Night & morning with my tears:
And I sunned it with smiles,
And with soft deceitful wiles.

And it grew both day and night,
Till it bore an apple bright.
And my foe beheld it shine,
And he knew that it was mine.

And into my garden stole,
When the night had veil'd the pole;
In the morning glad I see,
My foe outstretch'd beneath the tree.

William Blake

Drama

The Tempest

Miranda: If by your art, my dearest father, you have
Put the wild waters in this roar, allay them.
The sky, it seems, would pour down stinking pitch,
But that the sea, mounting to the welkin's cheek,
Dashes the fire out. O, I have suffered
With those that I saw suffer: a brave vessel,
Who had, no doubt, some noble creature in her,
Dash'd all to pieces. O, the cry did knock
Against my very heart. Poor souls, they perish'd.
Had I been any god of power, I would
Have sunk the sea within the earth or ere
It should the good ship so have swallow'd and
The fraughting souls within her.

Prospero: Be collected:
No more amazement: tell your piteous heart
There's no harm done.
Miranda: O, woe the day!
Prospero: No harm.
I have done nothing but in care of thee,
Of thee, my dear one, thee, my daughter, who
Art ignorant of what thou art, nought knowing
Of whence I am, nor that I am more better
Than Prospero, master of a full poor cell,
And thy no greater father.

William Shakespeare

2 Introducing Production

One aspect of GCSE English that many students enjoy is writing creatively, whether it is under examination conditions and with a particular purpose in mind, or writing at length as part of a coursework folder. At Advanced level, the types of imaginative writing that you will do will be both more demanding and require more preparation.

This A level Language and Literature specification has two opportunities for creative writing, both with exact yet quite different starting points. In Unit 1, you will be asked to use a particular aspect, theme, event or character as the starting point for your writing after having read a set text. This means that you will need a detailed knowledge of this text, so as to draw on it for accurate details of plot, style or voice. At A2 level, you will be engaged in imaginative writing of a particular type, where you will be asked to recast a specific section of another (non-fiction) set text for a particular audience and purpose. The art of textual recasting is dealt with later in this book; however, the principles of any creative and imaginative writing are very important and apply to both AS and A2 and are, indeed, a direct derivation from the writing that you did at GCSE level.

These principles are repeated and emphasized here for you. Any imaginative or creative writing of your own should always take careful note of, and vigilantly adhere to:

- audience
- purpose
- context
- style
- format.

As with any language production task, knowledge of different types of writing and familiarity with differing textual examples is very important. First, read carefully the different kinds of text that are given in this chapter, and then analyse them by using a framework to find out what gives each text its particular qualities. Second, look at the tasks linked to each piece and practise writing in response to the kinds of questions that might be set for Unit 1 of this specification.

The basics: purpose and audience

It is vital for you to recognize that any text that is produced always has a purpose and a particular audience in mind. These are two key terms, and they form the backbone of any framework for language production. To help you see at first hand the differences between these two, use the framework for textual analysis given in Chapter 1 when looking closely at the two texts printed on the next page.

Clockwork

Once upon a time (when time ran by clockwork), a strange event took place in a little German town. Actually, it was a series of events, all fitting together like the parts of a clock, and although each person saw a different part, no-one saw the whole of it; but here it is as well as I can tell it.

It began on a winter's evening, when the townsfolk were gathering in the White Horse Tavern. The snow was blowing down from the mountains, and the wind was making the bells shift restlessly in the church tower. The windows were steamed up, the stove was blazing brightly, Putzi the old black cat was snoozing on the hearth; and the air was full of the rich smell of sausage and sauerkraut, of tobacco and beer.

Philip Pullman

Captain Corelli's Mandolin

Dr Iannis had enjoyed a satisfactory day in which none of his patients had died or got any worse. He had attended a surprisingly easy calving, lanced one abscess, extracted a molar, dosed one lady of easy virtue with Salvarsan, performed an unpleasant but spectacularly fruitful enema, and had produced a miracle by a feat of medical prestidigitation.

He chuckled to himself, for no doubt this miracle was already being touted as worthy of St Gerasimos himself. He had gone to old man Stamatis' house, having been summoned to deal with an earache, and had found himself gazing down an aural orifice more dank, be-lichened, and stalagmatic even than the Drogarati cave.

Louis de Bernieres

Activity

These are the beginnings of two novels with distinct purposes and audiences in mind.

What does each writer concentrate on or aim to do (purpose) in the opening of each novel? You might like to focus on such matters as character, setting and plot when you look at each writer's purpose in this way.

What clues are there that help you to see who the readership (audience) is intended to be for each of these extracts? You should concentrate on lexis (the words used), grammatical and syntactic issues (the way the particular words are selected and then strung together) and phonological and stylistic features (sound and style devices).

In the activity above, you will no doubt come up with a variety of answers to each of the questions. You will have seen that the first extract is essentially a simple piece of writing that aims to set the scene, whereas the second piece is more complex and concentrates on establishing one of the central characters. You should have ascertained that *Clockwork* is aimed at a young audience and that *Captain Corelli's Mandolin* is much more adult in its appeal.

For the purposes of this book, we will use the following definitions of purpose and audience. As you work through this textbook, you may find it helpful to build up a critical vocabulary in an exercise book or note-book of your own, to use in your specific analytical frameworks.

Purpose

What the text is trying to communicate to its target audience and the responses it seeks from the reader(s) or listener(s).

Audience

Who the text is written for or aimed at; the audience can vary from the very general (such as adults) to the very specific (female twenty-somethings who work in the city).

Context and topic

Any text must have a purpose, and the purpose may be a combination of a number of ideas. But many students make the mistake, when analysing texts, of thinking that the purpose stands alone and there are no other elements to be considered. For instance, when students analyse texts, they commonly write that a text's purpose is 'to persuade' or 'to entertain'. However, they are missing a crucial point here – the text must have been written 'to persuade someone to do something' or 'to entertain a particular audience in some way'. In other words, it is a pointless exercise to look at the different purposes a text might have without considering the audience the text is aimed at, and the context within which it is produced. Any text will also have a certain amount of content or a central topic, which can also be linked to the context. Look closely at the two texts printed below and answer the questions in the activity, and you will see how these two features play a vital part in any text.

Adventure holiday advertisement

NEVER A DULL MOMENT

Abseiling, pony trekking, windsurfing, motorsports, canoeing, learning to drive, training to be a lifeguard – PGL offer over 60 different activities at 23 centres across the UK and France for 6–18 year olds.

Whether you have a young child or a teenager, they won't experience a single dull moment on a PGL holiday!

Football commentary from BBC local radio

An' the ball goes out of play for another throw-in to Darlo (1.0) just over twenty minutes remainin' (1.0) Darlington nil (1.0) Wolverhampton Wanderers two (1.5) an' it looks as if Wolves (.) are headin' to south London (0.5) to play Charlton (.) in the fourth round (.) in ten days' time (2.0) unless we see a mighty comeback (1.0) from Darlington (1.0) in these remainin' minutes.

Key

(1.5) indicates a pause in seconds

(.) indicates a micropause

Activity

Examine the two texts above closely.

- What evidence is there that these two texts are dependent upon their context?
- What pointers are given as to the subject matter of each text?
- Having answered the previous two questions, can you say what purpose each text has? Remember to make your estimation of the purpose transitive (in other words, consider the audience for whom it is intended to fulfil this purpose), and give sufficient evidence to account for each of your answers.

As you will no doubt have noticed, the place of production of each of the above texts is all-important. If the first text were found in the middle of a recipe for lasagne, it would be totally inappropriate; but it is part of a leaflet advertising a holiday company, so it is contextualized and we accept its appropriateness, even if we do not want to patronize the company. If we heard the second text in the middle of a dinner party, we would again find that the piece is out of context; but if we switched on the car radio and heard it, we would readily accept it.

The subject matter of these two texts is also obvious. In the advert, we see a number of nouns that are all part of the semantic field of sporting activities: *abseiling, windsurfing, canoeing*. In the second text, there are a number of terms that belong to the semantic field of soccer: *ball, throw-in, Wolverhampton Wanderers, fourth round*. It is easy, therefore, to recognize what the texts are about and that in turn helps us to put them into context.

There is one other crucial difference that you will have noted about these two texts: one is written and the other is spoken (it is represented here in the form of a transcript). These differences of mode will be discussed at length in Chapter 5, where you will examine the differences between speech and writing.

To add to our framework of the terminology used in analysing language production, we can define context and topic in the following way.

Context

The situation in which the text takes place, is used or is intended to happen.

Topic

What the text is about, its subject matter or 'topicality', which can be recognized by words used in a particular semantic field.

Form and style

As we have already noted, a number of other factors can affect textual production but do not always come into play. One of these matters is the form that the text takes, or the representation of the text. If we look at the following text, we can see simply by its appearance that it is an advertisement, despite the fact that there are no images. The layout, the use of words, the inclusion of a location, telephone number and website address all help to convey this.

OVERCOME SHYNESS

BUILD SELF-ESTEEM

Combat fear, conversation blocks and physical symptoms
in a new group, led by a skilled psychotherapist.

Achieve success and build self-confidence. Proven results.

CALL FOR FREE CONSULTATION

THE SHYNESS CLINIC

Somerset Place, W1
Tel: 0797 000 0000

www.bashfulpeople.com

So we can define form in the following way.

> **Form**
>
> The way that the text is represented, seen or heard; the recognized format of textual representation that is applied by the writer to the whole of the text.

One vital area we must also consider is the style in which a text is written (or spoken). This will be linked very closely to the purpose, and consequently to the audience, with any stylistic issues having been decided beforehand. Style is a term you will also come across when you study literary texts; indeed, you should already have a good grasp of what constitutes a writer's literary style from your study of literature at GCSE. We can define it for textual production purposes by breaking it down into five major areas.

> **Style**
>
> The way that the text is written. It includes such matters as **lexis** (the words used), **grammar** (the ways in which single words are organized into meaningful chunks of text), **phonology and style** (the way sounds and stylistic devices are used and combined to help convey textual meaning), **cohesion** (the way the text is ordered and hangs together) and **graphology** (what the text looks like).

Language production

It is essential that you take all of the above areas into consideration when you plan and produce texts (as well as when you analyse texts), and you must always ensure that you are able to justify your choice of any of them in your commentary.

The chart below is a diagrammatic representation of the issues that we have discussed so far.

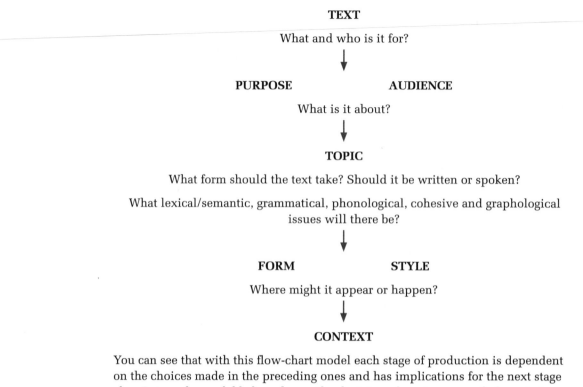

TEXT

What and who is it for?

↓

PURPOSE   **AUDIENCE**

What is it about?

↓

TOPIC

What form should the text take? Should it be written or spoken?

What lexical/semantic, grammatical, phonological, cohesive and graphological issues will there be?

↓

FORM   **STYLE**

Where might it appear or happen?

↓

CONTEXT

You can see that with this flow-chart model each stage of production is dependent on the choices made in the preceding ones and has implications for the next stage also. But, as the model below shows, the decisions do not necessarily have to be made in a linear fashion. We can also consider the text as being at the centre of a production 'circle', where each stage of production is linked to the other stages and the text needs all of them in order to work.

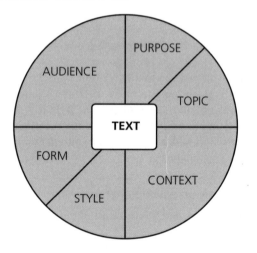

In this diagram we see that each segment must be suitable and all must be working together before the 'whole' can operate as a text.

Whichever of these models you feel is most appropriate and works for you is the 'framework' you should use when you come to write texts of your own, whatever they may be, either in response to a stimulus from your set text, or a piece of textual recasting.

In conclusion, you should be aware that no texts are produced in a vacuum; you should therefore always assume that any writing you do on this course has a practical angle to it and a particular purpose and audience at its heart. Once these two areas have been identified, considerations can be given to topic, form, style and context. If texts are produced without these considerations, it is likely that they will not be effective.

Purposes for language production in Unit 1

It is impossible to give an exhaustive list of the types of purposes for writing that you might be given in this unit. However, there are quite a few obvious and well-used writing frames which you should learn to use and practise for possible use in examination situations. The likelihood is that the tasks that you are given will fall into the four main areas for language production:

- writing to entertain and narrative writing
- argument-based writing and persuasive writing
- information-based writing and discursively-based writing
- expositional and instructional work

or any reasonable combination of these.

As you can see, this constitutes a vast range of purposes, and when you take all other considerations into account, such as audience and context, then it seems that a huge combination of tasks could be given to you. This is why there is so much written material in our world; and when you add in spoken texts, the weight of material becomes enormous! Bearing this in mind, we will look at some of the more common types of task you might be asked to do.

It is worth remembering here that the task you are given will be an imaginary one linked to your set text in some way. As already mentioned, you will therefore need to know your set text well so as to make informed and thoughtful choices about style, content, plot, characterization and so forth. Here is a list (not exhaustive) of possible writing scenarios that you may be given:

- a narrative continuation of the story
- an alternative narrative route
- the account of a minor character within the narrative
- a letter which may have been written within the plot of the text
- a series of diary entries from the viewpoint of a character within the text
- a newspaper report of a particular event from the text, either objectively or subjectively, depending on the style of newspaper
- a transformation of a particular section of text from one genre into another, such as prose into drama
- a report about a certain character or event for a specific audience
- a persuasive piece of writing where you are asked to support a particular character or issue
- a leaflet which informs a particular audience about a certain topic, event or issue from the text, real or imagined
- a web page that reports an explicit event in the text for a new audience and purpose
- a magazine article that discusses a particular aspect of the plot or character behaviour.

Writing to entertain (and divert) an audience

If you have to write in an entertaining fashion, you will be given a specific brief from which to write. You will still need to provide some ideas, perhaps to do with characterization or with plot (remembering the parameters of the text you have studied), but you will be given a specific starting point. You could use the framework cited earlier as a planning tool for your writing. It is likely, having studied your set book, that you will have a clear understanding of such aspects of the text as:

- character
- motivation
- theme
- plot and its outcomes
- any stylistic matters
- interesting or relevant issues
- historical background.

Your understanding of the text can be applied to the style of writing that you are asked to do.

Imaginative narrative writing: Possible story lines

Many writers have claimed that there are only a certain number of story lines and that any narrative is a variation on a theme. In an article in the *Guardian*, Rory Johnson outlines what he believes are the eight basic plot lines available to any writer. These are useful in that they can provide you with a structure, should you struggle to come up with one in the examination room. Don't forget, however, that your narrative does not need to be complete. There is a limit to what you can produce in 50–60 minutes!

Johnson's eight basic plots are:

1 The **Cinderella** story, where an unrecognized virtue is finally given due credit. Cinderella is not always female and a love interest does not have to be the basis for the plot. (Example: *Jane Eyre* by Charlotte Bronte)

2 The **Achilles** story, which highlights the fatal flaw that leads to inevitably tragic consequences. (Example: *King Lear* by William Shakespeare)

3 The **Orpheus** story, which shows what happens when apparent good fortune is taken away for a particular reason. (Example: *Vile Bodies* by Evelyn Waugh)

4 The **Romeo and Juliet** story, which shows what happens when strangers meet and fall in love. It does not have to be a tragic ending. (Example: *Pride and Prejudice* by Jane Austen)

5 The **Irrepressible Hero** story, where a series of hurdles are placed in front of the protagonist and he or she always succeeds. A variant of this is the David and Goliath story. (Example: Widmerpool in Anthony Powell's *A Dance to the Music of Time*)

6 The **Circe** story, where an unsuspecting character is drawn into a devious plot by a villain. (Example: Boxer in *Animal Farm* by George Orwell)

7 The **Tristan** story, which sets out the workings of the eternal triangle; this can be two men and one woman, or vice versa. (Example: *Far From the Madding Crowd* by Thomas Hardy)

8 The **Faust** story, where a pact is made with the devil, and the debt must finally be paid. (Example: *Macbeth* by Shakespeare)

Each of these plots can be styled in various fashions, such as given a comic or melodramatic treatment, or can shift the basic plot details around. They can also have various issues or themes superimposed upon them, to add interest to the narrative. If you feel you need to make overt use of any of the above ideas, you should try to fit the narration to the plot that you know from the text, not making it too unbelievable and rooting it in the text's original story line.

If you have to make a new outcome or narrative route out of the existing plot, you should consider what you can meaningfully do in 50–60 minutes. You should not need to establish character, given that you will be able to use characters already present in your text, so you will probably need to focus on structure and style. Remember that if you need to move the plot on in an original way, a good method to use is the following:

- introduce a new development or problem
- expand upon the problem
- solve the problem (or not)
- resolve the new situation (or not).

It will have probably become apparent to you that a plan or outline for a piece of writing such as this is absolutely vital. You need a plan to keep to your time limit as well as to keep within the bounds of your new story.

If you are asked to tackle an alternative plot line or continuation of a part of the story, once again take note of previously delineated character and themes. These should help to inform your writing and give you the basis on which to continue.

While not necessarily echoing the style of the original text, you should try to keep the original style in mind. For example, if you were to introduce flowery and romantic imagery into a text such as *Wuthering Heights*, it would run counter to the natural and often violent imagery that Emily Brontë uses in the original text.

Activity

Read the following extract from *Wuthering Heights*, in which Lockwood relates to Heathcliff his dream of seeing Catherine's ghost trying to come in through his window. Then answer the question below.

Imagine that you are Heathcliff and you are writing a detailed entry in your personal diary about what happens when Lockwood reports these events to you. You may introduce detail into your account after Lockwood has left the room.

You should give careful consideration to your language choice and style by incorporating Heathcliff's feelings and establishing his voice. You should not copy out large quantities of the printed text, however, when answering this question.

'The truth is, sir, I passed the first part of the night in –' Here I stopped afresh – I was about to say 'perusing those old volumes,' then it would have revealed my knowledge of their written, as well as their printed contents; so, correcting myself, I went on, 'in spelling over the name scratched on that window-ledge. A monotonous occupation, calculated to set me asleep, like counting, or –'

'What *can you* mean by talking in this way to *me*?' thundered Heathcliff with savage vehemence. 'How – how *dare* you, under my roof – God! he's mad to speak so!' And he struck his forehead with rage.

I did not know whether to resent this language, or pursue my explanation; but he seemed so powerfully affected that I took pity and proceeded with my dreams; affirming I had never heard the appellation of 'Catherine Linton' before, but, reading it often over produced an impression which personified itself when I had no longer my imagination under control.

Heathcliff gradually fell back into the shelter of the bed, as I spoke, finally, sitting down almost concealed behind it. I guessed, however, by his irregular and intercepted breathing, that he struggled to vanquish an access of violent emotion.

Not liking to show him that I heard the conflict, I continued my toilette rather noisily, looked at my watch, and soliloquized on the length of the night:

'Not three o'clock, yet! I could have taken oath it had been six – time stagnates here – we must surely have retired to rest at eight!'

'Always at nine in winter, and always rise at four,' said my host, suppressing a groan; and, as I fancied, by the motion of his shadow's arm, dashing a tear from his eyes.

'Mr Lockwood,' he added, 'you may go into my room; you'll only be in the way, coming down stairs so early; and your childish outcry has sent sleep to the devil for me.'

'And for me, too,' I replied. 'I'll walk in the yard till daylight, and then I'll be off; and you need not dread a repetition of my intrusion. I am now quite cured of seeking pleasure in society, be it country or town. A sensible man ought to find sufficient company in himself.'

'Delightful company!' muttered Heathcliff. 'Take the candle, and go where you please. I shall join you directly. Keep out of the yard, though, the dogs are unchained; and the house – Juno mounts sentinel there – and – nay, you can only ramble about the steps and passages – but, away with you! I'll come in two minutes.'

I obeyed, so far as to quit the chamber; when, ignorant where the narrow lobbies led, I stood still, and was witness, involuntarily, to a piece of superstition on the part of my landlord, which belied, oddly, his apparent sense.

He got on to the bed, and wrenched open the lattice, bursting, as he pulled at it, into an uncontrollable passion of tears.

'Come in! come in!' he sobbed. 'Cathy, do come. Oh do – *once* more! Oh! my heart's darling! hear me *this* time – Catherine, at last!'

The spectre showed a spectre's ordinary caprice; it gave no sign of being; but the snow and wind whirled wildly through, even reaching my station, and blowing out the light.

There was such anguish in the gush of grief that accompanied this raving, that my compassion made me overlook its folly, and I drew off, half angry to have listened at all, and vexed at having related my ridiculous nightmare, since it produced that agony; though *why*, was beyond my comprehension.

Writing to persuade or argumentative writing

You will also learn about persuasive and rhetorical techniques in the prepared speech section of Chapter 5 (see pages 121–128).

As you will no doubt remember from your GCSE English course, there are many techniques that can be employed to create persuasive or argumentative writing.

One of the best ways to practise these kinds of writing is to look at a variety of texts and try to emulate them by doing something similar yourself. Some of the techniques that you might try to help your writing are as follows:

- use of exaggeration to make a particular point; this is often useful when you want to accentuate a particular characteristic of a person within a narrative
- use of questions to raise particular issues; they may be rhetorical in nature in that they don't require an answer, as the answer is suggested within the question itself
- repetition of words, phrases or syntactic parallels which help to make a certain issue remain in your mind once it has been read
- use of emotional language, often in the form of strong verbs or powerful adjectives, to help convey an idea or attitude
- use of polar opposites or antithetical ideas to help make a contrast, again for the purpose of remembrance or recall
- use of appropriate imagery through simile, image or metaphor to help emphasize your point
- use of factual ideas or evidence (this may be in the form of factual plot information or realistic facts and figures which would fit into the task you are doing) to help drive your argument home
- phonological and sound effects to help to emphasize a point, especially careful use of assonance, consonance and alliteration.

You may be asked to write a review of one of the texts you have studied or a critique of one of the plays you have seen. You will need to carefully construct your views using the kinds of techniques listed above.

Below is the review of a recent production of *Hamlet* by the English Touring Theatre.

ETT has garnered an enthusiastic following in the York area. It was obvious from the pre-performance chat that many people had seen the company's three previous Shakespeare productions at the Theatre Royal and were looking forward to their fourth. Stephen Unwin's back-to-basics approach to the Bard – clear, fast-paced and uncluttered – seems to have struck a chord with playgoers, and his new period production of *Hamlet* has been eagerly awaited by those of us who were bowled over by his superb *King Lear*.

Elsinore, as designed by Michael Vale, is a forbiddingly dark, claustrophobic place – only candles and a couple of backlit windows break the Stygian gloom. Mark Bouman's costumes are rich (but not gaudy!) and the few items of Jacobean furniture on display were clearly not designed with comfort in mind. Malcolm Rippeth's atmospheric lighting helps to create a world in which 'something is rotten' and anything can happen.

The play, as we have come to expect from ETT, boasts a strong cast. In the title role Ed Stoppard's naturalistic delivery is occasionally a little too fast to be comprehensible, but he avoids the trap of making the part sound like a string of famous quotations. Stoppard's Hamlet is every inch 'the glass of fashion', an intelligent and sensitive young man trapped in a living nightmare, but he makes little of his character's black humour and feigned insanity. Still, it's abundantly clear that Stoppard has the potential to become a major Shakespearean star in the not too distant future.

It's a curious fact that with every new production of *Hamlet* Claudius seems to get nicer and Polonius nastier, as if there were a weird causal relationship between the two. However, just for a change Unwin gives us a coldly efficient Claudius (the excellent David Robb) and an affectionate Polonius (ETT regular Michael Cronin, who also makes a memorable appearance as the Gravedigger). Ben Warwick as Laertes and Alice Patten as Ophelia both make their marks as the ill-fated siblings – Warwick is genuinely devastated by his sister's pitiful fate, and in Ophelia's mad scene Patten never resorts to the clichéd drama school histrionics that so many young actresses find irresistible. The smaller roles are equally well cast, with an honourable mention for Richard Hansell as Reynaldo, Osric and a glamorous Player Queen.

The only disappointing performance comes, unfortunately, from the production's one big name – Anita Dobson as Gertrude. Although she speaks the part well enough there isn't a spark of erotic attraction between the Queen and Claudius, nor was I convinced by her repentance in the closet scene. Dobson's lack of response to Polonius' murder pushes the scene perilously close to comedy, and her own death was greeted by much suppressed giggling in the audience. Proof, if any were needed, that TV stardom and Shakespearean competence don't necessarily go hand in hand…

Although this production doesn't quite reach the heights of the company's *King Lear* it passed one test with flying colours – that of holding the attention of a large audience of sixth form students for over three hours. It's a clear and involving *Hamlet* which I would warmly recommend to anyone coming to Shakespeare for the first time.

J.D. Atkinson, britishtheatreguide.info

Activity

Write a review of a theatre production or film that you have recently seen. You should carefully consider your language choices and style; your audience is an adult one in a quality newspaper.

Another example of the kind of writing that you may be asked to do is letter writing. It will be likely that your letter will have to reflect the attitude or point of view of a character in the text you have studied. Once again, you will have to adopt a consistent voice that reflects the way the character might speak or reflects the character's attitudes and values. (You will not, however, be expected to replicate the style of the original writer.)

Activity

Devise a letter-writing task connected to one of the texts you are studying for Unit 1. For example, if you are studying *Murmuring Judges*, look closely at the final scene. Imagine that you are Sandra and that the Chief Superintendent has asked you to write a letter which helps explain what you have just said to him (your point of view and argument). Your letter will certainly be formal and will outline and explain your argument.

You should carefully consider your language choices, bearing in mind the very specific audience for your letter, and its purpose; in the example given above, it will almost certainly be used in any forthcoming investigation of the police.

Just as a reminder, letter writing should always take note of the following points. If the letter is formal you should always include:

- your address in the top right of the letter, properly punctuated
- the recipient's address diagonally below this and on the left
- a date, formally written, e.g. *17 October, 2008*
- a formal address to the recipient, e.g. *Dear Sir* or *Dear Mr Green*; if it is to a newspaper then the accepted from of address is *Sir*.

If you address the letter *Dear Sir/ Madam* (or just *Sir*) you should finish it with *Yours faithfully.* If you address the letter *using a name* you should finish it with *Yours sincerely.*

You should always be as concise as possible, which means that you should plan out your letter carefully, taking note of what you want to say in each paragraph. Don't use slang or informal lexis in a formal letter.

If your letter is informal you may:

- leave out the recipient's address
- address the recipient by his or her first name, e.g. *Dear Jan,* or *Hello Dave*
- finish the letter less formally, e.g. *Yours,* or *Kind regards*

Your writing can be friendlier and can certainly reflect a more subjective view and style. You should not, however, be over-wordy, and you should still use correct punctuation and grammar; remember, this is not an e-mail or a text message.

Information-based and discursive writing

There may be occasions with the writing that you need to do in this unit where you are required to pass on information within the wider context of writing for another purpose. Remember, your task might not be simply to write persuasively for a particular audience, but also to include some information from your set text.

If you think of the amount of informative writing that occurs around us in everyday life, you can get some idea of the range it covers:

- textbooks and printed factual information such as encyclopaedias
- newspapers (although there may be a slant on certain news items)
- signage of all kinds
- media forms such as magazines, journals, websites, e-zines and so on.

Activity

Research a couple of the separate areas listed above to find out the different features that they have in common. You could, for instance, look at the types of feature that appear in both a Wikipedia entry and a specialist magazine on the same subject, such as woodworking or bird watching.

When you come to tackle informative writing of your own, you should take the following features into account; you will have found some or all of these when you completed the above task.

Lexical issues:

- possible use of a particular semantic field
- jargon, specialist or technical language

Grammatical issues:

- declarative constructions
- precise adjectives

Stylistic issues:

- absence of imagery or metaphorical language
- formal tone
- quotations and references

Cohesive issues:

- objectivity
- subheadings to help structure certain types of informative writing
- careful control of structure

Graphological issues:

- bullet points
- shortened forms or abbreviations.

Activity

As a way of picking out the relevant information from a particular section of a text, read the following extract from *Property* by Valerie Martin. It describes the point in the story when a mill is burnt down. This section is a first-person account from the point of view of Manon. She relates what happens as she surfaces from sleep.

Write an objective account which passes on the precise information of what happens to Manon from the moment she wakes up to when she remembers sleeping in her mother's bed.

Property

I woke up with a start, thinking someone was standing next to my bed, but there was no one there. Had I heard a sound? The room was black. I could make out the curtains at the window but little else. At once I remembered the man. I pulled back the net and sat on the edge of the bed, groggy but determined, shaking my head to clear it. Then I went to the window.

It was like looking into the inkwell. I could make out the shape of the oak, but only as texture, like black velvet against black silk. Was there something among the roots? I dropped down to my knees, as I thought my white shift, my light hair, made me visible, and gazed long and hard. Still my eyes failed to penetrate the darkness. Did something move, there, near the house? Listen, I told myself and I closed my eyes, listening as what had seemed like silence unraveled into different sounds, the buzz of insects, the clock in the hall, something scratching in the wall, the rustling of leaves and branches, and then, just beyond my own heartbeat, not near or loud, but sudden and unmistakable, the sound of a rifle shot.

My eyes flew open. I jumped up and ran for the bedroom door, but I tripped over a footstool and fell headlong across the carpet. As I got to my feet, I heard a shout from outside, then my husband's voice, cursing. I opened my bedroom door just as his door was opened. A lamp sputtered, someone came out into the hall. It was Sarah. I stepped behind the door, laying my cheek against the wood, listening as she hurried toward the landing.

Another door opened, the doctor's. He spoke to her, she answered, but I couldn't make out what they said. There was more light, the heavy sound of my husband's boots, then his voice. 'They've set the mill on fire,' he said, and Dr Landry replied, 'I'll dress and join you.' My husband was halfway down the stairs. 'Stay in your bed,' he called back. 'There are hands enough.'

How could the mill be on fire? I'd just been looking toward it. I felt my way to my dresser, lit the lamp, and went to the window. It was true. There were no flames, but there was a deep red glow to the blackness in that direction. I heard shouts downstairs, my husband appeared on the lawn, running, and from the quarter two men bearing torches came running to meet him. The doctor's door opened again, his footsteps faded as he hurried downstairs. After a few moments he too appeared below me, walking briskly toward the fire.

My heart smote me. It was this way that night: the sounds of doors opening and closing, the clatter of boots on the stairs. But it was different too. It was clear and cold. When I woke up and looked out my window, I could see the flames and smoke billowing up above the trees. I never did see Father leave the house, and I never did see him again. I heard Mother's voice, then a man's voice I didn't recognize, more doors closing, someone riding away. I leaped from my bed and ran into the hall calling for Mother, but she didn't answer. I found her in the parlor with our housemaid Celeste; they had only one lamp lit between them and the room was cold. Mother's crochet hook glinted amid the lace she was frantically working. Celeste was darning a sock. I wanted to throw myself in Mother's lap, but I knew she would scold me. 'What is happening?' I said. Mother looked up, hollow-eyed, her mouth in a grim line, shadows from the lamp playing over her cheeks. She's frightened, I thought. She's more frightened than I am.

'They have murdered him,' she said.

'Father!' I cried and ran to the door.

'Manon,' Mother shouted, jumping to her feet. 'Don't go out there.' She came to me and took me in her arms and I wept. I couldn't understand what had happened. 'The driver has gone for your uncle,' Mother said, 'and we must stay inside until he comes.'

That night I slept in Mother's bed. In the morning she refused to get up, refused to eat, sobbed and muttered wild accusations by turns. 'She mad with grief,' Celeste said.

Valerie Martin

Instructional writing

It is likely that, as with informative writing, any instructional writing that you do, especially in Unit 1, will be within the context of another purpose or as part of a wider task. You are more likely to have to write in a straightforwardly informative or instructional way in the second part of Unit 3, when you have to recast some non-fiction writing.

As with the other types of writing that you have looked at in this chapter, there are certain features which help to define instructional writing and, as with informative writing, it is easy to find practical examples of writing to instruct in the real world:

- printed instructions for assembling or using certain products
- step-by-step guidance for tasks such as cooking, driving, travelling, etc.
- the text accompanying diagrams or other visual forms
- 'how to' guides and books.

Like informative writing, there are a number of features which you should already be familiar with from your GCSE work. These are listed below both as a reminder and for you to use as a checklist when producing this type of writing.

- Lexical features tend to be fairly simple and remain in one semantic field.
- Specialist language will occur but with glossing where necessary.
- Grammatical features tend to be simple.
- Short and precise chunks of language are used, with little subordination in the case of simple instructions.
- Conditional clauses are used for more complex instructions.
- Verbs tend to be in the imperative form, often with adverbs modifying them.
- Stylistic points tend to be minimal.
- Cohesive issues such as stepped or numbered points are often important.
- Question-and-answer formats may be used.

Activity

Read the following web page taken from the NHS Direct website. You will see there is both information and instruction in the text. Pick out the relevant instructions, showing what features are used and how they contribute to the overall effect of the piece.

Can I give my child painkillers?

Babies aged between two and three months can have paediatric paracetamol oral suspension (liquid paracetamol) for <u>fever</u> or mild to moderate <u>pain</u>. They can have one 2.5ml <u>dose</u> and another 2.5ml <u>dose</u> 4-6 hours later. After this, it is important to seek medical advice if the <u>fever</u> or mild to moderate <u>pain</u> has not cleared up. This advice only applies to babies who weigh over 4kg (9lb) and were not born before 37 weeks of pregnancy.

Children and babies over three months old can have paediatric paracetamol oral suspension (liquid paracetamol). Older children can take tablets or tablets dissolved in water. Do not give paracetamol if there is a history of any previous adverse reactions or sensitivity to paracetamol.

Children over one year old can have ibuprofen as long as they weigh over 7kg (15lb) and do not have a history of asthma, <u>heart</u> problems, <u>kidney</u> problems, <u>stomach ulcers</u> or <u>indigestion</u>. Do not give ibuprofen if there is a history of any previous adverse reactions or sensitivity to ibuprofen. Speak to your GP or pharmacist if you are not sure.

Do not give aspirin to children under sixteen.

- Always read the label to make sure you give the correct <u>dosage</u> for your child's age. Do not exceed the stated <u>dose</u>. Some medicines are only suitable for children over six or twelve.
- See your GP if your child is not better within a couple of days.
- Try not to give your children <u>painkillers</u> too often because over time they will have less of an effect on <u>pain</u>.
- Keep all medicines out of the reach of children and in a locked cupboard. Do not leave medicines out if you need to remind yourself, write yourself a note.
- Do not leave children unsupervised in the kitchen or bathroom.

For further information:

Painkillers

What temperature is a fever in children?

Can I take paracetamol and ibuprofen together?

Examination-style question

Read the following extract from Act II of *The Importance of Being Earnest*. You are asked to write two short diary extracts, one each for the characters Jack and Rev. Canon Chasuble, describing this encounter. You are therefore writing two quite different first-person accounts where you are reflecting on what has happened. You should take careful consideration of your language choices and style, especially in the way you reflect the different voices of each character.

(In case you do not know the play, it is important to be aware that Jack's 'brother Ernest' is really just a figment of his imagination; Jack has been mischievously using 'Ernest's' behaviour as cover for his own activities, and now, for complicated reasons, he needs to dispense with the fictitious brother and change his own name to Ernest.)

The Importance of Being Earnest

(*Enter* **Jack** *slowly from the back of the garden. He is dressed in the deepest mourning, with crape hatband and black gloves.*)

Miss Prism:	Mr Worthing!
Chasuble:	Mr Worthing?
Miss Prism:	This is indeed a surprise. We did not look for you till Monday afternoon.
Jack:	(*Shakes **Miss Prism**'s hand in a tragic manner.*) I have returned sooner than I expected. Dr Chasuble, I hope you are well?
Chasuble:	Dear Mr Worthing, I trust this garb of woe does not betoken some terrible calamity?
Jack:	My brother.
Miss Prism:	More shameful debts and extravagance?
Chasuble:	Still leading his life of pleasure?
Jack:	(*Shaking his head.*) Dead!
Chasuble:	Your brother Ernest dead?
Jack:	Quite dead.
Miss Prism:	What a lesson for him! I trust he will profit by it.
Chasuble:	Mr Worthing, I offer you my sincere condolence. You have at least the consolation of knowing that you were always the most generous and forgiving of brothers.
Jack:	Poor Ernest! He had many faults, but it is a sad, sad blow.
Chasuble:	Very sad indeed. Were you with him at the end?
Jack:	No. He died abroad; in Paris, in fact. I had a telegram last night from the manager of the Grand Hotel.
Chasuble:	Was the cause of death mentioned?
Jack:	A severe chill, it seems.
Miss Prism:	As a man sows, so shall he reap.
Chasuble:	(*Raising his hand.*) Charity, dear Miss Prism, charity! None of us are perfect. I myself am peculiarly susceptible to draughts. Will the interment take place here?

Jack: No. He seems to have expressed a desire to be buried in Paris.

Chasuble: In Paris! *(Shakes his head.)* I fear that hardly points to any very serious state of mind at the last. You would no doubt wish me to make some slight allusion to this tragic domestic affliction next Sunday. (**Jack** *presses his hand convulsively.)* My sermon on the meaning of the manna in the wilderness can be adapted to almost any occasion, joyful, or, as in the present case, distressing. *(All sigh.)* I have preached it at harvest celebrations, christenings, confirmations, on days of humiliation and festal days. The last time I delivered it was in the Cathedral, as a charity sermon on behalf of the Society for the Prevention of Discontent among the Upper Orders. The Bishop, who was present, was much struck by some of the analogies I drew.

Jack: Ah! that reminds me, you mentioned christenings I think, Dr Chasuble? I suppose you know how to christen all right? (**Dr Chasuble** *looks astounded.)* I mean, of course, you are continually christening, aren't you?

Miss Prism: It is, I regret to say, one of the Rector's most constant duties in this parish. I have often spoken to the poorer classes on the subject. But they don't seem to know what thrift is.

Chasuble: But is there any particular infant in whom you are interested, Mr Worthing? Your brother was, I believe, unmarried, was he not?

Jack: Oh yes.

Miss Prism: *(Bitterly.)* People who live entirely for pleasure usually are.

Jack: But it is not for any child, dear Doctor. I am very fond of children. No! the fact is, I would like to be christened myself, this afternoon, if you have nothing better to do.

Chasuble: But surely, Mr Worthing, you have been christened already?

Jack: I don't remember anything about it.

Chasuble: But have you any grave doubts on the subject?

Jack: I certainly intend to have. Of course I don't know if the thing would bother you in any way, or if you think I am a little too old now.

Chasuble: Not at all. The sprinkling, and, indeed, the immersion of adults is a perfectly canonical practice.

Jack: Immersion!

Chasuble: You need have no apprehensions. Sprinkling is all that is necessary, or indeed I think advisable. Our weather is so changeable. At what hour would you wish the ceremony performed?

Jack: Oh, I might trot round about five if that would suit you.

Chasuble: Perfectly, perfectly! In fact I have two similar ceremonies to perform at that time. A case of twins that occurred recently in one of the outlying cottages on your own estate. Poor Jenkins the carter, a most hard-working man.

Jack: Oh! I don't see much fun in being christened along with other babies. It would be childish. Would half-past five do?

Chasuble: Admirably! Admirably! *(Takes out watch.)* And now, dear Mr Worthing, I will not intrude any longer into a house of sorrow. I would merely beg you not to be too much bowed down by grief. What seem to us bitter trials are often blessings in disguise.

Miss Prism: This seems to me a blessing of an extremely obvious kind.

Oscar Wilde

- -

You have now examined the four main areas of production work that you are likely to find in Unit 1 of this specification. You should also use this chapter when studying the other major form of production, that is textual adaptation and recasting.

3 Analysing Prose Fiction

In the course you are studying you may encounter prose texts in Unit 1, Integrated Analysis and Text Production; Unit 2, Analysing Speech and its Representation; and possibly as an extract as part of the comparative analysis section of Unit 3. Also, you may write about a prose text in Unit 4 for the comparative coursework, should you choose the prose option for your second text.

In this chapter we will focus on the ways in which writers use language in fiction texts and the effects that they create through this language use. In the examination for Unit 1, this study of prose fiction texts will be closely linked to detailed language analysis and also imaginative textual production based on a fiction text. In looking at the language of prose fiction, both linguistic and literary issues will be examined, and you will need to prepare yourself by examining literary issues through the language of the texts you study, noting how writers use language to achieve and enhance literary effects and address issues. In the examination for Unit 2, the focus will be on the ways in which speech is used by the writer in the set text that you have studied.

In Unit 1 you will need to demonstrate your ability to:

- select and apply relevant concepts and approaches from integrated linguistic and literary study, using appropriate terminology and accurate, coherent written expression
- demonstrate detailed critical understanding in analysing the ways in which structure, form and language shape meanings.

In Unit 2 you will need to demonstrate the above and also your ability to:

- use integrated approaches to explore relationships between texts, analysing and evaluating the significance of contextual factors in their production and reception.

The nature of prose fiction

All the prose fiction texts that you are offered in the specification are of the kind we refer to as narrative prose – narrative in the sense that they all 'tell a story' in one way or another, usually in the form of a novel or short story. Narrative prose consists primarily in the telling of a sequence of connected events, by some kind of narrator. The events of the narrative are connected in the sense that they are linked in some way. Although narrative prose fiction can be difficult to place in specific categories as it can be wide-ranging in purpose and style, most prose fiction has certain features in common.

Activity

Think about the features of the prose fiction you have studied either during your AS course or for work you have done earlier. Make a list of the key features of narrative prose.

Here are some of the key features you might have listed.

- There is usually a narrator of some kind and therefore the story is told from a particular **point of view**.
- Narrative prose is usually **structured** so it has a 'beginning', a 'middle' and some kind of ending.
- It usually has a point – it is told for some kind of **purpose** – to develop or explore an idea or theme or offer some kind of view of something, or simply to tell an entertaining story.
- It usually contains **characters** that are presented in certain kinds of ways by the writer.

Although every novel or short story is different and each writer makes decisions about the **purpose** and **style** of his or her prose, most narrative prose has one function in common. This function is to entertain – although, of course, the vast majority of authors do much more than this. Narrative prose can raise readers' awareness of a particular theme or issue or group of ideas, and thus the prose may educate and inform as well as entertain.

Features of narrative prose

Theories of narrative usually identify two main levels of narrative. These are:

1 The basic events or actions of the narrative, given in the chronological order in which they are supposed to have happened, with the circumstances surrounding them – in basic terms, this level is often referred to as the **story** or the **plot**.
2 The techniques and devices used for telling the story. These are often called the **narrative techniques**.

The recognition of a distinction between the story itself and the way in which it is told is important because it acknowledges that the same story can be told in different ways depending on the **viewpoint** of the teller.

Point of view

The point of view is of central importance to narrative prose because the reader needs to know who is telling the story. The term can be used literally to describe the visual perspective from which the story is presented. It can also be used to indicate the ideological framework from which the story is told, or the bias contained in the text. This is what we are commenting on when, for example, we say that a text presents a 'female perspective', or the story is told from 'the point of view of the ordinary worker'.

A third way in which the term can be used is to describe basic types of narration – in other words, the relationship between the narrator of the story and the reader.

At a simple level we can make the distinction between the two basic and most common types of narration: **first-person narration** and **third-person narration**.

Let's have a closer look at these to begin with.

First-person narration

In a first-person narrative, the 'I' narrator tells of the events that he or she experiences. This kind of narration is found in a range of novels and short stories covering a wide variety of styles and periods; for example, Mary Shelley's *Frankenstein* (1818), Charlotte Brontë's *Jane Eyre* (1847), Alice Sebold's *The Lovely Bones* (2002),

Valerie Martin's *Property* (2003) and Khaled Hosseini's *The Kite Runner* (2003). Several features of first-person narrative are worth bearing in mind.

- First-person narrative allows the reader directly into the mind of the narrator.
- Sometimes the events of the novel can be viewed retrospectively, so the narrator's view of things can change as he or she matures. This is particularly evident in some novels. In *Great Expectations*, for example, the narrator, Pip, develops and changes as he grows into adulthood; Graham Swift, in *Waterland*, use the first-person form to create fictional autobiography.
- Sometimes there is more than one narrator. Emily Brontë uses multiple narrators to tell her story in *Wuthering Heights* and each presents the story from his or her own viewpoint, which can be biased or questionable. Sometimes these are referred to as unreliable narrators.
- Because this form of narration often gives only one person's view of the story, it can present a biased account of events and by its nature seems more subjective than third-person narration.

Third-person narration

In a third-person narrative the narrator is often omniscient – he or she 'sees all' and 'knows all' that is going on. There is no 'I' figure and so the story is related directly to the reader. There are two types of **omniscient narrator** – the **intrusive** and the **unintrusive**. The intrusive narrator enters into the novel by explicitly commenting on events and characters. Authors such as Thomas Hardy, Jane Austen and George Eliot do this frequently and, to some extent, Anita Shreve does this in *Eden Close*. On the other hand, the unintrusive narrator tells the story from a distance without the reader being aware that the narrator is making judgements or voicing opinions.

Third-person narration can also work in other ways. For example, the narrative point of view can be either **internal** or **external**. Third-person narration can simply describe events, characters, and so on as they are observed from the outside, but it can also describe them from the inside. Such a narrator can seem able to see into the minds of the characters and tell us about how they think and feel; hence the term 'omniscient' narrators.

Another distinction that can be made in third-person narration is between **restricted** and **unrestricted** narration. In some novels the narrator apparently has no restrictions on the knowledge he or she possesses concerning the characters and events. On the other hand, some writers deliberately give their narrators restricted knowledge. Such limitations are often signalled by phrases such as it *seemed/ appeared/ looked as if*.

Sometimes this restricting of the narration reflects the fact that the narrative identifies closely with a single character, while at the same time remaining in the third person. It is important to recognize this as it shows that sometimes third-person narration is not necessarily objective, and it can operate from more subjective and restricted viewpoints.

Other forms of narrative you might come across in your studies do not fit easily into either first- or third-person narration. For example, interior monologues can be used to reflect and develop the thoughts in a character's head. You may well be familiar with this form of writing through such works as Alan Bennett's *Talking Heads* and *Talking Heads 2*, but other writers frequently use this approach too, sometimes as a part of a larger narrative. Many nineteenth-century novelists use passages of interior monologue to allow the reader to see how a character's thoughts are developing.

Another form of narrative you might come across is **stream of consciousness** writing, in which thoughts are written randomly just as if they have been spilled out of the character's mind on to the page. One of the features of this kind of writing is that it appears unstructured, unpunctuated and chaotic. However, it is important to remember that the writer has deliberately structured it in this way to reflect the complex outpourings of the human mind. Perhaps the best-known writers to experiment with this style of writing are James Joyce and Virginia Woolf.

Activity

Look carefully at these two short extracts. The first is taken from *The Kite Runner* by Khaled Hosseini and the second from *Things Fall Apart* by Chinua Achebe. The first is written in the first person and the second in the third person. Try re-writing the first extract in the third person and the second extract in the first person. Make a note of any ways in which you feel your version changes the original. Also note any parts that you found difficult to 'translate' into the other narrative mode, and discuss why difficulties arose.

The Kite Runner

Over the years, I had seen a lot of guys run kites. But Hassan was by far the greatest kite runner I'd ever seen. It was downright eerie the way he always got to the spot the kite would land *before* the kite did, as if he had some sort of inner compass.

I remember one overcast winter day, Hassan and I were running a kite. I was chasing him through neighborhoods, hopping gutters, weaving through narrow streets. I was a year older than him, but Hassan ran faster than I did, and I was falling behind.

'Hassan! Wait!' I yelled, my breathing hot and ragged.

He whirled around, motioned with his hand. 'This way!' he called before dashing around another corner. I looked up, saw that the direction we were running was opposite to the one the kite was drifting.

'We're losing it! We're going the wrong way!' I cried out.

'Trust me!' I heard him call up ahead. I reached the corner and saw Hassan bolting along, his head down, not even looking at the sky, sweat soaking through the back of his shirt. I tripped over a rock and fell – I wasn't just slower than Hassan but clumsier too; I'd always envied his natural athleticism. When I staggered to my feet, I caught a glimpse of Hassan disappearing around another street corner. I hobbled after him, spikes of pain battering my scraped knees.

I saw we had ended up on a rutted dirt road near Isteqlal Midde School. There was a field on one side where lettuce grew in the summer, and a row of sour cherry trees on the other. I found Hassan sitting cross-legged at the foot of one of the trees, eating from a fistful of dried mulberries.

'What are we doing here?' I panted, my stomach roiling with nausea.

He smiled. 'Sit with me, Amir agha.'

I dropped next to him, lay on a thin patch of snow, wheezing. 'You're wasting our time. It was going the other way, didn't you see?'

Hassan popped a mulberry in his mouth. 'It's coming,' he said. I could hardly breathe and he didn't even sound tired.

'How do you know?' I said.

'I know.'

'How can you *know*?'

He turned to me. A few sweat beads rolled from his bald scalp. 'Would I ever lie to you, Amir agha?'

Khaled Hosseini

Things Fall Apart

It was not yet noon on the second day of the New Yam Festival. Ekwefi and her only daughter, Ezinma, sat near the fireplace waiting for the water in the pot to boil. The fowl Ekwefi had just killed was in the wooden mortar. The water began to boil, and in one deft movement she lifted the pot from the fire and poured the boiling water on to the fowl. She put back the empty pot on the circular pad in the corner, and looked at her palms, which were black with soot. Ezinma was always surprised that her mother could lift a pot from the fire with her bare hands.

'Ekwefi,' she said, 'is it true that when people are grown up, fire does not burn them?' Ezinma, unlike most children, called her mother by her name.

'Yes,' replied Ekwefi, too busy to argue. Her daughter was only ten years old but she was wiser than her years.

'But Nwoye's mother dropped her pot of hot soup the other day and it broke on the floor.'

Ekwefi turned the hen over in the mortar and began to pluck the feathers.

'Ekwefi,' said Ezinma, who had joined in plucking the feathers, 'my eyelid is twitching.'

'It means you are going to cry,' said her mother.

'No,' Ezinma said, 'it is this eyelid, the top one.'

'That means you will see something.'

'What will I see?' she asked.

'How can I know?' Ekwefi wanted her to work it out herself.

'Oho,' said Ezinma at last. 'I know what it is – the wrestling match.'

At last the hen was plucked clean. Ekwefi tried to pull out the horny beak but it was too hard. She turned round on her low stool and put the beak in the fire for a few moments. She pulled again and it came off.

Chinua Achebe

Narrative voice

Closely associated with the idea of narrative viewpoint is the idea of narrative voice. Different narrators and different narrative techniques change a story, affecting not just how we are told something but what we are told and how we respond to it. The feelings and attitudes of the narrator can be detected through the tone of voice adopted, thus providing the writer with another way of shaping the responses of the reader.

Activity

Read carefully the two extracts that follow. The first is from Jean Rhys's novel *Wide Sargasso Sea*, which creates an 'early life' of the Mrs Rochester who appears in Charlotte Brontë's novel, *Jane Eyre*. The second extract is taken from *Jane Eyre*.

Compare and contrast the two passages, focusing on the effects achieved by the differing points of view each writer has chosen to adopt. You should consider the following points:

- the narrative viewpoint and its effect on the reader
- the effect of the narrative voice of each text
- the perspectives that the writers create and the ways in which they sustain it.

Wide Sargasso Sea

In this room I wake early and lie shivering for it is very cold. At last Grace Poole, the woman who looks after me, lights a fire with paper and sticks and lumps of coal. She kneels to blow it with bellows. The paper shrivels, the sticks crackle and spit, the coal smoulders and glowers. In the end flames shoot up and they are beautiful. I get out of bed and go close to watch them and to wonder why I have been brought here. For what reason? There must be a reason. What is it that I must do? When I first came I thought it would be for a day, two days, a week perhaps. I thought that when I saw him and spoke to him I would be wise as serpents, harmless as doves. 'I give you all I have freely,' I would say, 'and I will not trouble you again if you will let me go.' But he never came.

The woman Grace sleeps in my room. At night I sometimes see her sitting at the table counting money. She holds a gold piece in her hand and smiles. Then she puts it all into a little canvas bag with a drawstring and hangs the bag round her neck so that it is hidden in her dress. At first she used to look at me before she did this but I always pretended to be asleep, now she does not trouble about me. She drinks from a bottle on the table then she goes to bed, or puts her arms on the table, her head on her arms, and sleeps. But I lie watching the fire die out. When she is snoring I get up and I have tasted the drink without colour in the bottle. The first time I did this I wanted to spit it out but managed to swallow it. When I got back into bed I could remember more and think again. I was not so cold.

There is one window high up – you cannot see out of it. My bed had doors but they have been taken away. There is not much else in the room. Her bed, a black press, the table in the middle and two black chairs carved with fruit and flowers. They have high backs and no arms. The dressing-room is very small, the room next to this one is hung with tapestry. Looking at the tapestry one day I recognised my mother dressed in an evening gown but with bare feet. She looked away from me, over my head just as she used to do. I wouldn't tell Grace this. Her name oughtn't to be Grace. Names matter, like when he wouldn't call me Antoinette, and I saw Antoinette drifting out of the window with her scents, her pretty clothes and her looking-glass.

There is no looking-glass here and I don't know what I am like now. I remember watching myself brush my hair and how my eyes looked back at me. The girl I saw was myself yet not quite myself. Long ago when I was a child and very lonely I tried to kiss her. But the glass was between us – hard, cold and misted over with my breath. Now they have taken everything away. What am I doing in this place and who am I?

The door of the tapestry room is kept locked. It leads, I know, into a passage. That is where Grace stands and talks to another woman whom I have never seen. Her name is Leah. I listen but I cannot understand what they say. So there is still the sound of whispering that I have heard all my life, but these are different voices.

When night comes, and she has had several drinks and sleeps, it is easy to take the keys. I know now where she keeps them. Then I open the door and walk into their world. It is, as I always knew, made of cardboard. I have seen it before somewhere, this cardboard world where everything is coloured brown or dark red or yellow that has no light in it. As I walk along the passages I wish I could see what is behind the cardboard. They tell me I am in England but I don't believe them. We lost our way to England. When? Where? I don't remember, but we lost it. Was it that evening in the cabin when he found me talking to the young man who brought me my food? I put my arms round his neck and asked him to help me. He said, 'I didn't know what to do, sir.' I smashed the glasses and plates against the porthole. I hoped it would break and the sea come in. A woman came and then an older man who cleared up the broken things on the floor. He did not look at me while he was doing it. The third man said drink this and you will sleep. I drank it and I said, 'It isn't like it seems to be.' – 'I know. It never is,' he said. And then I slept. When I woke it was a different sea. Colder. It was that night, I think, that we changed course and lost our way to England. This cardboard house where I walk at night is not England.

Jean Rhys

Jane Eyre

When we left the dining-room, she proposed to show me over the rest of the house; and I followed her upstairs and downstairs, admiring as I went; for all was well-arranged and handsome. The large front chambers I thought especially grand; and some of the third story rooms, though dark and low, were interesting from their air of antiquity. The furniture once appropriated to the lower apartments had from time to time been removed here, as fashions changed; and the imperfect light entering by their narrow casements showed bedsteads of a hundred years old; chests in oak or walnut, looking, with their strange carvings of palm branches and cherubs' heads, like types of the Hebrew ark; rows of venerable chairs, high-backed and narrow; stools still more antiquated, on whose cushioned tops were yet apparent traces of half-effaced embroideries, wrought by fingers that for two generations had been coffin-dust. All these relics gave to the third story of Thornfield Hall the aspect of a home of the past: a shrine of memory. I liked the hush, the gloom, the quaintness of these retreats in the day; but I by no means coveted a night's repose on one of those wide and heavy beds: shut in, some of them, with doors of oak; shaded, others, with wrought old English hangings encrusted with thick work, portraying effigies of strange flowers, and stranger birds, and strangest human beings, – all which would have looked strange, indeed, by the pallid gleam of moonlight.

'Do the servants sleep in these rooms?' I asked.

'No: they occupy a range of smaller apartments to the back; no one ever sleeps here: one would almost say that, if there were a ghost at Thornfield Hall, this would be its haunt.'

'So I think: you have no ghost, then?

'None that I ever heard of,' returned Mrs Fairfax, smiling.

'Nor any traditions of one? No legends or ghost stories?'

'I believe not. And yet it is said, the Rochesters have been rather a violent than a quiet race in their time: perhaps, though, that is the reason they rest tranquilly in their graves now.'

'Yes – "after life's fitful fever they sleep well,"' I muttered. 'Where are you going now, Mrs Fairfax?' for she was moving away.

'On to the leads; will you come and see the view from thence?' I followed still, up a very narrow staircase to the attics, and thence by a ladder and through a trap-door to the roof of the hall. I was now on a level with the crow colony, and could see into their nests. Leaning over the battlements and looking far down, I surveyed the grounds laid out like a map: the bright and velvet lawn closely girding the grey base of the mansion; the field, wide as a park, dotted with its ancient timber; the wood, dun and sere, divided by a path visibly overgrown, greener with moss than the trees were with foliage; the church at the gates, the road, the tranquil hills, all reposing in the autumn day's sun; the horizon bounded by a propitious sky, azure, marbled with pearly white. No feature in the scene was extraordinary, but all was pleasing. When I turned from it and repassed the trap-door, I could scarcely see my way down the ladder: the attic seemed black as a vault compared with that arch of blue air to which I had been looking up, and to that sunlit scene of grove, pasture, and green hill of which the hall was the centre, and over which I had been gazing with delight.

Mrs Fairfax stayed behind a moment to fasten the trap-door. I, by dint of groping, found the outlet from the attic, and proceeded to descend the narrow garret staircase. I lingered in the long passage to which this led, separating the front and back rooms of the third story: narrow, low, and dim, with only one little window at the far end, and looking, with its two rows of small black doors all shut, like a corridor in some Bluebeard's castle.

While I paced softly on, the last sound I expected to hear in so still a region, a laugh, struck my ear. It was a curious laugh; distinct, formal, mirthless. I stopped: the sound ceased, only for an instant; it began again, louder: for at first, though distinct, it was very low. It passed off in a clamorous peal that seemed to wake an echo in every lonely chamber; though it originated but in one, and I could have pointed out the door whence the accents issued.

'Mrs Fairfax!' I called out: for I now heard her descending the garret stairs. 'Did you hear that loud laugh? Who is it?'

'Some of the servants, very likely,' she answered: 'perhaps Grace Poole.'

'Did you hear it?' I again inquired.

'Yes, plainly; I often hear her; she sews in one of these rooms. Sometimes Leah is with her: they are frequently noisy together.'

The laugh was repeated in its low, syllabic tone, and terminated in an odd murmur.

'Grace!' exclaimed Mrs Fairfax.

I really did not expect any Grace to answer; for the laugh was as tragic, as preternatural a laugh as any I ever heard; and, but that it was high noon, and that no circumstance of ghostliness accompanied the curious cachination; but that neither scene nor season favoured fear, I should have been superstitiously afraid. However, the event showed me I was a fool for entertaining a sense even of surprise.

The door nearest me opened, and a servant came out, – a woman of between thirty and forty; a set, square-made figure, red-haired, and with a hard, plain face: any apparition less romantic or less ghostly could scarcely be conceived.

'Too much noise, Grace,' said Mrs Fairfax. 'Remember directions!' Grace curtseyed silently and went in.

'She is a person we have to sew and assist Leah in her housemaid's work,' continued the widow; 'not altogether unobjectionable in some points, but she does well enough. By-the-by, how have you got on with your new pupil this morning?'

The conversations, thus turned to Adèle, continued till we reached the light and cheerful region below. Adèle came running to meet us in the hall, exclaiming –

'Mesdames, vous êtes servies!' adding, 'J'ai bien faim, moi!'

We found dinner ready, and waiting for us in Mrs Fairfax's room.

Charlotte Brontë

- -

Here is how one student responded to this activity. Read her response carefully.

Student response

At first, it appears that the person narrating the story in *Wide Sargasso Sea* is a child as the language is simple and the descriptions of her surroundings are immature in their outlook. She refers to Grace Poole as 'the woman who looks after me', indicating that she herself is not yet a woman and also that she requires supervision. The narration of how the fire is built and how it looks when it has become established adds to this effect in the way it is lit with 'paper and sticks and lumps of coal'. The repetitive use of 'and' here indicates a child's view in the account of the chore. This theme continues to run throughout the piece as Grace is referred to as 'the woman' again and then the narrator 'pretended to be asleep' going on to describe the 'drink without colour'. The language is very matter of fact and logical in a simple way especially when she is negotiating with herself about the importance of having the right name. This simple descriptive language is later repeated when she looks out of her room into 'their world' and sees the corridor as 'made of cardboard' with 'no light in it'. At the same time she flits from subject to subject, never really settling on one object or subject for very long.

However, the reader is informed that the narrator is not a child with the words 'Long ago when I was a child', which gives a new twist to the story. The character of the storyteller takes on a new twist being portrayed as a wistful, trapped and lonely adult. It leads nicely to the correct viewpoint – that of a woman who is in some way retarded, hence the simple language.

The woman comes across as being confused about her situation – especially in the first paragraph with the rush of questions '... why I have been brought here. For what reason?... What is it that I must do?' and later on 'What am I doing in this place and who am I?' In the last paragraph, she feels as though they 'lost our way to England' followed by 'When? Where?' and again affirming in the last lines 'lost our way to England'. This all supports the confused tone created at the beginning of the piece.

It is touching the way she refers to the looking-glass and how she would watch herself brush her hair. The hint of loneliness created by the way her mother 'looked away from me, over my head' is affirmed as she saw herself as 'very lonely' and by the way she tried to kiss herself in the mirror. She described it as 'hard, cold and misted over', which is ironically how she now sees England.

There is an air of suspicion held through the writing too as she recounts, 'there is still the sound of whispering that I have heard all my life, but these are different voices.' This prompts the reader to wonder whether she is referring to real or imagined voices in the past, even though they are real at this point in time. However the narrator does not actually question this herself, she just accepts it as though she realizes deep down that she is 'different'.

The whole piece jumps from the past tense to the present tense and as mentioned before uses very basic language. This gives us a clue that perhaps Mrs Rochester was not well educated. All in all though the picture painted is one of a confused and sensitive adult – sensitive, in the way she views the fire as 'beautiful' and reaching out for affection when trying to kiss her reflection in the looking-glass; confused, in the way she does not understand why she is where she is and really cannot remember how she got there.

In contrast, *Jane Eyre* gives the viewpoint of an educated, well-balanced individual whose prose is far more detailed in its descriptions, using complex rather than simple sentence structure, and having a notably larger range of vocabulary. The writing also flows more fluently as opposed to being stilted and remains in the past tense – hence it does not have the confused childlike qualities of *Wide Sargasso Sea*. The speech at the end of *Jane Eyre* also gives credence to the sense that Jane is more educated when Mrs Fairfax asks her about her student who then appears speaking in French.

When looking at the objects and her surroundings, Jane uses many more adjectives and notes numerous intricate details about the different objects as well as metaphors to express her imaginative side. This is very apparent from the first paragraph when admiring the different rooms she passes through with Mrs Fairfax. She appears to be a very fair and kind person, referring to the third-storey rooms as 'interesting from their air of antiquity' despite being 'dark and low'. As a narrator she tries hard to avoid being too critical as shown when realizing the furniture was old yet regarding it as having been 'appropriated' to the upper rooms 'as fashions changed', giving the third storey a 'shrine of memory'. Particular attention is paid to the detail of the furniture and the embroideries. It is as though she could almost see them being sewn when she uses the term 'wrought by fingers'. This imagination rears again later, referring to the attic as 'black as a vault'.

In the centre of the piece there is a break where the viewpoint shifts, as there is some narrative dialogue, but then the viewpoint returns to Jane again, adding to the stable air of the piece.

The non-critical view arises again when Jane sees the beauty of the view from the battlements, using many adjectives such as 'bright... velvet... tranquil... propitious... azure' and 'pearly' all within a single sentence. These are punctuated by two similes, 'the grounds laid out like a map' and 'wide as a park' as well as being complemented by her comparison of the trees and the moss. Her following sentence reads, 'No feature in the scene was extraordinary, but all was pleasing.' How nice to see such detail in a view which is not 'extraordinary'.

The two writings do agree on a couple of points:

One is the appearance of the corridor in which Mrs Rochester is kept. The excerpt from *Jane Eyre* again shows the imaginative side by use of the simile 'like a corridor in some Bluebeard's castle' in contrast to Mrs Rochester's childlike and simple metaphor of 'cardboard'.

The other point is the fact that Grace was perhaps not a suitable name for the woman who 'looked after' Mrs Rochester. Again, Jane Eyre's version is far more descriptive: 'I really did not expect any Grace to answer' calling her laugh 'tragic' and 'preternatural' and her physical appearance an 'apparition less romantic or less ghostly could scarcely be conceived', whereas Mrs Rochester simply says 'Her name oughtn't to be Grace. Names matter.'

These two examples are typical of the different effects created by the differing points of view the pieces were written from.

Examiner's comments

This is a perceptive and sensitive response to the task. The student has read the passages thoroughly and has employed deductive skills, using the clues to work out what is happening. Note how the student is not thrown but re-assesses the situation when new information is found. For example, the original impression in the first extract that the character is a child is re-evaluated when textual clues make it clear that this is not the case.

The student shows a sound understanding of 'narrative voice' and draws contrasts and comparisons between the two extracts. Overall the writing shows a good level of sensitivity to the ways in which writers use language to create their effects, and the importance that 'narrative voice' can have in shaping the readers' perceptions and responses.

Register

The term 'register' is used to describe how language varies to suit the particular audience and purpose. For example, a solicitor might use a form of language containing many legal words and phrases, while a doctor could use language dominated by medical words and phrases. You might use formal language when attending a job interview, and an informal register when speaking to your friends. When you are asked to analyse a piece of writing containing spoken language it is important to make sure that you note three key areas related to register:

The mode

Either spoken or written (although there can be subdivision where a speech is written down, for example).

The manner

The particular level of formality of language used by the writer. In basic terms this can be either formal or informal.

The field

The way that the words used are linked to the subject matter being dealt with. For example, a writer dealing with a military theme is likely to use words such as *garrison*, *sergeant*, *unexploded*, *shell*, *artillery*, etc. The field, therefore, is closely related to lexis, and by examining it conclusions can be drawn about the topic or focus of the language being used.

Lexis

Lexis (sometimes called **lexicon**) is the term used to describe the vocabulary of a novel, poem, speech or other form of language use. You may find this feature referred to as **diction** in some books, particularly those dealing with literary criticism, although the term it is not used so much nowadays.

Lexis deals with the study of words and the way that they relate to one another, and it can take a variety of forms depending on the choices that writers make to achieve their purposes.

When examining the lexis of narrative prose, certain features or kinds of words are worth watching out for. Here is one way to approach the task:

Nouns

Abstract nouns may focus on describing states of mind, concepts, ideas.

Concrete nouns are used more to describe solid events, characters, etc.

Proper nouns are used to refer to specific characters, places, etc.

Verbs

Stative verbs (such as *know*, *believe*) may indicate a writer's interest is in describing states of mind, setting, etc.

Dynamic verbs (such as *go*, *say*) place the emphasis on what is currently happening.

Modifiers

Modifiers, such as adverbs and adjectives, can provide a whole range of added detail and writers use them a great deal to influence the reader's perceptions. They can add positive or negative connotations and shape readers' responses.

Here is a checklist of other features to look for when examining the word choice of a writer:

- levels of formality (i.e. formal or informal)
- technical and non-technical vocabulary
- non-standard vocabulary (e.g. colloquialisms, dialect words).

What sorts of vocabulary are being used? Are the words:

- short or long
- simple or complex
- concrete or abstract
- in everyday use or specialist and relating to a particular area
- literal or figurative
- heavily modified or presented with little modification?

Remember, though, that throughout your consideration of lexis you should always bear in mind the time and place in which the narrative is set. The writer's lexical choices will depend very much on the world he or she inhabits and the world he or she creates.

Activity

Read the following extract carefully. It is taken from *Great Expectations* by Charles Dickens and in it he describes the marshes of the Thames estuary, the setting for the central character Pip's encounter with an escaped convict.

Examine the lexical choices that Dickens has made here and discuss the effects that his choices create. Use specific examples from the text to illustrate your ideas.

Great Expectations

The man, after looking at me for a moment, turned me upside down, and emptied my pockets. There was nothing in them but a piece of bread. When the church came to itself – for he was so sudden and strong that he made it go head over heels before me, and I saw the steeple under my feet – when the church came to itself, I say, I was seated on a high tombstone, trembling, while he ate the bread ravenously.

'You young dog,' said the man, licking his lips, 'what fat cheeks you ha' got.'

I believe they were fat, though I was at that time undersized, for my years, and not strong.

'Darn Me if I couldn't eat 'em,' said the man, with a threatening shake of his head, 'and if I han't half a mind to't!'

I earnestly expressed my hope that he wouldn't, and held tighter to the tombstone on which he had put me; partly, to keep myself upon it; partly, to keep myself from crying.

'Now lookee here!' said the man. 'Where's your mother?'

'There, sir!' said I.

He started, made a short run, and stopped and looked over his shoulder.

'There, sir!' I timidly explained. 'Also Georgiana. That's my mother.'

'Oh!' said he, coming back. 'And is that your father alonger your mother?'

'Yes, sir,' said I; 'him too; late of this parish.'

'Ha!' he muttered then, considering. 'Who d'ye live with – supposin' you're kindly let to live, which I han't made up my mind about?'

'My sister, sir – Mrs Joe Gargery – wife of Joe Gargery, the blacksmith, sir.'

'Blacksmith, eh?' said he. And looked down at his leg.

After darkly looking at his leg and at me several times, he came closer to my tombstone, took me by both arms, and tilted me back as far as he could hold me; so that his eyes looked most powerfully down into mine, and mine looked most helplessly up into his.

'Now lookee here,' he said, 'the question being whether you're to be let to live. You know what a file is?'

'Yes, sir.'

'And you know what wittles is?'

'Yes, sir.'

After each question he tilted me over a little more, so as to give me a greater sense of helplessness and danger.

'You get me a file.' He tilted me again. 'And you get me wittles.' He tilted me again. 'You bring 'em both to me.' He tilted me again. 'Or I'll have your heart and liver out.' He tilted me again.

I was dreadfully frightened, and so giddy that I clung to him with both hands, and said, 'If you would kindly please to let me keep upright, sir, perhaps I shouldn't be sick, and perhaps I could attend more.'

He gave me a most tremendous dip and roll, so that the church jumped over its own weather-cock. Then, he held me by the arms, in an upright position on the top of the stone, and went on in these fearful terms:

'You bring me, to-morrow morning early, that file and them wittles. You bring the lot to me, at that old Battery over yonder. You do it, and you never dare to say a word or dare to make a sign concerning your having seen such a person as me, or any person sumever, and you shall be let to live. You fail, or you go from my words in any partickler, no matter how small it is, and your heart and your liver shall be tore out, roasted and ate. Now, I ain't alone, as you may think I am. There's a young man hid with me, in comparison with which young man I am a Angel. That young man hears the words I speak. That young man has a secret way pecooliar to himself, of getting at a boy, and at his heart, and at his liver. It is in wain for a boy to attempt to hide himself from that young man. A boy may lock his door, may be warm in bed, may tuck himself up, may draw the clothes over his head, may think himself comfortable and safe, but that young man will softly creep and creep his way to him and tear him open. I am a-keeping that young man from harming of you at the present moment, with great difficulty. I find it wery hard to hold that young man off of your inside. Now, what do you say?'

I said that I would get him the file, and I would get him what broken bits of food I could, and I would come to him at the Battery, early in the morning.

'Say Lord strike you dead if you don't!' said the man.

I said so, and he took me down.

'Now,' he pursued, 'you remember what you've undertook, and you remember that young man, and you get home!'

'Goo-good night, sir,' I faltered.

'Much of that!' said he, glancing about him over the cold wet flat. 'I wish I was a frog. Or a eel!'

At the same time, he hugged his shuddering body in both his arms – clasping himself, as if to hold himself together – and limped towards the low church wall. As I saw him go, picking his way among the nettles, and among the brambles that bound the green mounds, he looked in my young eyes as if he were eluding the hands of the dead people, stretching up cautiously out of their graves, to get a twist upon his ankle and pull him in.

When he came to the low church wall, he got over it, like a man whose legs were numbed and stiff, and then turned round to look for me. When I saw him turning, I set my face towards home, and made the best use of my legs. But presently I looked over my shoulder, and saw him going on again towards the river, still hugging himself in both arms, and picking his way with his sore feet among the great stones dropped into the marshes here and there, for stepping-places when the rains were heavy, or the tide was in.

The marshes were just a long black horizontal line then, as I stopped to look after him; and the river was just another horizontal line, not nearly so broad nor yet so black; and the sky was just a row of long angry red lines and dense black lines intermixed. On the edge of the river I could faintly make out the only two black things in all the prospect that seemed to be standing upright; one of these was the beacon by which the sailors steered – like an unhooped cask upon a pole – an ugly thing when you were near it; the other a gibbet, with some chains hanging to it which had once held a pirate. The man was limping on towards this latter, as if he were the pirate come to life, and come down, and going back to hook himself up again. It gave me a terrible turn when I thought so; and as I saw the cattle lifting their heads to gaze after him, I wondered whether they thought so too. I looked all round for the horrible young man, and could see no signs of him. But, now I was frightened again, and ran home without stopping.

Charles Dickens

Speech, dialogue and thought

Narrative prose very often contains speech, through which the characters communicate with the reader or with other characters. If the character is speaking alone, the speech is known as a **monologue**, but if one or more other characters are involved it becomes a **dialogue**. The thoughts of characters are sometimes treated in the same way as speech, as if the character is 'thinking aloud' in order to convey information to the reader.

Writers adopt a number of approaches to convey the speech of their characters through prose. It is worth remembering, though, that these techniques – which present something spoken and heard in the form of writing to be read – are doing something fundamentally artificial with language. Written speech tends to be very much more conventionalized and ordered than speech in real life. Just compare a transcript of a real conversation with a conversation from a novel to convince yourself of this. The writer's talent, however, lies in convincing the reader of the reality of this artificial dialogue, so that disbelief is suspended.

Direct speech

Direct speech presents the reader with an exact copy of the words spoken. They are enclosed within quotation marks and accompanied by a reporting clause such as *he shouted/ said/ called/ demanded.*

Wuthering Heights

'It is well you are out of my reach,' he exclaimed. 'What fiend possesses you to stare back at me, continually, with those infernal eyes? Down with them! and don't remind me of your existence again. I thought I had cured you of laughing.'

'It was me,' muttered Hareton.

'What did you say?' demanded the master.

Emily Brontë

- -

The use of direct speech gives a prominence and emphasis to the speaker's point of view. It also allows writers to vary spelling, vocabulary, word order and so on in order to give an accurate phonological, lexical and syntactical version to represent a character's accent, dialect or individual manner of speaking.

Indirect speech

Indirect speech presents the material from a slightly different perspective, away from that of the speaker and towards the narrator. For example, if we take the above speech from *Wuthering Heights*, this could be represented in indirect speech in the following way:

He exclaimed that it was well she was out of his reach and asked her what fiend possessed her to stare back at him continually with those infernal eyes. He told her to look down and not to remind him of her existence again and that he thought he had cured her of laughing. Hareton then muttered that it was him.

Activity

Look carefully at the two versions and identify the changes that have taken place.

Check your points against the following:

1 The quotation marks around the speech, which indicate that direct quotation is taking place, have been dropped.

2 A subordinating conjunction – *that* – is used.

3 There is a change from first- and second-person pronouns (*I*, *you*) to third-person (*he*, *she*, *her*).

4 There is a shift in the tense 'backwards' in time (*you are* to *she was*).

Activity

Look at the following extract.

Try re-writing the passage in indirect speech. Make a note of the changes that you need to make to the language in order to convert it. What has changed in your new version? Think about the differences between the two versions.

'Mrs Heathcliff,' I said, earnestly, 'you must excuse me for troubling you. I presume, because, with that face, I'm sure you cannot help being good-hearted. Do point out some landmarks by which I may know my way home: I have no more idea how to get there than you would have how to get to London!'

'Take the road you came,' she answered, ensconcing herself in a chair, with a candle, and the long book open before her. 'It is brief advice, but as sound as I can give.'

'Then, if you hear of me being discovered dead in a bog or a pit full of snow, your conscience won't whisper that it is partly your fault?'

'How so? I cannot escort you. They wouldn't let me go to the end of the garden-wall.'

'*You*! I should be sorry to ask you to cross the threshold, for my convenience, on such a night,' I cried. 'I want you to *tell* me my way, not to *show* it; or else to persuade Mr Heathcliff to give me a guide.'

'Who? There is himself, Earnshaw, Zillah, Joseph, and I. Which would you have?'

'Are there no boys at the farm?'

'No; those are all.'

'Then, it follows that I am compelled to stay.'

'That you may settle with your host. I have nothing to do with it.'

'I hope it will be a lesson to you to make no more rash journeys on these hills,' cried Heathcliff's stern voice from the kitchen entrance. 'As to staying here, I don't keep accommodations for visitors: you must share a bed with Hareton or Joseph, if you do.'

Emily Brontë

Free direct speech

Direct speech has two features which show evidence of the presence of the narrator:

- the quotation marks
- the reporting clause (*she said*, etc.)

In free direct speech the reference to the speaker is not always made. Many writers use this approach when creating speech in their narratives. Here is an example from *Beloved* where Toni Morrison uses only the occasional supporting clause indicating who is speaking.

Patience, something Denver had never known, overtook her. As long as her mother did not interfere, she was a model of compassion, turning waspish, though, when Sethe tried to help.

'Did she take a spoonful of anything today?' Sethe inquired.

'She shouldn't eat with cholera.'

'You sure that's it? Was just a hunch of Paul D's.'

'I don't know, but she shouldn't eat anyway just yet.'

'I think cholera people puke all the time.'

'That's even more reason, ain't it?'

'Well she shouldn't starve to death either, Denvery.'

'Leave us alone, Ma'am. I'm taking care of her.'

Toni Morrison

- -

Sometimes a writer might use a mixture of direct and free direct speech to create an effect. Dickens adopts this technique in *Bleak House*:

'This won't do, gentlemen!' says the Coroner, with a melancholy shake of the head.

'Don't you think you can receive his evidence, sir?' asks an attentive Juryman.

'Out of the question,' says the Coroner. 'You have heard the boy. "Can't exactly say" won't do, you know. We can't take *that*, in a Court of Justice, gentlemen. It's terrible depravity. Put the boy aside.'

Boy put aside; to the great edification of the audience; – especially of Little Swills, the Comic Vocalist.

Now. Is there any other witness? No other witness.

Very well, gentlemen! Here's a man unknown, proved to have been in the habit of taking opium in large quantities for a year and a half, found dead of too much opium. If you think you have any evidence to lead you to the conclusion that he committed suicide, you will come to that conclusion. If you think it is a case of accidental death, you will find a Verdict accordingly.

Verdict accordingly. Accidental death. No doubt. Gentlemen, you are discharged. Good afternoon.

Charles Dickens

Activity

Think about these examples. Why do you think some writers choose to adopt this free direct speech technique? What effect does it have on the narrative?

Here are some possible effects:

- the removal of the distinction between speech and narrative creates the impression that they are inseparable aspects of one unified piece
- Dickens's switch to the free direct form allows him to speed up the usually lengthy concluding processes of the court. This free direct form allows him to focus on the essentials while at the same time retaining the narrative line and the sense of the direct voice.

Occasionally some writers remove the quotation marks entirely. James Joyce, for example, runs speech and narrative together throughout *A Portrait of the Artist as a Young Man*.

Free indirect speech

This is a form of indirect speech in which the main reporting clause (such as *She said that...*) is missed out, but the tense and pronoun selection are those associated with indirect speech. The effect of this is to merge the approach of both direct and indirect speech.

This form of speech is often used in third-person narratives where the third-person narrator presents the speech (or thoughts) of the characters.

Here, the writer, after a straightforward narrative lead-in, goes into free direct and then free indirect speech mode:

In the Conservatory

She scarcely knew Nancy at all, she had gone to the party in place of her husband, Boris, to whom the invitation was addressed. Boris never went to parties of any kind, but that did not stop the invitations coming. And she had gone with this purpose in mind – to meet someone. For she had decided some weeks beforehand that it ought to be her next experience. I am thirty-two years old, she told herself, eight years married and childless, what else is there for me? I am not unattractive, not unintelligent, yet I have never had any sort of an affair, before marriage or since, there is a whole world about which my friends talk and people write, and about which I know nothing. There are emotions, passions, jealousies and anxieties, which I do not understand. It is time, surely it is time...

Perhaps, after all, it was not as clear-cut, as fully conscious as that, perhaps there were many doubts and moments of disillusionment. But the decision was in some sort made, and afterwards, she felt herself to be suddenly more vulnerable, more aware, she was receptive to glances and questions and implications. And then, it was only a question of time.

Susan Hill

Activity

Think about how this form varies from the others you have looked at. In what ways do you think it differs from the others? What particular effects do you think could be achieved through its use?

Here are some points for you to think about.

- Free indirect speech blurs the distinction between a character's speech and the narrative voice.

- It offers a way for writers to present words that seem to come both from inside and outside a character at the same time.

- It can give speech the emotional power of coming from the character's perspective while at the same time preserving some narrative distance or detachment from the character.

- It is often used to convey irony because it allows for the introduction of two points of view – the character's and the narrator's – simultaneously.

The presentation of thoughts

In many ways 'thought' can be considered a kind of 'inner speech', and the categories available to a writer in presenting the thoughts of characters are the same as for the presentation of speech. For example:

a He wondered, 'Is the train on time?' (direct thought)

b Is the train on time? (free direct thought)

c He wondered if the train was on time. (indirect thought)

d Was the train on time? (free indirect thought)

Many narratives use these various methods of telling the reader what is in the minds of characters and many writers, particularly of the nineteenth and twentieth centuries, have experimented with the portrayal of 'internal speech'. One reason for this is the fact that writers have become more and more concerned with ways of presenting vividly the flow of thought through a character's mind. Taken to its extreme this led to the development of what has become known as **stream of consciousness** writing, in which the character's thoughts are poured out in a constant stream, often without punctuation, just as if they were flowing from the character's mind.

Activity

Read the following passage carefully. It is from Jane Gardam's 'Stone Trees' and describes the experiences of a bereaved woman.

1 How does Gardam's use of language here differ from a straightforward description of the scene?

2 What details do you gather from the text that a straightforward description of the scene would not have given you?

3 What details are missed out that a straightforward description would have given you?

4 What effects do you think Gardam wanted to create here?

Stone Trees

The boat crosses. Has crossed. Already. Criss-cross deck. Criss-cross water. Splashy sea and look –! Lovely clouds flying (now that you are dead) and here's the pier. A long, long pier into the sea and gulls shouting and children yelling here and there and here's my ticket and there they stand. All in a row – Tom, Anna, the two children solemn. And smiles now – Tom and Anna. Tom and Anna look too large to be quite true. Too good. Anna who never did anything wrong. Arms stretch too far forward for a simple day.

They stretch because they want. They would not stretch to me if you were obvious and not just dead. Then it would have been, hullo, easy crossing? Good. Wonderful day. Let's get back and down on the beach. Great to see you both.

So now that you are dead –

We paced last week. Three.

Tom. Anna. I.

And other black figures wood-faced outside the crematorium in blazing sun, examining shiny black-edged tickets on blazing bouquets. 'How good of Marjorie – fancy old Marjorie. I didn't even know she –' There was that woman who ran out of the so-called service with handkerchief at her eyes. But who was there except you my darling and I and the Robertsons and the shiny cards and did they do it then? Were they doing it then as we read the flowers? Do they do it at once or stack it up with other coffins and was it still inside waiting as I paced with portly Tom? Christian Tom – Tom we laughed at so often and oh my darling now that you are dead –

Jane Gardam

- -

Overall, we can summarize the presentation of speech and thought in the following points:

- speech presentation is more than a mere technical feature
- different modes present different viewpoints and different relationships with the narrator
- each variation has a different effect, allowing the character to speak as if in his or her 'own words' or filtering them through the perspective of the narrator
- different kinds of interplay between the voice of the narrator and the speech of a character are closely connected to the idea of point of view.

Grammar

In narrative prose, the grammar will reflect the kind of world the writer creates and the viewpoint adopted. Analysing the grammar of a text can be useful in establishing how the text works. The writer of narrative prose has a good deal of scope as non-standard grammar and lexis are acceptable.

In examining a piece of prose, look out for the following grammatical features.

- **Tense** – most narrative is written in the simple past tense but other tenses are sometimes used to create different effects.
- **Mood** can be reflected through the use of grammar – the declarative mood is the most common, but the use of imperatives and interrogatives can influence the pace and change the focus.
- **Sentence structure** (syntax) can also be used to achieve different effects. Simple sentences are often used to give emphasis, while more complex structures can create various effects. Most writers tend to vary their sentence structure to help give the reader variety and therefore sustain interest.

Syntax

Syntax simply means sentence structure. Basically, the term 'sentence' can be applied to any group of words that makes complete sense, and the usual visual markers of the sentence are a capital letter at the beginning and a full stop at the end. In spoken language a meaningful utterance may not seem to be a sentence, but could be easily understood. In fact, if you look at a transcript of spontaneous speech you will find few complete sentences in the grammatical sense, although meaning may be communicated perfectly effectively. For example, in response to the question 'What are you doing?' the answer could be 'Going out.' This is perfectly acceptable. The context enables us to supply the missing parts, and so it is unnecessary to say 'I am going out.' However, in many ways the rules for written and spoken language are different. In grammatical terms, a complete sentence must have two things:

a a **subject** – the person or thing the sentence is about

b a **predicate** – describing what the subject is doing.

In some sentences the predicate may consist of a verb only, as in 'James runs'. Or there may be an additional element known as the **adjunct**. This could be an adverb (or modifier) as in 'James runs quickly' or a noun phrase, 'James runs to the house'. All subjects will include a noun or pronoun – 'James' or 'he' – or they can be lengthened by **determiners** (*a*, *the*, *that*, etc.), adjectives (modifiers), and so on.

Sentences can be divided into three basic kinds:

1 Simple sentences have one main clause (one subject and one verb).

2 Compound sentences have two (or more) main clauses, i.e. two subjects and two verbs which are linked by co-ordinating words or conjunctions (*and*, *but*, *or*, *nor*, *either*, *neither*).

3 Complex sentences, like compound sentences, consist of two or more clauses, but these are linked together by subordination using words such as *because*, *when*, *although*. This kind of sentence is the most complicated and in prose usually signals a fairly sophisticated style.

In analysing a writer's stylistic technique, however, it is of no use to simply be able to recognize whether he or she uses simple, compound or complex sentences. The real questions are 'What purpose do the sentences serve?' and 'What effect do they have on the piece of writing concerned?'

In answer to this first question, a sentence may perform various **functions**.

For example:

- **Declarative** sentences state things (make statements, if you prefer).
- **Interrogative** sentences ask questions.
- **Imperative** sentences issue commands.
- **Exclamatory** sentences always end with an exclamation mark and contain exclamations.

When analysing prose it is important to be able to say something about the syntax, but it is not sufficient to simply say things like 'this piece uses long and short sentences' or 'a lot of hard sentences are used here'. You need to be able to recognize why the writer has chosen to use particular sentence structures, and what effect they have on the tone, mood and impact of the writing overall.

Here are some general pointers:

- **Declarative** sentences could be used to create a sense of drama.
- **Interrogative** sentences may produce a questioning, probing effect in the prose.
- **Imperative** sentences could be used to create an attacking, critical or off-hand effect.
- **Exclamatory** sentences could heighten drama, express shock or communicate surprise.
- Short, **simple** sentences could be used to give the sense of action speeding up, or a sense of breathlessness.
- Longer, **compound** sentences could produce a slowing effect on the narrative.
- **Complex** sentences might create a contemplative, philosophical mood.

Remember that these are just some examples of the effects different sentence types can create. In reality, each type of sentence can create a whole variety of different effects, so to determine exactly what effects the syntax has on a piece of prose you must assess it within the context of the individual piece you are examining.

Literal and non-literal language

A piece of writing has potentially two different sorts of meaning:

a a literal meaning

b a non-literal or implied meaning.

Literal meaning is a meaning that is fixed for a particular word or group of words. Many groups of words, however, also have a non-literal meaning or an implied meaning.

Literary devices that are used to create particular effects through non-literal meaning are known collectively as **figurative language**, and include **metaphors**, **similes** and **symbolism**.

Activity

Read the following extract from *Hard Times* by Charles Dickens, describing Mr Bounderby. Discuss Dickens's use of non-literal language here, explaining what it contributes to the effect of the description.

Hard Times

Why, Mr Bounderby was as near being Mr Gradgind's bosom friend, as a man perfectly devoid of sentiment can approach that spiritual relationship towards another man perfectly devoid of sentiment. So near was Mr Bounderby – or, if the reader should prefer it, so far off.

He was a rich man: banker, merchant, manufacturer, and what not. A big, loud man, with a stare and a metallic laugh. A man made out of a coarse material, which seemed to have been stretched to make so much of him. A man with a great puffed head and forehead, swelled veins in his temples, and such a strained skin to his face that it seemed to hold his eyes open and lift his eyebrows up. A man with a pervading appearance on him of being inflated like a balloon, and ready to start. A man who could never sufficiently vaunt himself a self-made man. A man who was always proclaiming, through that brassy speaking-trumpet of a voice of his, his old ignorance and his old poverty. A man who was the Bully of humility.

A year or two younger than his eminently practical friend, Mr Bounderby looked older; his seven or eight and forty might have had the seven or eight added to it again, without surprising anybody. He had not much hair. One might have fancied he had talked it off; and that what was left, all standing up in disorder, was in that condition from being constantly blown about by his windy boastfulness.

Charles Dickens

Rhetorical techniques

Writers can also make use of rhetoric in their writing, to persuade readers and shape their responses in various ways. Various rhetorical devices can be used, and an examination of a particular writer's stylistic techniques should take account of these. The rhetorical techniques of planned speech, which are very similar to those used in writing, are discussed in Chapter 5. Here are some of the features you should watch out for:

- repetition, of sounds, words, sentence structures, etc.
- juxtaposition
- listing
- parallelism
- hyperbole
- the rhetorical question.

Cohesion

Structure is given to prose by cohesion. In most texts there is some kind of connection, in terms of ideas expressed or actions described, which holds the piece of writing together. The sentences normally link together in a structured way to convey the meaning of a piece of writing to the reader. This structure is called **cohesion** or **coherence**.

Writers can create coherence in their texts in different ways in order to create particular effects. Understanding how a writer creates coherence can help you to understand more fully the effects created through the writing.

Normally some of the 'connectedness' of a text comes from the topic or subject matter of the piece of writing. This prompts a key question: 'How do you know what a text is about?' In some cases the answer to this may be obvious – you understand what a text is about because of the knowledge you already possess about the topic it deals with, and the words used relate to that topic. For example, if we note in the lexis of a piece that words like *surgery*, *doctor*, *nurse*, *scalpel*, *stretcher*, and *ward* are used, it is likely that the piece is in some way connected to a hospital or medical situation. These are **collocations** of words – clusters of words that may occur in texts of a similar kind. Words that are generally less common, such as specialist or technical terms, tend to suggest more specialized contexts. Collocations are sometimes referred to as **semantic fields**, and through the use of vocabulary related to particular 'fields', the subject matter is reflected in the patterns of words it is made up of.

Besides subject matter and vocabulary, there are other forms of connections between sentences. They can indicate relations of sequence, such as **causality** (one thing leads to another), **exemplification** (giving an example), **implication** (suggesting something) and so on. Sometimes particular words signal connections between sentences and therefore cohesion in a text. Such markers can be of various kinds.

- Words and phrases co-refer in that they refer to people, situations, or things already mentioned. **Pronouns** such as *he, she, they, it* refer back to people or things already introduced.
- Words like *the, this*, etc. refer back to earlier mentions of things.
- Verbs that have already been used are repeated in condensed, or substitute forms, e.g. *She thought she might be late. If so* [be late] *she would have to get a taxi.*
- Connective words and phrases primarily signal directions, e.g.

  consequence: *therefore, because of this*
  ordering: *firstly, finally*
  continuation: *furthermore, then*
  simultaneity: *meanwhile, in the meantime*
  concession: *admittedly, yet*
  opposition: *nevertheless, in spite of this.*

Taken together, these various elements create what is often known as the texture of a text – presenting it as a unified and connected whole rather than as a random selection of sentences.

Activity

Examine the following passage and make notes on the writer's use of syntax and the ways in which language give a sense of coherence and texture to the piece.

Notes from a Small Island

I rose early the next day and attended to my morning hygiene in a state of small excitation because I had a big day ahead of me. I was going to walk across Windsor Great Park. It is the most splendid park I know. It stretches over 40 enchanted square miles and incorporates into its ancient fabric every manner of sylvan charm: deep primeval woodlands, bosky dells, wandering footpaths and bridleways, formal and informal gardens and a long, deeply fetching lake. Scattered picturesquely about are farms, woodland cottages, forgotten statues, a whole village occupied by estate workers and things that the Queen has brought back from trips abroad and couldn't think of anywhere else to put – obelisks and totem poles and other curious expressions of gratitude from distant outposts of the Commonwealth.

The news had not yet come out there was oil under the park and that it all soon might turn into a new Sullom Voe (but don't be alarmed; the local authority will make them screen the derricks with shrubs), so I didn't realize that I ought to drink things in carefully in case the next time I came this way it looked like an Oklahoma oilfield. At this time, Windsor Great Park continued to enjoy a merciful obscurity, which I find mystifying in an open space so glorious on the very edge of London. Only once could I remember any reference to the park in the newspapers, a couple of years before when Prince Philip had taken a curious disliking to an avenue of ancient trees and had instructed Her Majesty's Tree-Choppers to remove them from the landscape.

I expect their branches had imperilled the progress through the park of his horses and plus-four, or whatever it is you call those creaking contraptions he so likes to roam around in. You often see him and other members of the royal family in the park, speeding past in assorted vehicles on their way to polo matches or church services in the Queen Mother's private compound, the Royal Lodge. Indeed, because the public aren't allowed to drive on the park roads, a significant portion of the little traffic that passes is generated by royals. Once, on Boxing Day when I was ambling along in a paternal fashion beside an offspring on a shiny new tricycle, I became aware with a kind of sixth sense that we were holding up the progress of a car and turned to find that it was being driven by Princess Diana. As I hastened myself and my child out of the way, she gave me a smile that melted my heart, and since that time I have never said a word against the dear sweet girl, however pressed by those who think that she is a bit off her head because she spends £28,000 a year on leotards and makes occasional crank phone calls to hunky military men. (And who among us hasn't? is my unanswerable reply.)

Bill Bryson

Authorial intentions

In your examination of narrative prose it is important that you are able to identify what the writer is trying to achieve at various points in the narrative. Authorial intention can take various forms, but here are some possible kinds:

- creating characters
- describing or presenting a scene
- creating a particular mood or atmosphere
- experimenting with language.

Creating characters

We have already looked at ways in which writers can use first- or third-person narrative to reveal character. In both these types of narrative, other linguistic and stylistic techniques also have a part to play in the creation of the overall effect.

The most obvious way a character can be created is through physical description. In analysing such description, it is important to establish from the outset whose view is being given, the writer's, another character's, or the narrator's, in order to make some assessment of its reliability.

Activity

Read this description carefully. It is from *Great Expectations* and describes Pip's first meeting with Miss Havisham.

How does Dickens use language to make his description of character effective here? You should pay particular attention to his use of nouns and modifiers, syntax, the connotations of the lexis and any symbolic value you might find in the physical details listed.

Great Expectations

She was dressed in rich materials – satins, and lace, and silks – all of white. Her shoes were white. And she had a long white veil dependent from her hair, and she had bridal flowers in her hair, but her hair was white. Some bright jewels sparkled on her neck and on her hands, and some other jewels lay sparkling on the table. Dresses, less splendid than the dress she wore, and half-packed trunks, were scattered about. She had not quite finished dressing, for she had but one shoe on – the other was on the table near her hand – her veil was but half arranged, her watch and chain were not put on, and some lace for her bosom lay with those trinkets, and with her handkerchief, and gloves, and some flowers, and a Prayer-book, all confusedly heaped about the looking-glass.

It was not in the first few moments that I saw all these things, though I saw more of them in the first moments than might be supposed. But, I saw that everything within my view which ought to be white, had been white long ago, and had lost its lustre, and was faded and yellow. I saw that the bride within the bridal dress had withered like the dress, and like the flowers, and had no brightness left but the brightness of her sunken eyes. I saw that the dress had been put upon the rounded figure of a young woman, and that the figure upon which it now hung loose, had shrunk to skin and bone. Once, I had been taken to see some ghastly waxwork at the Fair, representing I know not what impossible personage lying in state. Once, I had been taken to one of our old marsh churches to see a skeleton in the ashes of a rich dress, that had been dug out of a vault under the church pavement. Now, waxwork and skeleton seemed to have dark eyes that moved and looked at me. I should have cried out, if I could.

Charles Dickens

Describing or presenting scenes

Scene setting is obviously very important to narrative prose if the writer wants to convince the reader of the fictional world created. Physical details of time and place can help to enable the reader to visualize the background against which the action takes place. Although separate from atmosphere, the setting could be closely linked to the atmosphere and mood the writer wishes to create.

Activity

Read the following extract carefully. it is from *Great Expectations* and describes Pip taking a boat down the Thames in an attempt to help Magwitch escape.

How does Dickens use language to make his description of the scene effective here? Make a note of specific details of language you find particularly effective and say why.

Great Expectations

The air felt cold upon the river, but it was a bright day, and the sunshine was very cheering. The tide ran strong, I took care to lose none of it, and our steady stroke carried us on thoroughly well. By imperceptible degrees, as the tide ran out, we lost more and more of the nearer woods and hills, and dropped lower and lower between the muddy banks, but the tide was yet with us when we were off Gravesend. As our charge was wrapped in his cloak, I purposely passed within a boat or two's length of the floating Custom House, and so out to catch the stream, alongside of two emigrant ships, and under the bows of a large transport with troops on the forecastle looking down at us. And soon the tide began to slacken, and the craft lying at anchor to swing, and presently they had all swung round, and the ships that were taking advantage of the new tide to get up to the Pool, began to crowd upon us in a fleet, and we kept under the shore, as much out of the strength of the tide now as we could, standing carefully off from low shallows and mud-banks.

Charles Dickens

Creating a mood or atmosphere

The creation of different atmospheres can be very important to the overall impact of a novel. If readers are to be convinced of the fictional world created it is important that the writer successfully arouses the reader's emotions. By creating various atmospheres and moods the writer can persuade the reader to feel things in certain ways, perhaps evoking a sympathy for one of the characters or anger at a particular situation, for example.

> ### Activity
>
> Read the following extract carefully and analyse the techniques the writer uses to set the scene and evoke atmosphere. You should pay particular attention to the following: the ways in which the writer conveys a feeling of the place; the effects of such features of language as lexical, grammatical and phonological aspects.

Hard Times

Coketown, to which Messrs Bounderby and Gradgrind now walked, was a triumph of fact; it had no greater taint of fancy in it than Mrs Gradgrind herself. Let us strike the key-note, Coketown, before pursuing our tune.

It was a town of red brick, or of brick that would have been red if the smoke and ashes had allowed it; but, as matters stood it was a town of unnatural red and black like the painted face of a savage. It was a town of machinery and tall chimneys, out of which interminable serpents of smoke trailed themselves for ever and ever, and never got uncoiled. It had a black canal in it, and a river that ran purple with ill-smelling dye, and vast piles of buildings full of windows where there was a rattling and a trembling all day long, and where the piston of the steam-engine worked monotonously up and down, like the head of an elephant in a state of melancholy madness.

It contained several large streets all very like one another, and many small streets still more like one another, inhabited by people equally like one another, who all went in and out at the same hours, with the same sound upon the same pavements, to do the same work, and to whom every day was the same as yesterday and tomorrow, and every year the counterpart of the last and the next.

These attributes of Coketown were in the main inseparable from the work by which it was sustained; against them were to be set off, comforts of life which found their way all over the world, and elegancies of life which made, we will not ask how much of the fine lady, who could scarcely bear to hear the place mentioned. The rest of its features were voluntary, and they were these.

You saw nothing in Coketown but what was severely workful. If the members of a religious persuasion built a chapel there – they made it a pious warehouse of red brick, with sometimes (but this only in highly ornamented examples) a bell in a bird-cage on the top of it. The solitary exception was the New Church; a stuccoed edifice with a square steeple over the door, terminating in four short pinnacles like florid wooden legs. All the public inscriptions in the town were painted alike, in severe characters of black and white. The jail might have been the infirmary, the infirmary might have been the jail, the town-hall might have been either, or both, or anything else, for anything that appeared to the contrary in the graces of their construction.

Charles Dickens

Experimenting with language

Writers often experiment with non-standard language in order to intensify a particular aspect or aspects of the fictional world that they have created. By using variations of language for different characters, the writer can make them seem more realistic and individual and can place them more specifically in a time or place. Often this is a technique that can be seen in the writer's use of dialogue, reflecting the accents and dialects of characters.

Activity

Read the following extract. How does Walker use language here to achieve her effects? What is the impact of this non-standard use of language?

The Color Purple

Dear God,

Harpo ast his daddy why he beat me. Mr _____ say,

Cause she my wife. Plus, she stubborn. All women good for – he don't finish. He just tuck his chin over the paper like he do. Remind me of Pa.

Harpo ast me, How come you stubborn? He don't ast How come you his wife? Nobody ast that.

I say, Just born that way, I reckon.

He beat me like he beat the children. Cept he don't never hardly beat them. He say, Celie, git the belt. The children be outside the room peeking through the cracks. It all I can do not to cry. I make myself wood. I say to myself, Celie, you a tree. That's how come I know trees fear man.

Harpo say, I love Somebody.

I say, Huh?

He say, A Girl.

I say, You do?

He say, Yeah. Us plan to marry.

Marry, I say. You not old enough to marry.

I is, he say. I'm seventeen. She fifteen. Old enough.

What her mama say, I ast.

Ain't talk to her mama.

What her daddy say?

Ain't talk to him neither.

Well, what she say?

Us ain't never spoke. He duck his head. He ain't so bad looking. Tall and skinny, black like his mama, with great big bug eyes.

Where yall see each other? I ast. I see her in church, he say. She see me outdoors.

She like you?

I don't know. I wink at her. She act like she scared to look.

Where her daddy at while all this going on?

Amen corner, he say.

Alice Walker

So far in this chapter we have suggested some aspects of language present in prose writing and you have looked at some examples of these features in the extracts you have worked on. However, the question is how this will help you in the analysis of the texts you have studied. Merely being able to identify features of language is meaningless unless you link it to a wider explanation of the **purpose** for using language in a particular kind of way to create specific **effects**.

In order to approach an examination question, it can be useful to have a checklist of features of language that you could look for in the piece of writing in order to analyse its purpose and effects.

Checklist of language features of prose

This may help you to identify key features, but be aware that not every example of prose will contain all these features.

- **Point of view**
  First-person narrative
  Third-person narrative
  Narrative voice

- **Register**
  Mode
  Manner
  Field

- **Lexis**
  Nouns
  Verbs
  Modifiers

- **Speech, dialogue and thought**
  Direct speech
  Indirect speech
  Free direct speech
  Free indirect speech
  The presentation of thoughts

- **Grammar**
  Tense
  Mood
  Sentence structure

- **Syntax**
  Sentence types
  Effects

- **Literal and non-literal language**
  Metaphor
  Simile
  Symbolism

- **Rhetorical features**
  Repetition
  Juxtaposition
  Listing
  Parallelism
  Hyperbole
  Rhetorical questions

- **Coherence and cohesion**

- **Authorial intention**
  To characterize
  To set the scene
  To evoke atmosphere
  To experiment with language

Examination-style questions

In your AS course the questions on prose texts can take several forms. Here are some examples.

Unit 1

In this unit you will study two texts. You do not have to study a prose text for this unit but if you do you could study either one or two prose texts. (It is likely, if you are studying in a school or college, that the texts you study will depend on the choices made by your teacher or lecturer.) In this unit you will answer two questions – **one** analytical question (Question A) and **one** production question (Question B) on different texts.

Here are some examples of questions in Question A style and Question B style. You are advised to spend 40 minutes on the analytical question (A) and 50 minutes on the production question (B).

You can take the texts into the exam with you.

These questions will test the following Assessment Objectives:

AO1   Select and apply relevant concepts and approaches from integrated linguistic and literary study, using appropriate terminology and accurate, coherent written expression.

AO2   Demonstrate detailed critical understanding in analysing the ways in which structure, form and language shape meanings in a range of spoken and written texts.

AO4   Demonstrate expertise and creativity in using language appropriately for a variety of purposes and audiences, drawing on insights from linguistic and literary studies.

Things Fall Apart – Chinua Achebe

Either

A   How does Achebe portray Ezinma's relationship with Okonkwo?

In your answer you should consider:

- Achebe's language choices
- narrative viewpoint

Or

B   In Chapter 4 Okonkwo breaks the peace of the sacred Peace Week by beating his youngest wife, Ojiugo. Write about Okonkwo's feelings at this point and afterwards from his point of view.

You should give careful consideration to your language choices and style, and create a sense of Okonkwo's voice.

Wuthering Heights – Emily Brontë

Either

A   How does Brontë portray Ellen Dean's relationship with Catherine during the course of the novel?

In your answer you should consider:

- Brontë's language choices
- narrative viewpoint

Or

B   Imagine that Edgar Linton keeps a diary and in it he records his thoughts and feelings during the days of Catherine's illness and death. Write his diary entries during this period revealing his inner thoughts at this time.

You should give careful consideration to your language choices and style, which should achieve a sense of Edgar's voice.

The Kite Runner – Khaled Hosseini

Either

A   How does Hosseini portray the relationship between Amir and Hassan?

In your answer you should consider:

- Hosseini's language choices
- narrative viewpoint

Or

B   In Chapter 7 Hosseini describes the attack on Hassan in the alleyway. Write about Amir's feelings at this point and afterwards, from his point of view.

Unit 2

The prose option question in Section B of Unit 2 is completely different in format from that of Unit 1. On this paper you will be given an extract from the text you have studied and you will be asked to analyse some aspect of the dialogue and other narrative techniques in the extract printed on the examination paper and **one** other episode in the text.

Here is an example of a question on a prose set text for Unit 2.

You may not take the text you have studied for this unit into the exam.

You are recommended to spend 40 minutes on this question.

These questions will test the following Assessment Objectives:

AO1   Select and apply relevant concepts and approaches from integrated linguistic and literary study, using appropriate terminology and accurate, coherent written expression.

AO2   Demonstrate detailed critical understanding in analysing the ways in which structure, form and language shape meanings in a range of spoken and written texts.

Great Expectations – Charles Dickens

How does Dickens use dialogue and other stylistic techniques to reveal Joe's character?

In your answer you should refer closely to the extract printed below and to **one** other episode in the novel.

One Sunday when Joe, greatly enjoying his pipe, had so plumed himself on being 'most awful dull,' that I had given him up for the day, I lay on the earthwork for some time with my chin on my hand, descrying traces of Miss Havisham and Estella all over the prospect, in the sky and in the water, until at last I resolved to mention a thought concerning them that had been much in my head.

'Joe,' said I; 'don't you think I ought to make Miss Havisham a visit?'

'Well, Pip,' returned Joe, slowly considering. 'What for?'

'What for, Joe? What is any visit made for?'

'There is some wisits, p'r'aps,' said Joe, 'as for ever remains open to the question, Pip. But in regard of wisiting Miss Havisham. She might think you wanted something – expected something of her.'

'Don't you think I might say that I did not, Joe?'

'You might, old chap,' said Joe. 'And she might credit it. Similarly she mightn't.'

Joe felt, as I did, that he had made a point there, and he pulled hard at his pipe to keep himself from weakening it by repetition.

'You see, Pip,' Joe pursued, as soon as he was past that danger, 'Miss Havisham done the handsome thing by you. When Miss Havisham done the handsome thing by you, she called me back to say to me as that were all.'

'Yes, Joe. I heard her.'

'ALL,' Joe repeated, very emphatically.

'Yes, Joe. I tell you, I heard her.'

'Which I meantersay, Pip, it might be that her meaning were – Make a end on it! – As you was! – Me to the North, and you to the South! – Keep in sunders!'

I had thought of that too, and it was very far from comforting to me to find that he had thought of it; for it seemed to render it more probable.

'But, Joe.'

'Yes, old chap.'

'Here am I, getting on in the first year of my time, and, since the day of my being bound, I have never thanked Miss Havisham, or asked after her, or shown that I remember her.'

'That's true, Pip; and unless you was to turn her out a set of shoes all four round – and which I meantersay as even a set of shoes all four round might not act acceptable as a present, in a total wacancy of hoofs –'

'I don't mean that sort of remembrance, Joe; I don't mean a present.'

But Joe had got the idea of a present in his head and must harp upon it. 'Or even,' said he, 'if you was helped to knocking her up a new chain for the front door – or say a gross or two of shark-headed screws for general use – or some light fancy article, such as a toasting-fork when she took her muffins – or a gridiron when she took a sprat or such like –'

'I don't mean any present at all, Joe,' I interposed.

'Well,' said Joe, still harping on it as though I had particularly pressed it, 'if I was yourself, Pip, I wouldn't. No, I would *not*. For what's a door-chain when she's got one always up? And shark-headers is open to misrepresentations. And if it was a toasting-fork, you'd go into brass and do yourself no credit. And the oncommonest workman can't show himself oncommon in a gridiron – for a gridiron IS a gridiron,' said Joe, steadfastly impressing it upon me, as if he were endeavouring to rouse me from a fixed delusion, 'and you may haim at what you like, but a gridiron it will come out, either by your leave or again your leave, and you can't help yourself –'

'My dear Joe,' I cried in desperation, taking hold of his coat, 'don't go on in that way. I never thought of making Miss Havisham any present.'

'No, Pip,' Joe assented, as if he had been contending for that, all along; 'and what I say to you is, you are right, Pip.'

'Yes, Joe; but what I wanted to say, was, that as we are rather slack just now, if you would give me a half-holiday to-morrow, I think I would go up-town and make a call on Miss Est – Havisham.'

'Which her name,' said Joe, gravely, 'ain't Estavisham, Pip, unless she have been rechris'ened.'

'I know, Joe, I know. It was a slip of mine. What do you think of it, Joe?'

In brief, Joe thought that if I thought well of it, he thought well of it. But he was particular in stipulating that if I were not received with cordiality, or if I were not encouraged to repeat my visit as a visit which had no ulterior object but was simply one of gratitude for a favour received, then this experimental trip should have no successor.

– –

4 Analysing Drama

In the course you are studying you may encounter drama texts in Unit 1, Integrated Analysis and Text Production; Unit 2, Analysing Speech and its Representation; and possibly as part of the Comparative Analysis section of Unit 3. Also, you may write about a drama text in Unit 4 for the comparative coursework, should you choose the drama option for your second text.

In this chapter we will focus on the ways in which language is used in drama texts and the interrelationship between that language and the effects created on the audience. In looking at the language of drama, both linguistic and literary issues will be examined, and the aim of your studies will be to develop a full understanding of the ways in which dramatists use language in their plays to create a whole range of effects, which in turn provoke responses in the audience.

The nature of drama

Drama is different from other forms of literature that you have studied in a number of respects. One key difference is that by its very nature drama focuses on the spoken word rather than the written word. Sometimes we lose sight of this, because very often in studying drama for examination purposes the focus is on the written text of a play rather than the spoken performance of it. It is important, even when sitting at a desk with only the written text in front of you, that you consider the 'performance' aspect of drama. In many respects a play can be fully appreciated only when seen in performance, and this is why it is so important to try to see a live performance of the play or plays you are studying. If you cannot see the play on the stage, try to get hold of a video or film performance of it. Sometimes it is impossible to see any kind of performance of a play, in which case you will need to rely on your own imagination to re-create a performance of the play inside your head.

Another difference between drama and other literary forms is the fact that drama relies upon certain conventions – it has distinct rules of structure, format and presentation. We will look at these conventions in more detail a little later.

As a drama text presents the core for a 'performance', it is often a more 'public' form of literary communication than other forms. As such, its audience is a particularly important element. When seen live on stage, the experience of a performance is a shared activity and there is a direct relationship between the way the dramatist writes, the way that this is put into performance, and the response of the audience.

If a dramatist's work is to survive, his or her works must be performed, and therefore the expectations of the audience need to be taken into account. Sometimes, when presented with something that doesn't meet their expectations, audiences can make their feelings felt and this can lead the dramatist to make alterations to the text. For example, when *The Rivals* was first performed the audience response to it was so hostile that Sheridan withdrew it after the first night and substantially re-wrote a large proportion of it.

Shakespeare often deliberately includes things in his plays that he knows will appeal to and gain the approval of his audience. Although a dramatist does write about and explore themes and ideas that he or she is interested in and wants to present to the audience, no dramatist can afford to lose sight of the audience being written for and the fact that plays must contain some appeal for that audience.

Activity

Think about a dramatization (stage play, video, film or television) of a novel you have read. Write about the strengths and weaknesses of the dramatization. If you had been the producer, how would you have made your dramatization different?

Now think about plays that you have read and those that you have seen. What do you feel are the main advantages to be gained from:

- seeing a play in performance
- reading a play on your own or as part of a group?

Features of drama

Conflict

At the centre of all drama is a sense of conflict, in one form or another. This could consist of conflict in the conventional sense where characters fight one another. Equally, conflict could be between individual characters and their ideals or values. The conflict could stem from within a character, perhaps torn between certain courses of action, or it could be spiritual or moral in nature. Whatever form it takes, this conflict will be ever present throughout the play and form the basis for sustaining the dramatic tension and the interest of the audience.

Of course this is explored and exploited in different ways by different dramatists. In *Othello*, for example, we see the emotional conflicts set up within Othello himself by Iago sowing the seeds of jealousy in his mind. A more subtle use of conflict can be found in the comedy *As You Like It*, in the opposition between court and countryside. In a more modern drama such as *Murmuring Judges*, conflicts operate in different ways. We have the conflict of views about the role of the barrister as represented by the attitudes of Irina and Sir Peter, or the conflict of views on the right way of policing as seen through the characters of Sandra and Barry, for example.

Activity

Think about any plays that you have studied in the past or are currently studying. Draw up a table for each of them showing what conflicts occur within each drama and how important each is to the overall effects of the play.

Realism

The question of realism is one that is often raised in relation to drama, and it has provoked much debate. One view of realism in drama is that put forward by the poet and philosopher Samuel Taylor Coleridge, who felt that in watching a play the audience are prepared to 'willingly suspend disbelief' and believe in the reality of the characters and the action they see before them on the stage. Some drama does work like this, and in the 1950s a whole style of drama, including plays such as *Look Back in Anger* by John Osborne, became known as 'kitchen sink dramas' because of their portrayals of 'real life' in the colloquial language of everyday speech.

It's quite clear, though, that not all drama sets out to be 'realistic' in that sense and some dramatists deliberately present a different picture from the world we know. In Shakespeare's *Hamlet*, for example, the starting point for the action is the appearance of a ghost, and in *The Tempest* Prospero deals in magic, and spirits of the air do his bidding. In the plays of Samuel Beckett all kinds of strange things happen, such as in *Endgame* where the characters live in dustbins, or *Waiting for Godot* where two men wait for a character they know nothing about and who never comes.

In reconciling these apparent opposites we come to the understanding that there are two kinds of realism – one is the surface or physical realism where the characters, the things they say and do, the language they use and so on are immediately recognizable as representing 'real life'. The other kind of realism is psychological realism, in which the dramatist focuses on the feelings, thoughts, emotions, fears, inner desires and life of the characters. Both kinds of drama, or varying degrees of each, are open to the dramatist depending on the effect and appeal to the audience he or she wishes to create.

The theatre

One final consideration when studying a play, as opposed to other kinds of literature, is the fact that, as we have said, a play is meant to be seen on the stage. The dramatist will have given thought to the mechanics of performing the play in the theatre. Some dramatists give little guidance in this respect, while others give detailed stage directions to do with things like the set and lighting. These features are integral to the play and are generally designed to enhance the performance, the visual effect or the impact of the spoken language of the play. The spoken language of the play is still the heart of the drama but you need to be aware of how it interrelates with the other elements of drama that bring language to life.

Plot and structure

The plot is obviously of central importance to most plays, although there are certain kinds of plays (those of Samuel Beckett, for example) where the lack of a conventional plot is essential for the overall effect of the drama. However, in much of the drama you have encountered you will probably have found that the plot is a key element. The plot, however, is much more than simply the 'story' of the play. The way plot develops is an essential part of the way a play is put together – in other words, its structure. From a dramatist's point of view this structure is something that needs careful thought and planning, because ultimately it can have a bearing on whether the play is a successful one or not.

Activity

From an audience's point of view, what features do you think a successful play should have in terms of plot?

Here are some points you might have thought about. An effective plot should:

- capture the audience's interest and attention right from the start
- maintain the interest of the audience from beginning to end
- move the action on from one episode to the next
- arouse the interest of the audience in character and situation
- create high points or moments of crisis at intervals
- create expectation and surprise.

Generally speaking, if a play contains most or all of these features, it is likely to be well received by an audience.

In studying plays you will see that most of them follow a particular pattern in the way that they are structured, and it is possible to identify the following key elements.

1 **Exposition:** This opens the play, often introduces the main characters and provides background information.

2 **Dramatic incitement:** This is an incident that provides the starting point for the main action of the play.

3 **Complication:** This usually forms the main action of the play – the characters respond to the dramatic incitement and other developments that stem from it.

4 **Crisis:** This constitutes the climax of the play.

5 **Resolution:** This is the final section of the play, where things are worked out and some kind of conclusion is arrived at.

Activity

Examine the structure of a play you are studying. Draw a diagram to represent the way the action of the play develops and the way it fits into this pattern. Make a note of the 'key moments' in the development of the plot.

This is how the above pattern applies to Shakespeare's *As You Like It*.

1 **Exposition:** The play begins with the audience being given the information that a good duke has been usurped by his ruthless brother, Frederick, and has taken to the forest with a few faithful courtiers. There they live simply but happily. Rosalind, the good duke's daughter, has stayed behind at court to be with her friend and cousin, Celia, who is Frederick's daughter.

2 **Dramatic incitement:** Rosalind displeases Frederick, who banishes her from court.

3 **Complication:** Rosalind disguises herself as a boy and leaves to search for her father, taking with her Celia and the court jester, Touchstone. Another character, Orlando, leaves to seek his brother, Oliver, who has withheld his inheritance and treats him cruelly. Various complications ensue.

4 **Crisis:** Rosalind realizes she must find a way to reveal her true self to Orlando.

5 **Resolution:** All the exiles meet together and the love affairs are happily resolved. Duke Frederick resigns his usurped position and everyone gets what is rightfully theirs.

The language of drama

The type of language used in a play – formal, serious, colloquial, slang, and so on – will depend on the kind of effects that the dramatist wants to achieve, and the functions language is to perform. For example, we can learn about characters through their language, or language can add colour to a scene, create atmosphere, and alter the tone and mood of a play.

Dialogue

The most obvious way in which dramatists use language in their plays is in dialogue, through which the characters convey information and interact with each other. There are dialogues of all kinds in plays and the language the dramatist uses will be chosen carefully to reflect the tone, atmosphere and content of the particular scene. Dialogue is a verbal exchange between two or more characters but it can take many forms – for example, it could present the tender exchange of love between two characters, it could involve characters plotting an evil deed together or it could be an argument.

Read the following extracts carefully. Extract 1 is from *The Rivals* by Richard Sheridan. The servant, Fag, talks to Captain Absolute about meeting the officer's father in Bath. Extract 2 is from *Othello* by Shakespeare. In it Iago talks to Cassio about Othello's wife Desdemona. Extract 3 is from *A Streetcar Named Desire* by Tennessee Williams. Stanley has his friends round for a card game but is irritated by his wife's sister in the next room.

Extract 1 The Rivals

Act II Scene 1

(Captain Absolute's *lodgings.* **Captain Absolute** *and*
Fag*)*

Fag: Sir, while I was there, Sir Anthony came in. I told him you had sent me to inquire after his health, and to know if he was at leisure to see you.

Absolute: And what did he say, on hearing I was at Bath?

Fag: Sir, in my life I never saw an elderly gentleman more astonished! He started back two or three paces, rapped out a dozen interjectural oaths, and asked, what the devil had brought you here!

Absolute: Well, sir, and what did you say?

Fag: Oh, I lied, sir. I forget the precise lie; but you may depend on't, he got no truth from me. Yet, with submission, for fear of blunders in future, I should be glad to fix what *has* brought us to Bath, in order that we may lie a little consistently. Sir Anthony's servants were curious, sir, very curious indeed.

Absolute: You have said nothing to them?

Fag: O, not a word, sir, not a word. Mr Thomas, indeed, the coachman (whom I take to be the discreetest of whips) –

Absolute: 'Sdeath, you rascal! You have not trusted him!

Fag: O, *no*, sir – no, no, not a syllable, upon my veracity! He was, indeed, a little inquisitive; but I was sly, sir, devilish sly. 'My master', said I, 'honest Thomas' – you know, sir, one says 'honest' to one's inferiors – 'is come to Bath to *recruit*' – yes, sir, I said 'to *recruit*' – and whether for men, money, or constitution, you know, sir, is nothing to him, nor any one else.

Absolute: Well, '*recruit*' will do. Let it be so.

Fag: O, sir, '*recruit*' will do surprisingly. Indeed, to give the thing an air, I told Thomas that your honour had already enlisted five disbanded chairmen, seven minority waiters, and thirteen billiard-markers.

Absolute: You blockhead, never say more than is necessary.

Fag: I beg pardon, sir; I beg pardon. But, with submission, a lie is nothing unless one supports it. Sir, whenever I draw on my invention for a good current lie, I always forge endorsements as well as the bill.

Absolute: Well, take care you don't hurt your credit by offering too much security. Is Mr Faulkland returned?

Fag: He is above, sir, changing his dress.

Absolute: Can you tell whether he has been informed of Sir Anthony's and Miss Melville's arrival?

Fag: I fancy not, sir; he has seen no one since he came in, but his gentleman, who was with him at Bristol. I think, sir, I hear Mr Faulkland coming down.

Absolute: Go, tell him I am here.

Fag: *(going)* Yes, sir. – I beg pardon, sir, but should Sir Anthony call, you will do me the favour to remember that we are '*recruiting*', if you please.

Absolute: Well, well.

Extract 2 Othello

Act II Scene 3

*(Enter **Iago**)*

Cassio: Welcome, Iago; we must to the watch.

Iago: Not this hour, lieutenant; 'tis not yet ten o' the clock. Our general cast us thus early for the love of his Desdemona; who let us not therefore blame: he hath not yet made wanton the night with her; and she is sport for Jove.

Cassio: She's a most exquisite lady.

Iago: And, I'll warrant her, full of game.

Cassio: Indeed, she's a most fresh and delicate creature.

Iago: What an eye she has! methinks it sounds a parley of provocation.

Cassio: An inviting eye; and yet methinks right modest.

Iago: And when she speaks, is it not an alarum to love?

Cassio: She is indeed perfection.

Iago: Well, happiness to their sheets! Come, lieutenant, I have a stoup of wine; and here without are a brace of Cyprus gallants that would fain have a measure to the health of black Othello.

Cassio: Not to-night, good Iago: I have very poor and unhappy brains for drinking: I could well wish courtesy would invent some other custom of entertainment.

Iago: O, they are our friends; but one cup: I'll drink for you.

Cassio: I have drunk but one cup to-night, and that was craftily qualified too, and, behold, what innovation it makes here: I am unfortunate in the infirmity, and dare not task my weakness with any more.

Iago: What, man! 'tis a night of revels: the gallants desire it.

Cassio: Where are they?

Iago: Here at the door; I pray you, call them in.

Cassio: I'll do't; but it dislikes me.

Extract 3 A Streetcar Named Desire

Scene 3

Stella: No. Stanley's the only one of his crowd that's likely to get anywhere.

Blanche: What makes you think Stanley will?

Stella: Look at him.

Blanche: I've looked at him.

Stella: Then you should know.

Blanche: I'm sorry, but I haven't noticed the stamp of genius even on Stanley's forehead.
(She takes off her blouse and stands in her pink silk brassiere and white skirt in the light through the portieres. The game has continued in undertones.)

Stella: It isn't on his forehead and it isn't genius.

Blanche: Oh. Well, what is it, and where? I would like to know.

Stella: It's a drive that he has. You're standing in the light, Blanche!

Blanche: Oh, am I?

(She moves out of the yellow streak of light. Stella has removed her dress and put on a light blue satin kimono.)

Stella: *(with girlish laughter)* You ought to see their wives.
Blanche: *(laughingly)* I can imagine. Big, beefy things, I suppose.
Stella: You know that one upstairs? *(More laughter.)* One time *(laughing)* the plaster – *(laughing)* cracked –
Stanley: You hens cut out that conversation in there!
Stella: You can't hear us.
Stanley: Well, you can hear me and I said to hush up!
Stella: This is my house and I'll talk as much as I want to!
Blanche: Stella, don't start a row.
Stella: He's half drunk! – I'll be out in a minute.

*(She goes into the bathroom. **Blanche** rises and crosses leisurely to a small white radio and turns it on.)*

Stanley: Awright, Mitch, you in?
Mitch: What? Oh! – No, I'm out!

*(**Blanche** moves back into the streak of light. She raises her arms and stretches, as she moves indolently back to the chair. Rhumba music comes over the radio. **Mitch** rises at the table.)*

Stanley: Who turned that on in there?
Blanche: I did. Do you mind?
Stanley: Turn it off!
Steve: Aw, let the girls have their music.
Pablo: Sure, that's good, leave it on!
Steve: Sounds like Xavier Cugat!

*(**Stanley** jumps up and, crossing to the radio, turns it off. He stops short at sight of **Blanche** in the chair. She returns his look without flinching. Then he sits again at the poker table. Two of the men have started arguing hotly.)*

Steve: I didn't hear you name it.
Pablo: Didn't I name it, Mitch?
Mitch: I wasn't listenin'.
Pablo: What were you doing, then?
Stanley: He was looking through them drapes. *(He jumps up and jerks roughly at curtains to close them.)* Now deal the hand over again and let's play cards or quit. Some people get ants when they win.

Activity

Examine each of these examples of dialogue and compare the ways in which language is used in each one, bearing in mind the following features:

- the lexis
- the tone created
- metaphorical and rhetorical features
- the overall effects created.

Here are some points you might have noted:

Extract 1 This exchange between Fag and his master Absolute is direct and the short-question-and-response format appears naturalistic, but it is carefully contrived to provide the audience with information. The language contains the mannered formality typical of drama of the eighteenth century.

Extract 2 Notice how in this dialogue between Iago and Cassio, in which Desdemona is discussed, two things are going on. Iago is provocatively trying to draw Cassio with his smutty and suggestive comments about Desdemona's sexuality, while Cassio's gentlemanly responses show that he will not be drawn and has a great respect for her. Note the contrast in the vocabulary used by Iago and Cassio.

Extract 3 Tennessee Williams creates a sense of underlying tension which focuses primarily on Stanley and how he responds to Stella and Blanche. Note Stanley's belligerent tone and use of imperatives, particularly directed towards the women but also towards his friends playing cards. He uses short, sharp phrases which suggest his ill-tempered mood, made worse by the fact he has been drinking.

Activity

From the play you are studying, pick three examples where the dramatist uses dialogue in different ways to create different effects. Analyse closely the language use in each example.

Presenting character

A key element in the overall effectiveness of a play is the extent to which the dramatist is successful in creating interesting and convincing characters. Although characters on the stage can be revealed through what they do, language has a key role to play in developing our perceptions of them. Sometimes dramatists (such as Tennessee Williams and David Hare) make extensive use of stage directions to tell us how they intend a character to appear to the audience. Of course, when watching a play on stage you will be seeing these directions translated into actions, rather than reading them.

Other dramatists, Shakespeare included, tend to provide little information of this type, but rely almost entirely on the other methods of revealing characters to the audience that dramatists can use. These methods include:

- what characters say
- how characters speak
- how characters are described by others and what is said about them
- how characters behave.

Characters in plays usually have distinctive voices, which the dramatist creates in order to shape the kind of response he or she wants from the audience. In simple terms this can present a single dimension of a character. For example, read the following extract from *Othello* which reveals things about the characters of both Iago and Roderigo.

Activity

Examine how Shakespeare uses language here to give an impression of the characters of Iago and Rodrigo. What kind of impression of each character do you get?

Othello

Roderigo: Iago!

Iago: What say'st thou, noble heart?

Roderigo: What will I do, thinkest thou?

Iago: Why, go to bed, and sleep.

Roderigo: I will incontinently drown myself.

Iago: If thou dost, I shall never love thee after. Why, thou silly gentleman!

Roderigo: It is silliness to live when to live is torment; and then have we a prescription to die when death is our physician.

Iago: O villainous! I have looked upon the world for four times seven years; and since I could distinguish betwixt a benefit and an injury, I never found man that knew how to love himself. Ere I would say, I would drown myself for the love of a guinea-hen, I would change my humanity with a baboon.

Roderigo: What should I do? I confess it is my shame to be so fond; but it is not in my virtue to amend it.

Iago: Virtue! a fig! 'tis in ourselves that we are thus or thus. Our bodies are our gardens, to the which our wills are gardeners: so that if we will plant nettles, or sow lettuce, set hyssop and weed up thyme, supply it with one gender of herbs, or distract it with many, either to have it sterile with idleness, or manured with industry, why, the power and corrigible authority of this lies in our wills. If the balance of our lives had not one scale of reason to poise another of sensuality, the blood and baseness of our natures would conduct us to most preposterous conclusions: but we have reason to cool our raging motions, our carnal stings, our unbitted lusts, whereof I take this that you call love to be a sect or scion.

Roderigo: It cannot be.

Iago: It is merely a lust of the blood and a permission of the will. Come, be a man. Drown thyself! drown cats and blind puppies. I have professed me thy friend and I confess me knit to thy deserving with cables of perdurable toughness; I could never better stead thee than now. Put money in thy purse; follow thou the wars; defeat thy favour with an usurped beard; I say, put money in thy purse. It cannot be that Desdemona should long continue her love to the Moor,– put money in thy purse,– nor he his to her: it was a violent commencement, and thou shalt see an answerable sequestration:– put but money in thy purse. These Moors are changeable in their wills: fill thy purse with money:– the food that to him now is as luscious as locusts, shall be to him shortly as bitter as coloquintida. She must change for youth: when she is sated with his body, she will find the error of her choice: she must have change, she must: therefore put money in thy purse. If thou wilt needs damn thyself, do it a more delicate way than drowning. Make all the money thou canst: if sanctimony and a frail vow betwixt an erring barbarian and a supersubtle Venetian be not too hard for my wits and all the tribe of hell, thou shalt enjoy her; therefore make money. A pox of drowning thyself! it is clean out of the way: seek thou rather to be hanged in compassing thy joy than to be drowned and go without her.

- -

Immediately the contrast between the two is apparent and there is no doubt that Iago is the dominant character. Roderigo appears weak and feeble as he talks childishly of drowning himself. Iago clearly has little patience or sympathy for him and mocks him, calling him 'silly'. Iago's cynical view of life and of love is clear to see in the views he expresses to bolster up Roderigo. Notice the imagery he uses to describe Othello's love for Desdemona; it is expressed in terms of physical appetite – 'the food that to him now is as luscious as locusts'. The vocabulary he use in connection with love – 'carnal stings', 'unbitted lusts', 'sated' – all emphasizes the contempt and cynicism he feels towards the notion of love.

Most major characters in drama have different sides to their personalities and behave in different ways in different situations. In *Othello*, for example, the changes that come about in Othello's personality are reflected in his language as he changes from a noble and assured leader with a rich and poetic language to a character eaten up with jealousy. At the end of the play, however, we once again see a glimpse of his noble nature before he kills himself. Look carefully at the following three extracts.

Activity

Examine Othello's language in each of the three extracts below, focusing on the following aspects of each:

- the lexis
- the ways in which the language reflects Othello's mood and state of mind
- the impression you get of Othello.

As you think about these points, look out for particular features of language – are there any key words or phrases? Is imagery used? If so, what is its effect? What about the rhythm and syntax of the speech – does it flow smoothly, or is it disjointed?

Act I Scene 1

Othello: Her father loved me; oft invited me;
Still question'd me the story of my life,
From year to year, the battles, sieges, fortunes,
That I have passed.
I ran it through, even from my boyish days,
To the very moment that he bade me tell it;
Wherein I spake of most disastrous chances,
Of moving accidents by flood and field
Of hair-breadth scapes i' the imminent deadly breach,
Of being taken by the insolent foe
And sold to slavery, of my redemption thence
And portance in my travels' history:
Wherein of antres vast and deserts idle,
Rough quarries, rocks and hills whose heads touch heaven
It was my hint to speak, – such was the process;
And of the Cannibals that each other eat,
The Anthropophagi and men whose heads
Do grow beneath their shoulders. This to hear
Would Desdemona seriously incline:
But still the house-affairs would draw her thence:
Which ever as she could with haste dispatch,
She'ld come again, and with a greedy ear
Devour up my discourse: which I observing,
Took once a pliant hour, and found good means
To draw from her a prayer of earnest heart
That I would all my pilgrimage dilate,
Whereof by parcels she had something heard,
But not intentively: I did consent,
And often did beguile her of her tears,
When I did speak of some distressful stroke

That my youth suffer'd. My story being done,
She gave me for my pains a world of sighs:
She swore, in faith, 'twas strange, 'twas passing strange,
'Twas pitiful, 'twas wondrous pitiful:
She wish'd she had not heard it, yet she wish'd
That heaven had made her such a man: she thank'd me,
And bade me, if I had a friend that loved her,
I should but teach him how to tell my story
And that would woo her. Upon this hint I spake:
She loved me for the dangers I had pass'd,
And I loved her that she did pity them.
This only is the witchcraft I have used:
Here comes the lady; let her witness it.

Act IV Scene 1

Othello: What hath he said?
Iago: 'Faith, that he did – I know not what he did.
Othello: What? what?
Iago: Lie –
Othello: With her?
Iago: With her, on her; what you will.
Othello: Lie with her! lie on her! We say lie on her, when they belie her. Lie with her!
that's fulsome. – Handkerchief – confessions – handkerchief! – To confess, and
be hanged for his labour; – first, to be hanged, and then to confess. – I tremble
at it. Nature would not invest herself in such shadowing passion without some
instruction. It is not words that shake me thus. Pish! Noses, ears, and lips. – Is't
possible? – Confess – handkerchief! – O devil! –

Act V Scene 2

Othello: Soft you; a word or two before you go.
I have done the state some service, and they know't.
No more of that. I pray you, in your letters,
When you shall these unlucky deeds relate,
Speak of me as I am; nothing extenuate,
Nor set down aught in malice: then must you speak
Of one that loved not wisely but too well;
Of one not easily jealous, but being wrought
Perplex'd in the extreme; of one whose hand,
Like the base Indian, threw a pearl away
Richer than all his tribe; of one whose subdued eyes,
Albeit unused to the melting mood,
Drop tears as fast as the Arabian trees
Their medicinal gum. Set you down this;
And say besides, that in Aleppo once,
Where a malignant and a turban'd Turk
Beat a Venetian and traduced the state,
I took by the throat the circumcised dog,
And smote him, thus.

(Stabs himself)

- -

Here is how one student responded to these three extracts.

Student response

In this first speech Shakespeare presents Othello as a noble and dignified character. He speaks with complete confidence that evokes admiration of his character. His language is impressive and persuasive and full of rich description as he describes some of the details of his past life that Brabantio loved to listen to and which captured the heart of Desdemona. Although he does not use metaphors and similes to describe his experiences his language if full of rich visual description and his use of repetition such as here, where he talks of the effect his words had on Desdemona, add emphasis to his speech –

> My story being done,
> She gave me for my pains a world of sighs:
> She swore, in faith, 'twas strange, 'twas passing strange,
> 'Twas pitiful, 'twas wondrous pitiful:
> She wish'd she had not heard it, yet she wish'd
> That heaven had made her such a man:

The poetic rhythms created through his speech give it a formal dignity which reflects his calm, dignified nature and the fact that he is a character clearly in control.

In the second speech Othello's language is a complete contrast. Here Iago's insinuations about Desdemona's unfaithfulness has clearly had a marked effect. Iago's calculated use of the word 'lie' with his double meaning immediately plants an image in Othello's mind of Desdemona and Cassio having sex together – an image spurred on by Iago –

Iago: With her, on her; what you will.
Othello: Lie with her! lie on her! We say lie on her, when they belie her. Lie with her! that's fulsome.

The short sentences, use of exclamation and repetition of 'lie' shows the torment that this thought is putting Othello through.

This is emphasized further through the fragmentation of Othello's language – his repetition of 'handkerchief' (Othello had given this to Desdemona as a love token and Iago had planted it in Cassio's room to make him seem guilty) coupled with the ideas of Desdemona confessing her guilt reveal the ideas that he has become obsessed with –

> – Handkerchief – confessions – handkerchief! – To confess, and be hanged for his labour; – first, to be hanged, and then to confess. – I tremble at it.

At the end of this extract the complete breakdown of his language in both structure and sense reflects how his mind has been overwhelmed with the power of the jealousy and anger –

> It is not words that shake me thus. Pish! Noses, ears, and lips. – Is't possible?
> – Confess – handkerchief! – O devil! –

In the third extract Othello, realizing the huge mistake he has made in murdering Desdemona, as she was innocent all along, regains some of his old nobility. His language has become composed once again and he speaks with a calm dignity as he is resigned to do what he knows he must do next – end his life.

Although he does not try to make excuses for what he has done he does try to explain it. No one is more aware than he is of what he has lost and he expresses this in an apt and poetic image as he explains that he was –

> wrought
> Perplex'd in the extreme; of one whose hand,
> Like the base Indian, threw a pearl away
> Richer than all his tribe;

His use of poetic language continues and he dramatizes his own suicide through the use of another image –

> Set you down this;
> And say besides, that in Aleppo once,
> Where a malignant and a turban'd Turk
> Beat a Venetian and traduced the state,
> I took by the throat the circumcised dog,
> And smote him, thus.
>
> *(Stabs himself)*

therefore making his death appear a noble and tragic action.

Examiner's comments

The student begins by going straight to the point, making an assessment of how Othello's character is perceived through this extract. She makes some perceptive points to do with Othello's dignity and nobility and the admiration that he inspires in others, linking this idea effectively to the rich and poetic language which he uses. She is clearly aware of the persuasive effects that this use of language is likely to have on both his audience within the play and the broader audience watching the drama. She also picks up on the fact that the poetic qualities of Othello's language here derive more from his vocabulary and visual description than his use of imagery. She comments on his use of repetition as a rhetorical device and the poetic rhythm of the lines which contributes to the calm and dignified impression Othello creates here.

The student rightly identifies the complete contrast presented by the second extract, commenting on Iago's insinuations, and she makes a good point about the double meaning in his use of the word 'lie'. Further perceptive points are made concerning the use of techniques such as the repetition of key words, the use of exclamation and the general fragmentation of Othello's language reflecting his emotional breakdown – a point reinforced in her final comments concerning the breakdown of both the structure of Othello's language and the actual sense of his words.

There is a clear understanding that in the third extract we see a return, to some extent, of the Othello seen in the first extract. Some perceptive comments are made about the use of poetic language here and the effect that this has in restoring some of Othello's nobility. The student also makes a good point about the use of imagery here, both to show Othello's awareness of what he has thrown away and the dramatic effect of his death.

Overall these are perceptive comments and the student clearly illustrates her ideas with well-chosen references to specific detail of language.

Activity

Now think about the play you are studying. Choose one of the main characters and find three speeches he or she makes in the play where language is used differently in each one. Analyse the ways in which language is used in each speech, and describe the effects created.

Soliloquies

The soliloquy is another way that the dramatist can develop character through the language of the play. The soliloquy is a speech that a character delivers when alone on the stage. Through this device the dramatist has much scope for allowing characters to express their thoughts and feelings aloud, and therefore to let the audience know what is going on in their minds. It is often used to allow characters to reveal their true feelings, plans or motives.

In *Othello*, Shakespeare gives the villainous Iago soliloquies in which he reveals his thoughts on some of the other characters, and on his own plans and motives.

Activity

Look carefully at the following two soliloquies. The first one is from *Othello* and in it Iago reveals his intentions to the audience. The second one is from *Murmuring Judges* by David Hare, and in it Sandra speaks about the nature of policing.

What do you learn from the first soliloquy about:

- the character of Iago
- his view of other characters?

Think about the tone of the soliloquy. Do you detect any shifts of tone here?

What do you learn from the second soliloquy about:

- Sandra's view of police work
- her attitude towards her job?

Think about the tone of the soliloquy. What do you think the dramatist's purpose was in including this soliloquy?

Othello

Act II Scene 3

Iago: And what's he then, that says I play the villain,
When this advice is free I give, and honest,
Probal to thinking, and indeed the course
To win the Moor again? For 'tis most easy
Th'inclining Desdemona to subdue
In any honest suit. She's framed as fruitful
As the free elements; and then for her
To win the Moor, were't to renounce his baptism,
All seals and symbols of redeemed sin,
His soul is so enfettered to her love,
That she may make, unmake, do what she list,
Even as her appetite shall play the god
With his weak function. How am I then a villain
To counsel Cassio to this parallel course
Directly to his good? Divinity of hell!
When devils will their blackest sins put on,
They do suggest at first with heavenly shows
As I do now. For while this honest fool
Plies Desdemona to repair his fortunes
And she for him pleads strongly to the Moor,
I'll pour this pestilence into his ear:
That she repeals him for her body's lust,

And by how much she strives to do him good,
She shall undo her credit with the Moor.
So will I turn her virtue into pitch,
And out of her own goodness make the net
That shall enmesh them all.

Murmuring Judges

(**Sandra Bingham** *has appeared. She is in a uniform, a WPC, in her mid-twenties with neat, dyed-blond short hair. She is quite small and tidy. She speaks directly to us. As she does so, the gaol is replaced by the charge room of a large inner-London police station. A long desk dominates the room, and opposite it is a self-locking door, which gives on to the outside world. To one side of the long room is a passage which leads to the cells; to the other, the front desk of the police station. You are aware of the activity in the room behind as* **Sandra** *speaks to us, but the emphasis of the light is on her.*)

Sandra: You see, it's all mess. That's what it is, mostly. If you take the charge room for instance, there's maybe thirty or forty people arrested in a day. Most of them are people who simply can't cope. They've been arrested before – petty thieving, deception, stealing car radios, selling stolen credit cards in pubs. Or not even that. Disturbing the peace. Failing to appear on a summons. Failing to carry out conditions of bail. Failing to produce a current car licence. Failing to fulfil Community Service. Getting drunk. Getting drunk and going for a joyride. Getting drunk and then driving home. Attacking your wife. Who then won't testify. Trying to cash a stolen cheque, only being so stupid you don't even try to make the signatures match. Opening telephone boxes. Fifty-fifty fights in clubs which are nobody's fault. Crimes of opportunity. Not being able to resist it. Then going back, thinking I got away with it last time. Possession. One acid tab. One Ninja Turtle sticker containing LSD. One smoke. One sniff. One toke. One three-quid packet. (*She smiles.*) That's the basic stuff. It's the stuff of policing. All you have to do with it is be a ledger clerk. You fill in bits of paper. Every officer carries thirty-six bits of paper about their person at any one time.

(**Sandra** *starts to move round the room to collect the boy she has just arrested. She stops a moment, before the scene begins.*)

Policing's largely the fine art of getting through biros. And keeping yourself ready for the interesting bits.

Activity

Now think about the play that you are studying. Make a list of each soliloquy in the play and for each one note down the following details:

- who is speaking
- the context of the soliloquy
- what is being said
- why the dramatist uses a soliloquy at that point in the drama.

Asides

Asides are also used to reveal character and motivation. The 'aside' is a kind of 'stage whisper', or behind-the-hand comment. Sometimes it is directed to another character but often it is aimed at the audience or the character is apparently speaking to himself or herself. For example, in *Othello* the effect is disquieting when Othello speaks in asides while eavesdropping on Cassio.

Othello

Act IV Scene 1

Othello: *(Aside)* Look, how he laughs already!

Iago: I never knew a woman love man so.

Cassio: Alas, poor rogue! I think i'faith she loves me.

Othello: *(Aside)* Now he denies it faintly, and laughs it out.

Iago: Do you hear, Cassio?

Othello: *(Aside)* Now he importunes him to tell it o'er.
          Go to, well said, well said!

Iago: She gives it out that you shall marry her.
          Do you intend it?

Cassio: Ha, ha, ha!

Othello: *(Aside)* Do you triumph, Roman? Do you triumph?

Cassio: I marry her! What! A customer! Prithee bear some charity to my wit: do not think it so
          unwholesome. Ha, ha, ha!

Othello: *(Aside)* So, so, so, so: they laugh that win.

Iago: Faith, the cry goes that you shall marry her.

Cassio: Prithee, say true.

Iago: I am a very villain else.

Othello: *(Aside)* Have you scored me? Well.

Cassio: This is the monkey's own giving out. She is persuaded I will marry her out of her own love
          and flattery, not out of my promise.

Othello: *(Aside)* Iago beckons me. Now he begins the story.

Activity

In the drama text you are studying, find three or four examples of the use of
the aside.

In each case make a note of:

- who is speaking
- what is being said
- what the purpose of the aside is.

Creating atmosphere

Until recent times, the theatres in which plays were first performed obviously
did not have the sophisticated technology and elaborate sets that are available to
modern dramatists. Much of the creation of scene, atmosphere and mood was done
through the language of the play. In the Elizabethan theatre, for example, the plays
were performed in daylight with no sets, and so all effects were created in the
imagination of the audience through the words of the play.

Look at the following example from *Othello*. The fleet in which Othello and his
entourage are travelling to Cyprus has been hit by a violent storm and the ships
scattered. Some of them have landed but as yet no one knows what has happened to
Othello's ship. Read it carefully.

Activity

Analyse the ways in which Shakespeare's language here creates an impression
of a storm.

Othello

Act II Scene 1

(A Sea-port in Cyprus. An open place near the quay)
*(Enter **Montano** and two Gentlemen)*

Montano: What from the cape can you discern at sea?

First Gentleman: Nothing at all: it is a highwrought flood;
I cannot, 'twixt the heaven and the main,
Descry a sail.

Montano: Methinks the wind hath spoke aloud at land;
A fuller blast ne'er shook our battlements:
If it hath ruffian'd so upon the sea,
What ribs of oak, when mountains melt on them,
Can hold the mortise? What shall we hear of this?

Second Gentleman: A segregation of the Turkish fleet:
For do but stand upon the foaming shore,
The chidden billow seems to pelt the clouds;
The wind-shaked surge, with high and monstrous mane,
Seems to cast water on the burning bear,
And quench the guards of the ever-fixed pole:
I never did like molestation view
On the enchafed flood.

Montano: If that the Turkish fleet
Be not enshelter'd and embay'd, they are drown'd:
It is impossible they bear it out.

(Enter a third Gentleman)

Third Gentleman: News, lads! our wars are done.
The desperate tempest hath so bang'd the Turks,
That their designment halts: a noble ship of Venice
Hath seen a grievous wreck and sufferance
On most part of their fleet.

Montano: How! is this true?

Third Gentleman: The ship is here put in,
A Veronesa; Michael Cassio,
Lieutenant to the warlike Moor Othello,
Is come on shore: the Moor himself at sea,
And is in full commission here for Cyprus.

Montano: I am glad on't; 'tis a worthy governor.

Third Gentleman: But this same Cassio, though he speak of comfort
Touching the Turkish loss, yet he looks sadly,
And prays the Moor be safe; for they were parted
With foul and violent tempest.

- -

Here are some things you might have thought about:

- The lexis creates a vivid impression of the violence of the storm: 'highwrought flood', 'blast', 'foaming shore', 'wind-shaked surge', 'drown'd', 'desperate tempest' all build to create a sense of the violence of the storm.

- The use of personification and metaphors, e.g. 'the wind hath spoke aloud', 'mountains melt on them', 'the wind-shaked surge... ever-fixed pole', builds up a strong physical image of the violence of the storm.
- Shakespeare creates this vivid impression of the storm through the dialogue between the gentlemen. What is the effect of the arrival of the Third Gentleman?

Activity

Select two contrasting passages from the play you are studying and examine the ways in which language is used to create a sense of atmosphere and mood.

Remember to use specific examples from each passage to illustrate your comments.

Opening scenes

We have already seen that plays usually begin with some kind of exposition, which sets the scene and gives the audience information. This can be important in order for them to understand what is going on, or to inform them of events that happened before the play starts. As we have also seen, one way of doing this is to start the play with a soliloquy in which a character gives the audience information indirectly, and another way is for information to be disclosed through conversation between two or more characters. Very often the seeds of the later action are sown in the opening scene.

However dramatists choose to begin their plays, it is vital that the drama captures the interest and imagination of the audience from the start. The central conflict must be introduced quickly, and the audience must become eager to know what happens next. In creating this atmosphere of expectancy and anticipation, the dramatist's use of language is central.

Look at the following opening scenes.

Activity

Compare the ways in which the dramatists open their plays in these extracts. What information do you learn from each, and what effect do you think each would have on the audience?

Hamlet

(Elsinore)
*(Enter **Barnardo** and **Francisco**, two sentinels)*

Barnardo: Who's there?
Francisco: Nay, answer me. Stand and unfold yourself.
Barnardo: Long live the King.
Francisco: Barnardo?
Barnardo: He.
Francisco: You come most carefully upon your hour.
Barnardo: 'Tis now struck twelve. Get thee to bed, Francisco.

Francisco: For this relief much thanks. 'Tis bitter cold,
    And I am sick at heart.
Barnardo: Have you had quiet guard?
Francisco: Not a mouse stirring.
Barnardo: Well, good night.
    If you do meet Horatio and Marcellus,
    The rivals of my watch, bid them make haste.

(Enter **Horatio** *and* **Marcellus**)

Francisco: I think I hear them. Stand, ho! Who is there?
Horatio: Friends to this ground.
Marcellus: And liegemen to the Dane.
Francisco: Give you good night.
Marcellus: O, farewell honest soldier,
    Who hath relieved you?
Francisco: Barnardo hath my place.
    Give you good night.

(Exit)

Marcellus: Holla, Barnardo!
Barnardo: Say,
    What, is Horatio there?
Horatio: A piece of him.
Barnardo: Welcome, Horatio. Welcome, good Marcellus.
Marcellus: What, has this thing appeared again tonight?
Barnardo: I have seen nothing.
Marcellus: Horatio says 'tis but our fantasy,
    And will not let belief take hold of him
    Touching this dreaded sight, twice seen of us.
    Therefore I have intreated him along
    With us to watch the minutes of this night,
    That, if again this apparition come,
    He may approve our eyes and speak to it.
Horatio: Tush, tush, 'twill not appear.
Barnardo: Sit down awhile,
    And let us once again assail your ears,
    That are so fortified against our story,
    What we have two nights seen.
Horatio: Well, sit we down,
    And let us hear Barnardo speak of this.
Barnardo: Last night of all,
    When yon same star that's westward from the pole,
    Had made his course t'illume that part of heaven
    Where now it burns, Marcellus and myself,
    The bell then beating one –

(Enter Ghost)

Marcellus: Peace, break thee off. Look where it comes again!
Barnardo: In the same figure like the King that's dead.
Marcellus: Thou art a scholar, speak to it Horatio.

Murmuring Judges

An empty stage. Then suddenly from nowhere they're all there – the judge, the jury, the battery of lawyers in wigs, the public, the police, the press, the ushers, the guards, and at the centre of the forward-facing court, the defendants. The entire company of the law has appeared in the blinking of an eye.

*At the centre, the three defendants of whom **Gerard McKinnon** is conspicuously the youngest, barely in his twenties, thin, wiry, tall, his dark hair down to his shoulders. Beside him, crop-haired, pale, in suits, two other defendants, **Travis** and **Fielding**. But the emphasis of the light is on **McKinnon**, and before you're ready he begins to speak. He has an Irish accent.*

Gerard: I'm standing here, I'm thinking, oh God, it's coming, it *is* coming, it's finally happening, hold on, remember, this is happening to me. After it going so slowly, *slowly*, the standing, the waiting – God, is there anything in the world slower than a lawyer? – after all that, now suddenly, stop, hold on, suddenly it's going so fast...

*(The lights change to favour the whole court as the **Usher** calls to make everyone stand.)*

Clerk: Has the jury reached a verdict upon which you are all agreed?
Juryman: We have.
Clerk: Do you find the defendant James Arthur Travis guilty or not guilty?
Juryman: Guilty.
Clerk: Do you find the defendant Michael Fielding guilty or not guilty?
Juryman: Guilty.
Clerk: Do you find the defendant Gerard Thomas McKinnon guilty or not guilty?

(A slight pause.)

Juryman: Guilty.

*(The lights change again as **Gerard** struggles to interrupt.)*

Gerard: And I want to say, yes, hold on, just a moment, take me back, I did meet these men, yes, I did, but I thought at the time, part of me thought, this is stupid, I mean, I'm not *really* doing this, there's a part of me which isn't standing on this freezing pavement, thinking how did I get myself into this? So why is it now, only now, yes, *now*, why is everything finally real?

(The lights change back to favour the court.)

Judge: And now I will turn to the sentencing. Please, will the prisoners attend?

*(The lights focus on **Gerard**, his speech more insistent than ever.)*

Gerard: Finally I get it, yes, it *is* happening, these men, every one of them silver-haired, judicious, informed, they will go home to their wives, to wine in fine glasses and the gossip of the Bar, they will walk the streets and complain about their lives, and I... *(He stops. More insistently.)* And I...

(The court is lit again.)

Judge: For Travis, eight years and six years to run concurrently. For Fielding, eight years and six concurrently also. For McKinnon... *(A pause.)* Five years.

*(The lights change, as if **Gerard** were at last alone. He is quiet.)*

Gerard: And I... the stuff of their profession... I will go to my gaol.

Here are some ideas about these opening scenes.

One of the important elements in the opening of *Hamlet* is the atmosphere that is created. It is midnight, bitterly cold and we are on the battlements of a castle. The guards are clearly on edge, expecting something to happen. Horatio and Marcellus arrive and we learn that for the past two nights a ghost has appeared. Horatio has dismissed this as imagination, but he has come to see for himself. Tension mounts as the ghost appears – it looks just like the king who recently died.

If you can imagine being in a theatre, you will see that this is an effective opening. The atmosphere of fear and tension would immediately capture the interest of the audience, and when the ghost appears the audience learns about the dead king.

The seeds of the whole drama are sown here, as the appearance of Hamlet's father's ghost begins the train of events that eventually lead to the tragic conclusion of the play.

Murmuring Judges opens in a different way. Obviously there are quite a few stage directions but in performance, of course, you would simply see these on the stage. The main difference between the opening of this play and *Hamlet* is that in *Hamlet* much of the information about what is going on is given to the audience through the dialogue between Barnardo, Francisco, Marcellus and Horatio. In *Murmuring Judges*, though, we gain information mainly through the internal monologue of Gerard set against the background of the dialogue of the court sentencing him to imprisonment. The internal monologue allows the audience to experience what is going through Gerard's mind at this point and his mental detachment from what is going on around him. The reality of the court and the words of the Juryman, Clerk and Judge give us the clinical details of his sentence. Like *Hamlet*, though, this scene both immediately captures the interest of the audience and at the same time gives them essential information about what is happening, thus preparing them for what is to come.

Activity

Look at the opening of the play you are studying. What kind of opening does the dramatist create? How does the dramatist:

- hold the attention of the audience?
- create atmosphere?
- convey important information?
- create a sense of character?

Themes

Plays address particular themes that the dramatist is interested in exploring and presenting to an audience. Although dramatists may make use of visual effects to examine these themes, the language of the play is the key element through which they are drawn to the attention of the audience. As plays usually contain more than one theme, the language can become a complex structure in which various thematic strands are woven together to present a unified whole.

The following extract is taken from *Translations* by Brian Friel. Read it through carefully.

Activity

From this extract, what key themes do you think the play might deal with? Give reasons for your answer.

Translations

Yolland: I mean – I feel so cut off from the people here. And I was trying to explain a few minutes ago how remarkable a community this is. To meet people like yourself and Jimmy Jack who actually converse in Greek and Latin. And your place names – what was the one we came across this morning? – Termon, from Terminus, the god of boundaries. It – it – it's really astonishing.

Hugh: We like to think we endure around truths immemorially posited.

Yolland: And your Gaelic literature – you're a poet yourself –

Hugh: Only in Latin, I'm afraid.

Yolland: I understand it's enormously rich and ornate.

Hugh: Indeed, Lieutenant. A rich language. A rich literature. You'll find, sir, that certain cultures expend on their vocabularies and syntax acquisitive energies and ostentations entirely lacking in their material lives. I suppose you could call us a spiritual people.

Owen: *(Not unkindly; more out of embarrassment before* **Yolland***)* Will you stop that nonsense, Father.

Hugh: Nonsense? What nonsense?

Owen: Do you know where the priest lives?

Hugh: At Lis na Muc, over near...

Owen: No, he doesn't. Lis na Muc, the Fort of the Pigs, has become Swinefort. *(Now turning the pages of the Name-Book, a page per name.)* And to get to Swinefort you pass through Greencastle and Fair Head and Strandhill and Gort and Whiteplains. And the new school isn't at Poll na gCaorach – it's at Sheepsrock. Will you be able to find your way? (**Hugh** *pours himself another drink. Then.*)

Hugh: Yes, it is a rich language, Lieutenant, full of the mythologies of fantasy and hope and self-deception – a syntax opulent with tomorrows. It is our response to mud cabins and a diet of potatoes; our only method of replying to... inevitabilities.
(To **Owen***.)* Can you give me the loan of half-a-crown? I'll repay you out of the subscriptions I'm collecting for the publication of my new book. *(To* **Yolland***.)* It is entitled: 'The Pentaglot Preceptor or Elementary Institute of the English, Greek, Hebrew, Latin and Irish Languages; Particularly Calculated for the Instruction of Such Ladies and Gentlemen as may Wish to Learn without the Help of a Master'.

Yolland: *(Laughs)* That's a wonderful title!

Hugh: Between ourselves – the best part of the enterprise. Nor do I, in fact, speak Hebrew. And that last phrase – 'without the Help of a Master' – that was written before the new national school was thrust upon me – do you think I ought to drop it now? After all you don't dispose of the cow just because it has produced a magnificent calf, do you?

Yolland: You certainly do not.

Hugh: The phrase goes. And I'm interrupting work of moment. *(He goes to the door and stops there.)* To return briefly to that other matter, Lieutenant. I understand your sense of exclusion, of being cut off from a life here; and I trust you will find access to us with my son's help. But remember that words are signals, counters. They are not immortal. And it can happen – to use an image you'll understand – it can happen that a civilisation can be imprisoned in a linguistic contour which no longer matches the landscape of... fact. Gentlemen. *(He leaves.)*

Owen: 'An *expeditio* with three purposes': the children laugh at him: he always promises three points and he never gets beyond A and B.

Yolland: He's an astute man.

Owen: He's bloody pompous.

Yolland: But so astute.

Owen: And he drinks too much. Is it astute not to be able to adjust for survival? Enduring around truths immemorially posited – hah!

Yolland: He knows what's happening.

Owen: What is happening?

Yolland: I'm not sure. But I'm concerned about my part in it. It's an eviction of sorts.

Owen: We're making a six-inch map of the country. Is there something sinister in that?

Yolland: Not in...

Owen: And we're taking place-names that are riddled with confusion and...

Yolland: Who's confused? Are the people confused?

Owen: ... and we're standardising those names as accurately and as sensitively as we can.

Yolland: Something is being eroded.

Activity

Look at the play you are studying. What themes does your play explore? For each theme you have identified, find four or five examples to show how the dramatist uses the language of the play to draw attention to and explore these themes.

Metaphorical techniques

Like other writers, dramatists make use of imagery, metaphor, simile and symbolism to create effects through the language of their plays. Sometimes dramatists use the technique of repeating similar images in order to build up a certain sense or a particular effect. For example, read the following two extracts from *Othello*. In the first, Othello has been led to believe from Iago's insinuation that his wife, Desdemona, has been unfaithful to him. He is struggling not to believe it but nevertheless the thought has brought unpleasant images to mind. In the second extract, Othello's jealousy has taken over completely and he charges his innocent wife with adultery.

Read the extracts through carefully.

Activity

Examine the ways in which Shakespeare uses imagery to create a sense of Othello's state of mind and mood in each extract. You should pay particular attention to the use of:

- metaphor
- simile
- symbolism
- repeated images.

Othello

Act III Scene 3

Othello: This fellow's of exceeding honesty,
And knows all qualities with a learned spirit
Of human dealings. If I do prove her haggard,
Though that her jesses were my dear heart-strings,
I'd whistle her off, and let her down the wind
To prey at fortune. Haply, for I am black
And have not those soft parts of conversation
That chamberers have; or for I am declined
Into the vale of years – yet that's not much –
She's gone: I am abused, and my relief
Must be to loathe her. O, curse of marriage!
That we can call these delicate creatures ours
And not their appetites! I had rather be a toad
And live upon the vapour of a dungeon
Than keep a corner in the thing I love
For others' uses. Yet 'tis the plague of great ones;
Prerogatived are they less than the base.
'Tis destiny unshunnable, like death:
Even then this forked plague is fated to us
When we do quicken. Desdemona comes:

(Enter **Desdemona** *and* **Emilia**)

If she be false, O, then heaven mocks itself!
I'll not believe't.

Act IV Scene 2

Desdemona: Upon my knees, what doth your speech import?
I understand a fury in your words,
But not the words.
Othello: Why, what art thou?
Desdemona: Your wife, my lord; your true and loyal wife.
Othello: Come, swear it; damn thyself;
Lest being like one of heaven, the devils themselves
Should fear to seize thee. Therefore be double-damned:
Swear thou art honest.
Desdemona: Heaven doth truly know it.
Othello: Heaven truly knows that thou art false as hell.
Desdemona: To whom, my lord? With whom? How am I false?
Othello: Ah, Desdemona! Away, away, away!
Desdemona: Alas, the heavy day! Why do you weep?
Am I the motive of these tears my lord?
If haply you my father do suspect
An instrument of this your calling back,
Lay not your blame on me. If you have lost him,
I have lost him too.
Othello: Had it pleased heaven
To try me with affliction, had they rained
All kind of sores and shames on my bare head,

Steeped me in poverty to the very lips,
Given to captivity me and my utmost hopes,
I should have found in some place of my soul
A drop of patience. But alas, to make me
A fixed figure for the time of scorn
To point his slow unmoving finger at!
Yet could I bear that too, well, very well:
But there where I have garnered up my heart,
Where either I must live, or bear no life,
The fountain from the which my current runs,
Or else dries up – to be discarded thence
Or keep it as a cistern for foul toads
To knot and gender in! Turn thy complexion there,
Patience, thou young and rose-lipped cherubin,
Ay, there look grim as hell!

- -

Here is how one student responded to these extracts.

Student response

Othello's state of mind in the extracts is one of anger and depression focused on his wife, Desdemona. In the first extract there is a mood of uncertainty and confusion over whether or not he believes she has betrayed him. Further in the extract, however, violent imagery is applied through Othello's soliloquy that emphasizes his feelings clearly. By the time Desdemona arrives and converses with him on the matter, in the second extract, Othello's mood and state of mind is distinct. He is extremely angry, and fails to recognize her truths by not permitting her to explain herself. Shakespeare mixes the strong imagery in Othello's speeches and a sense of anguish towards his wife is created.

At the beginning of the first extract, Othello is not entirely sure as to whether these 'crimes' allegedly committed by Desdemona are true, as he has still to 'prove her haggard'. Yet, as he continues to contemplate the possibility Shakespeare uses extraordinary and very strong, harsh images that seem to push Othello into the belief that Desdemona has been unfaithful to him:

> I am abused, and my relief
> Must be to loathe her.

By the use of the words 'abused' and 'loathed' Shakespeare has created an image of a torn, decayed figure in the form of Othello who must turn to abhor the woman he loved. The word 'abused' signifies Othello's distress and indicates that his mind must have been in a distraught and delicate state. Additionally Shakespeare uses a paradox in the form of 'O, curse of marriage!' Whilst metaphorically this suggests that his marriage has been cursed, the statement is also a paradox because 'curse' symbolizes woe and tribulations, while 'marriage' signifies hope and expectation. This image, therefore, further enhances the idea of Othello's instability. Further on in the first extract, Othello's anger seems accentuated through the use of intense imagery. For example he claims:

> Yet 'tis the plague of great ones.

The use of 'plague' suggests terror, pain and death, thus showing the way that Othello's mind is suffering torment.

Towards the end of the first extract the idea of 'death' is introduced, showing again the feelings of anguish that Othello is suffering and the power of his rage against Desdemona:

> 'Tis destiny unshunnable, like death.

This simile shows that Othello is placing his wife's betrayal (as he perceives it) on a parallel with death itself. There is also a sense here in which he seems to accept all this as a kind of destiny.

In the second extract there is a repetition of many of the images of the first. For example, Shakespeare again introduces the image of the plague and affliction is used again:

> Had it pleased heaven
> To try me with affliction, had they rained
> All kinds of sores and shames on my bare head

Similarly he feels that he could have coped with 'poverty to the very lips' or being put into captivity and it would have hurt less than Desdemona's infidelity to him. Through this imagery Shakespeare seems to portray Othello as almost suicidal. This combination of Othello's thoughts implies that he is now certain that his wife has betrayed him.

Perhaps the most powerful image that reflects Othello's state of mind occurs in both extracts. In the first extract he says:

> I had rather be a toad
> And live upon the vapour of a dungeon
> Than keep a corner in the thing I love
> For others' uses.

The image of the toad here creates a sense of baseness and bleakness through the imagery of the dungeon and this emphasizes the strength of Othello's feeling in that he would rather be this than allow another man to sleep with his wife. In the second extract the image of the toad is used again, but rather differently this time. Othello says:

> ... where I have garnered up my heart,
> Where either I must live, or bear no life,
> The fountain from the which my current runs,
> Or else dries up – to be discarded thence
> Or keep it as a cistern for foul toads
> To knot and gender in!

The image has become more intense here. The 'toad' has now become 'foul toads' and an unpleasant sexual element has been introduced with 'knot and gender' – as the thought of Desdemona with another man eats away at Othello's mind.

Examiner's comments

Overall the student has handled the task quite well. She is clearly aware of Othello's state of mind and mood in each extract, and she is also aware of some of the ways in which Shakespeare creates a sense of this mood. The response begins with a clear statement of Othello's state of mind and, although there are one or two minor technical infelicities, the sense of understanding is here.

From stating the more general points the student then begins to look at specific examples of the lexis of the two extracts and comments on the connotations and effects of individual words. The response develops with an analysis of the effects of the repeated use of the 'toad' as an image. Although the essay does lack analysis at a deeper level and the idea of the symbolic use of language is not really taken up, the response does cover a range of relevant points.

> **Activity**
>
> Now think about the play you are studying.
>
> 1 Make a list of any groups of images the dramatist uses, and within each group find examples of specific images used in the play. Remember to make a note of where these come from (Act, Scene and line number).
>
> 2 Choose two passages from the play where the dramatist uses imagery, and write an analysis of each showing how language is used in each in order to create the effects desired.

Rhetorical techniques

Dramatists also make use of rhetorical techniques in their writing, and give to their characters the kind of language that can be used to persuade the audience or shape their responses in a particular way. Here are some of the features that you will find in the language of plays:

- repetition of sounds, words, sentence structures, etc.
- listing
- alliteration
- onomatopoeia
- assonance
- hyperbole
- puns
- antithesis.

For example, in *Measure for Measure*, Shakespeare uses **repetition** as Isabella calls for justice against the corrupt Angelo, who has used his powers and position to try to blackmail her into sleeping with him.

Measure for Measure

Act V Scene 1

Isabella: Justice, justice, justice, justice!
  Duke: Relate your wrongs: in what? By whom? Be brief.
      Here is Lord Angelo shall give you justice;
      Reveal yourself to him.
Isabella: Oh worthy Duke,
      You bid me seek redemption of the devil.
      Hear me yourself: for that which I must speak
      Must either punish me, not being believed,
      Or wring redress from you. Hear me, oh hear me, here!
  Angelo: My Lord, her wits I fear me are not firm;
      She hath been a suitor to me for her brother
      Cut off by course of justice.
Isabella: By course of justice!
  Angelo: And she will speak most bitterly and strange.
Isabella: Most strange, but yet most truly will I speak.
      That Angelo's forsworn, is it not strange?
      That Angelo's a murderer, is't not strange?

That Angelo is an adulterous thief,
An hypocrite, a virgin-violator,
Is it not strange, and strange?

Duke: Nay, it is ten times strange.

Isabella: It is not truer he is Angelo
Than this is all as true as it is strange;
Nay, it is ten times true, for truth is truth
To th'end of reck'ning.

- -

Note here how the almost ritualistic, incantatory effect of the repetition adds power to Isabella's words.

Listing can also be used to accumulate words or phrases like a list, to add impact as in this example from *The Merchant of Venice*:

The Merchant of Venice

Act III Scene 1

Shylock: Hath not a Jew eyes? Hath not a Jew hands, organs, dimensions, senses, affections, passions, fed with the same food, hurt with the same weapons, subject to the same diseases, healed by the same means, warmed and cooled by the same winter and summer as a Christian is?

Activity

If necessary, remind yourself of alliteration, assonance and onomatopoeia (see pages 171–4). Now look at the play you are studying and find five or six examples of each. In each case, describe what effect the particular feature adds to the overall impact of the language.

Antithesis is a technique very commonly used in drama; it involves contrasting ideas or words balanced against one another. Some of Shakespeare's most famous lines are examples of antithesis:

To be, or not to be
(*Hamlet*)
Fair is foul, and foul is fair
(*Macbeth*)
My only love sprung from my only hate
(*Romeo and Juliet*)

We mentioned earlier that conflict is at the heart of drama and that language expresses the conflict, of whatever kind it might be. The opposition of words in antithesis often reflects the oppositions or conflicts at the centre of the drama. The fact that Othello's jealousy has taken him to the extremes of love and hate is summed up in the antithesis in his final lines of the play, which are addressed to the dead Desdemona:

Othello: I kissed thee, ere I killed thee: no way but this,
Killing myself, to die upon a kiss.

Activity

Look at the play you are studying and see whether you can find some examples of antithesis. Describe the effects created.

Another rhetorical technique you are likely to find used in the play you study is that of **hyperbole**. Hyperbole means an exaggerated and extravagant use of language in order to create a particular effect or impact. For example, the passage recited by Hamlet from one of his favourite plays is full of extravagant and exaggerated rhetorical language.

Hamlet: One speech in it I chiefly loved, 'twas Aeneas' tale to Dido, and thereabout of it especially where he speaks of Priam's slaughter. If it live in your memory, begin at this line – let me, see, let me see –

'The rugged Pyrrhus; like th' Hyrcanian beast' –
'Tis not so, it begins with Pyrrhus –
'The rugged Pyrrhus, he whose sable arms,
Black as his purpose, did the night resemble
When he lay couched in th' ominous horse,
Hath now this dread and black complexion smeared
With heraldry more dismal; head to foot
Now is he total gules, horridly tricked
With blood of fathers, mothers, daughters, sons,
Baked and impasted with the parching streets,
That lend a tyrannous and a damned light
To their lord's murder. Roasted in wrath and fire,
And thus o'er-sized with coagulate gore,
With eyes like carbuncles, the hellish Pyrrhus
Old grandsire Priam seeks.'

- -

Puns were particularly popular with Elizabethan audiences, but it is likely that you will find some in any pre-twentieth-century text that you study. A pun is a play on words – when a word has two or more different meanings, the ambiguity can be used for a witty or amusing effect.

For example, Mercutio in *Romeo and Juliet*, although mortally wounded by Tybalt, keeps up his reputation for word-play to the end by telling his friends:

Ask for me tomorrow, and you will find me a grave man.

Activity

Look through the play you are studying and make notes on the use of hyperbole and punning. Identify what these elements add to the drama.

Irony in drama

A dramatist might use two types of irony. In both types, the irony lies in the fact that the audience knows something that a character or characters on stage do not know.

Dramatic irony occurs when what is said by a character contrasts with what happens elsewhere in the action. Look at this example from Hamlet:

Hamlet

Act III Scene 3

King Claudius: O, my offence is rank, it smells to heaven;
It hath the primal eldest curse upon't –
A brother's murder. Pray can I not,
Though inclination be as sharp as will,
My stronger guilt defeats my strong intent,
And, like a man to double business bound,
I stand in pause where I shall first begin,
And both neglect. What if this cursed hand
Were thicker than itself with brother's blood,
Is there not rain enough in the sweet heavens
To wash it white as snow? Whereto serves mercy
But to confront the visage of offence?
And what's in prayer but this twofold force,
To be forestalled ere we come to fall
Or pardon'd being down? Then I'll look up.
My fault is past – but O, what form of prayer
Can serve my turn? 'Forgive me my foul murder'?
That cannot be, since I am still possess'd
Of those effects for which I did the murder –
My crown, mine own ambition, and my queen.
May one be pardon'd and retain th'offence?
In the corrupted currents of this world
Offence's gilded hand may shove by justice,
And oft 'tis seen the wicked prize itself
Buys out the law. But 'tis not so above:
There is no shuffling, there the action lies
In his true nature, and we ourselves compell'd
Even to the teeth and forehead of our faults
To give in evidence. What then? What rests?
Try what repentance can. What can it not?
Yet what can it, when one cannot repent?
O wretched state! O bosom black as death!
O limed soul, that struggling to be free
Art more engag'd! Help, angels! Make assay.
Bow, stubborn knees; and heart with strings of steel,
Be soft as sinews of the new-born babe.
All may be well.

(He kneels)
*(Enter **Hamlet**)*

Hamlet: Now might I do it pat, now a is a-praying.
And now I'll do't. *(Draws his sword)*
                    And so a goes to heaven;
And so am I reveng'd. That would be scann'd:
A villain kills my father, and for that
I, his sole son, do this same villain send
To heaven.
Why, this is hire and salary, not revenge.
A took my father grossly, full of bread,
With all his crimes broad blown, as flush as May;
And how his audit stands who knows save heaven?
But in our circumstance and course of thought
'Tis heavy with him. And am I then reveng'd,
To take him in the purging of his soul,
When he is fit and season'd for his passage?
No.
Up, sword, and know thou a more horrid hent:
When he is drunk asleep, or in his rage,
Or in th'incestuous pleasure of his bed,
At game a-swearing, or about some act
That has no relish of salvation in't,
Then trip him, that his heels may kick at heaven
And that his soul may be as damn'd and black
As hell, whereto it goes. My mother stays.
This physic but prolongs thy sickly days.

(Exit)

King Claudius: My words fly up, my thoughts remain below.
Words without thoughts never to heaven go.

(Exit)

Activity

This is an example of dramatic irony. Explain why this situation is ironical.

Verbal irony occurs when a character says one thing but means another. For example, again in *Hamlet*, Claudius says that he is sending Hamlet to England for safety's sake when in fact the audience knows (and Hamlet guesses) that he is really planning to have him killed.

Activity

Look at the play you are studying and find three or four examples of the use of irony. Explain what the irony consists of, and its significance in the play.

Drama and contextual variation

In terms of studying a drama text for A level, **contextual variation** can refer to two quite separate elements of the play.

First, the language of the play can vary depending on the context of the particular scene, groupings of character, and so on. For example, in *The Rivals*, Sir Anthony Absolute uses language in different ways according to the context in which he is speaking – who he is speaking to, for what purpose, and so on.

Activity

Look at the following extracts from the play which show Sir Anthony using language in different ways.

The first comes from an early part of the play where Sir Anthony speaks to Mrs Malaprop. The two are keen to create a match between Sir Anthony's son Jack and Mrs Malprop's niece Lydia. Lydia, however, who is very wilful, is not co-operating with her elders' plan. This prompts Sir Anthony to air his theories on the dangers of teaching women to read.

What first impression do you get of the character of Sir Anthony from the way he speaks to Mrs Malaprop?

The Rivals

Act I Scene 2

Mrs Malaprop: There's a little intricate hussy for you!

Sir Anthony: It is not to be wondered at, ma'am; all this is the natural consequence of teaching girls to read. Had I a thousand daughters, by heaven, I'd as soon have them taught the black art as their alphabet!

Mrs Malaprop: Nay, nay, Sir Anthony, you are an absolute misanthropy.

Sir Anthony: In my way hither, Mrs Malaprop, I observed your niece's maid coming forth from a circulating library! She had a book in each hand; they were half-bound volumes, with marble covers! From that moment I guessed how full of duty I should see her mistress!

Mrs Malaprop: Those are vile places, indeed!

Sir Anthony: Madam, a circulating library in a town is as an evergreen tree of diabolical knowledge! It blossoms through the year! And depend on it, Mrs Malaprop, that they who are so fond of handling the leaves will long for the fruit at last.

...

Mrs Malaprop: Fie, fie, Sir Anthony, you surely speak laconically!

Sir Anthony: Why, Mrs Malaprop, in moderation now, what would you have a woman know?

Mrs Malaprop: Observe me, Sir Anthony. I would by no means wish a daughter of mine to be a progeny of learning; I don't think so much learning becomes a young woman. For instance, I would never let her meddle with Greek, or Hebrew, or algebra, or simony, or fluxions, or paradoxes, or such inflammatory branches of learning. Neither would it be necessary for her to handle any of your mathematical, astronomical, diabolical instruments. But, Sir Anthony, I would send her, at nine years old, to a boarding-school, in order to learn a little ingenuity and artifice. Then, sir, she should have a supercilious knowledge in accounts; and as she grew up, I would have her instructed in geometry, that she might know something of the contagious countries. But above all, Sir Anthony, she should be mistress of orthodoxy, that she might not misspell, and mispronounce words so shamefully as girls usually do, and likewise that she might reprehend the true meaning of what she is saying. This, Sir Anthony, is what I would have a woman know; and I don't think there is a superstitious article in it.

Sir Anthony: Well, well, Mrs Malaprop, I will dispute the point no further with you; though I must confess that you are a truly moderate and polite arguer, for almost every third word you say is on my side of the question. But, Mrs Malaprop, to the more important point in debate. You say you have no objection to my proposal.

Mrs Malaprop: None, I assure you. I am under no positive engagement with Mr Acres, and as Lydia is so obstinate against him, perhaps your son may have better success.

Sir Anthony: Well, madam, I will write for the boy directly. He knows not a syllable of this yet, though I have for some time had the proposal in my head. He is at present with his regiment.

Mrs Malaprop: We have never seen your son, Sir Anthony; but I hope no objection on his side.

Sir Anthony: Objection! Let him object if he dare! No, no, Mrs Malaprop, Jack knows that the least demur puts me in a frenzy directly. My process was always very simple. In their younger days, 'twas 'Jack, do this'. If he demurred, I knocked him down; and if he grumbled at that, I always sent him out of the room.

Mrs Malaprop: Ah, and the properest way, o' my conscience! Nothing is so conciliating to young people as severity. Well, Sir Anthony, I shall give Mr Acres his discharge, and prepare Lydia to receive your son's invocations; and I hope you will represent *her* to the captain as an object not altogether illegible.

Sir Anthony: Madam, I will handle the subject prudently. Well, I must leave you. And let me beg you, Mrs Malaprop, to enforce this matter roundly to the girl. Take my advice; keep a tight hand. If she rejects this proposal, clap her under lock and key; and if you were just to let the servants forget to bring her dinner for three or four days, you can't conceive how she'd come about!

In the next extract, Sir Anthony has told his son of his plans for him and we see the consequences when Jack objects to them. In the final extract, though, we see a very different Sir Anthony when all seems to be turning out well.

> ## Activity
>
> Compare Sir Anthony's language in these two extracts. How does his language change? What clues can you find in the language to tell you how he is feeling here?
>
> Make a list of specific examples to illustrate your points.

Act II Scene 1

Sir Anthony: Hark'ee, Jack. I have heard you for some time with patience. I have been cool, quite cool; but take care. You know I am compliance itself, when I am not thwarted – no one more easily led, when I have my own way; but don't put me in a frenzy!

Absolute: Sir, I must repeat. In this I cannot obey you.

Sir Anthony: Now, damn me, if ever I call you Jack again while I live!

Absolute: Nay, sir, but hear me.

Sir Anthony: Sir, I won't hear a word; not a word! Not one word! So give me your promise by a nod, and I'll tell you what, Jack – I mean, you dog – if you don't, by –

Absolute: What, sir, promise to link myself to some mass of ugliness! To –

Sir Anthony: Zounds, sirrah, the lady shall be as ugly as I choose. She shall have a hump on each shoulder. She shall be as crooked as the Crescent. Her one eye shall roll like the bull's in Cox's Museum. She shall have a skin like a mummy and the beard of a Jew. She shall be all this, sirrah! Yet I will make you ogle her all day, and sit up all night to write sonnets on her beauty.

Absolute: This is reason and moderation indeed!

Sir Anthony: None of your sneering, puppy! No grinning, jackanapes!

Absolute: Indeed, sir, I never was in a worse humour for mirth in my life.

Sir Anthony: 'Tis false, sir! I know you are laughing in your sleeve. I know you'll grin when I am gone, sirrah!

Absolute: Sir, I hope I know my duty better.

Sir Anthony: None of your passion, sir! None of your violence, if you please! It won't do with me, I promise you.

Absolute: Indeed, sir, I never was cooler in my life.

Sir Anthony: 'Tis a confounded lie! I know you are in a passion in your heart; I know you are, you hypocritical young dog! But it won't do.

Absolute: Nay, sir, upon my word.

Sir Anthony: So you will fly out! Can't you be cool like me? What the devil good can *passion* do! *Passion* is of no service, you impudent, insolent, overbearing reprobate! There, you sneer again! Don't provoke me! But you rely upon the mildness of my temper. You do, you dog! You play upon the meekness of my disposition! Yet take care. The patience of a saint may be overcome at last! But mark! I give you six hours and a half to consider of this. If you then agree, without any condition, to do everything on earth that I choose, why, confound you, I may in time forgive you. If not, zounds, don't enter the same hemisphere with me! Don't dare to breathe the same air, or use the same light with me; but get an atmosphere and a sun of your own! I'll strip you of your commission; I'll lodge a five-and-threepence in the hands of trustees, and you shall live on the interest. I'll disown you, I'll disinherit you, I'll unget you! And damn me, if ever I call you Jack again!

Act IV Scene 2

Sir Anthony: Well, I am glad you are not the dull, insensible varlet you pretended to be, however! I'm glad you have made a fool of your father, you dog; I am. So this was your *penitence*, your *duty*, and *obedience*! I thought it was damned sudden! You 'never heard their names before', not you! 'What, the Languishes of Worcestershire', hey? 'If you could please me in the affair, 'twas all you desired!' Ah! you dissembling villain! (*Pointing to* **Lydia**) What, she squints don't she? A little red-haired girl! Hey? Why, you hypocritical young rascal, I wonder you a'n't ashamed to hold up your head!

Absolute: 'Tis with difficulty, sir. I *am* confused, very much confused, as you must perceive.

Mrs Malaprop: O lud! Sir Anthony! A new light breaks in upon me! Hey! How! What! Captain, did *you* write the letters then? What! Am I to thank *you* for the elegant compilation of 'an old weather-beaten she-dragon', hey? O mercy! Was it *you* that reflected on my parts of speech?

Absolute: Dear sir, my modesty will be overpowered at last, if you don't assist me. I shall certainly not be able to stand it!

Sir Anthony: Come, come, Mrs Malaprop. We must forget and forgive. Od's life, matters have taken so clever a turn all of a sudden, that I could find in my heart to be so good-humoured, and so gallant! Hey, Mrs Malaprop!

Mrs Malaprop: Well, Sir Anthony, since you desire it, we will not anticipate the past. So mind, young people. Our retrospection will be all to the future.

Sir Anthony: Come, we must leave them together; Mrs Malaprop, they long to fly into each other's arms, I warrant! – Jack, isn't the *cheek* as I said, hey? And the eye, you rogue! And the lip, hey? – Come, Mrs Malaprop, we'll not disturb their tenderness; theirs is the time of life for happiness! (*Sings*) 'Youth's the season made for joy.' Hey! Od's life, I'm in such spirits. I don't know what I couldn't do! (*Gives his hand to* **Mrs Malaprop**) Permit me, ma'am (*Sings*) 'Tol-de-rol!' Gad, I should like to have a little fooling myself (*Sings*) 'Tol-de-rol! de-rol!'

- -

The **context** of the play is also the larger cultural frame of reference within which the play came about – for example, the kind of society and the historical period within which the work was produced. In studying a Shakespeare play it can be useful to have an understanding of the kind of theatres they were originally performed in or the kind of beliefs the people of that time held. Similarly, in studying a play like *The Rivals*, an understanding of the life style and social etiquette of late-eighteenth-century England can be useful in helping you to a full understanding of the play.

Examination-style questions

In your AS course the questions on drama can take several forms. Here are some examples.

Unit 1

In this unit you will study two texts. You do not have to study drama for this unit but if you do you could study either one or two drama texts. (It is likely, if you are studying in a school or college, that the text choices will be made by your teacher or lecturer.) In this unit you will answer two questions – **one** analytical question (Question A) and **one** production question (Question B) from different texts.

Below are examples of Question A and Question B. You are advised to spend 40 minutes on the analytical question and 50 minutes on the production question.

You can take the texts into the exam with you.

These questions will test the following Assessment Objectives:

AO1 Select and apply relevant concepts and approaches from integrated linguistic and literary study, using appropriate terminology and accurate, coherent expression.

AO2 Demonstrate detailed critical understanding in analysing the ways in which structure, form and language shape meanings in a range of spoken and written texts.

AO4 Demonstrate expertise and creativity in using language appropriately for a variety of purposes and audiences, drawing on insights from linguistic and literary studies.

Murmuring Judges by David Hare

Either

A How does Hare present the nature of police work through his portrayal of Sandra Bingham?

In your answer you should consider:

- Hare's language choices
- dramatic techniques

Or

B The play ends with Sandra asking to speak to the Chief Superintendent. Imagine what Sandra has to say to him.

You should give careful consideration to your language choices and style. Write in an appropriate speech form from Sandra's point of view.

Unit 2

The drama option question in Section B of Unit 2 is completely different in format from that of Unit 1. On this paper you will be given an extract from the text you have studied and you will be asked to analyse some aspect of the dialogue and other dramatic techniques in the extract printed on the examination paper and **one** other episode in the play.

Here is an example of a question on a drama set text for Unit 2.

You may not take the text you have studied into the exam.

You are recommended to spend 40 minutes on this question.

These questions will test the following Assessment Objectives:

AO1 Select and apply relevant concepts and approaches from integrated linguistic and literary study using appropriate terminology and accurate, coherent expression

AO2 Demonstrate detailed critical understanding in analysing the ways in which structure, form and language shape meanings in a range of spoken and written texts

How does Shakespeare use dialogue and other dramatic techniques to convey Iago's purpose and Othello's reaction?

In your answer you should refer closely to the extract printed below and to **one** other episode in the play.

Iago: My noble lord –
Othello: What dost thou say, Iago?
Iago: Did Michael Cassio, when you woo'd my lady,
Know of your love?
Othello: He did, from first to last: why dost thou ask?
Iago: But for a satisfaction of my thought;
No further harm.
Othello: Why of thy thought, Iago?
Iago: I did not think he had been acquainted with her.
Othello: O, yes; and went between us very oft.
Iago: Indeed!
Othello: Indeed! ay, indeed: discern'st thou aught in that?
Is he not honest?
Iago: Honest, my lord!
Othello: Honest! ay, honest.
Iago: My lord, for aught I know.
Othello: What dost thou think?
Iago: Think, my lord!
Othello: Think, my lord!
By heaven, he echoes me,
As if there were some monster in his thought
Too hideous to be shown. Thou dost mean something:
I heard thee say even now, thou likedst not that,
When Cassio left my wife: what didst not like?
And when I told thee he was of my counsel
In my whole course of wooing, thou criedst 'Indeed!'
And didst contract and purse thy brow together,
As if thou then hadst shut up in thy brain

Some horrible conceit: if thou dost love me,
Show me thy thought.

Iago: My lord, you know I love you.

Othello: I think thou dost;
And, for I know thou'rt full of love and honesty,
And weigh'st thy words before thou givest them breath,
Therefore these stops of thine fright me the more:
For such things in a false disloyal knave
Are tricks of custom, but in a man that's just
They are close delations, working from the heart
That passion cannot rule.

Iago: For Michael Cassio,
I dare be sworn I think that he is honest.

Othello: I think so too.

Iago: Men should be what they seem;
Or those that be not, would they might seem none!

Othello: Certain, men should be what they seem.

Iago: Why, then, I think Cassio's an honest man.

Othello: Nay, yet there's more in this:
I prithee, speak to me as to thy thinkings,
As thou dost ruminate, and give thy worst of thoughts
The worst of words.

Iago: Good my lord, pardon me:
Though I am bound to every act of duty,
I am not bound to that all slaves are free to.
Utter my thoughts? Why, say they are vile and false;
As where's that palace whereinto foul things
Sometimes intrude not? who has a breast so pure,
But some uncleanly apprehensions
Keep leets and law-days and in session sit
With meditations lawful?

- -

Here is how one student responded to this question.

Student response

Throughout this extract Shakespeare uses many techniques to convey the idea that Iago wants to make Othello suspicious and is succeeding.

One way that Shakespeare does this is that Iago uses lots of small sentences and exclamations, showing that he is choosing his words carefully in order to heighten Othello's sense of suspicion. For example, when Iago uses the exclamation 'Indeed!'

He chooses this so that it looks like a natural reaction from Othello, who says 'Indeed! ay, indeed: discern'st thou ought in that?' That shows that Othello is curious to know what Iago is thinking.

Another clear way that we can see Iago's purpose and Othello's reaction is through the tone of the piece, particularly the first few lines. Just looking at the punctuation used, it is clear to see that it is Othello who is asking all the questions, which demonstrates that he is becoming increasingly desperate to know what is on Iago's mind. This means that Iago is succeeding in his purpose of planting the seeds of jealousy in Othello's mind.

In this section of the play, Shakespeare shows that for the time being Othello has faith in Cassio, saying that he thinks he is honest and taking an almost defensive stance when

Iago asks him questions about him. For example he replies 'He did, from first to last' rather than simply 'He did'. By showing Othello's reaction as such, Shakespeare then goes on to show the audience how Iago changes his methods to fulfil his purpose. That is to say, after Othello defends Cassio, Iago knows that he must be careful and not say too much to avoid incriminating himself or Othello rejecting his idea straight away. In this passage this is evident because of the fact that it is Othello who does the majority of the speaking. The only time Iago really speaks is to assure Othello that he is a faithful friend.

The phrase 'As if there were some monster in his thought/ Too hideous to be shown', used by Othello shows that Iago has had the exact effect on Othello that he wants. The word 'monster' gives the sense that something big and awful is about to happen. Iago wants Othello to think that Cassio's feelings for Desdemona are playing on his mind, but that he dare not voice his concerns. As Othello trusts Iago, this means he does not believe Iago would not say anything without due cause and so this concerns him. Othello says 'I know thou'rt full of love and honesty,/ And weigh'st thy words before thou givest them breath,/ Therefore these stops of thine fright me the more.'

Another device that Shakespeare uses to show Othello's reaction is by changing the tone of his lines from inquisitive to imperative. For example, at first Othello simply asks questions such as 'why dost thou ask?' and 'Why of thy thought?' to show that he wants to know. However, as Iago keeps holding back, it becomes apparent to the reader that Othello is becoming increasingly desperate to know, and it is here when Othello uses imperatives such as 'Show me thy thought' and 'speak to me as to thy thinkings'. This tone is harsher, and so shows that Iago is making him curious.

By saying 'I dare be sworn I think that he is honest' about Michael Cassio, Iago is in effect backtracking upon what he has implied. The effect of this upon Othello is that he is left to think about what Iago is implying and draw his own conclusions. Othello uses lots of words and phrases such as 'thy worst of thoughts/ The worst of words' which show that he is assuming the worst.

Iago also uses a lot of language with negative connotations such as 'vile' and 'false' which make it seem like he is having second thoughts about bringing up this terrible thing. He also uses rhetorical questions such as 'Utter my thoughts?' which shows that he supposedly has doubts. Overall the dialogue in this extract reveals the clever subtlety that Iago uses to arouse feelings of uncertainty and jealousy and Othello's responses show how effective his technique is.

Later in the play, through Iago's clever trickery, after Othello has seen Cassio with the handkerchief Othello is convinced of his wife's unfaithfulness. In this part of the play Iago is much more confident of his ground as he knows that Othello is now totally convinced. At this point he no longer need to insinuate but he can speak outright. Othello is determined to kill both Desdemona and Cassio and he wants to make Cassio suffer – 'I would have him nine years a-killing' and as far as Desdemona goes he will 'chop her into messes'. Even now, though, he is torn between hatred for his wife and love for her, and this time Iago openly urges him to forget any feelings he once had for Desdemona and it is he who suggests he 'strangle her in her bed'. Again, as in the extract, Iago leads and Othello follows – the language shows the extent of the control Iago has over him.

Examiner's comments

The student begins her response directly by clearly identifying Iago's purpose and his success in achieving it. She follows up on this introduction by identifying Shakespeare's use of short sentences and exclamations and the effects these have, and supports her ideas with an apt example to illustrate the point. Othello's response to Iago's words is then examined, again using appropriate examples to illustrate her points.

The student then goes on to comment on the tone of the dialogue and the effects of the use of questions to show Othello's increasing anxiety. He longs to know what Iago is thinking, which reveals his success in planting suspicion in Othello's mind. However, the student is also aware of the trust that Othello still has in Cassio and how this is evident from Othello's responses.

There are some perceptive comments on the balance of speech between Iago and Othello in the dialogue and the fact that Othello does most of the talking. She rightly understands that by saying little and apparently being reluctant to reveal to Othello what is in his mind, Iago increases the effectiveness of his insinuations. The student again uses well-chosen references from the extract, such as her comment on the use of the word 'monster', to support her ideas. Her comments on Othello's use of imperatives and rhetorical questions are also well made.

The references to another episode in the text are quite brief although some relevant points are made. This section of the response would benefit from further development. Overall, though, this is a perceptive analysis of the extract and the student shows a good understanding of the effects created through the dialogue.

5 Analysing Speech and Speech Representation

Whichever specification you study at AS and A2 level in English Language and Literature, you will have to examine speech and the way it is represented in a variety of situations. This is a new departure for students of English Literature, although English Language students may well be familiar with the conventions of speech and discourse. However, by studying speech you will be in a much stronger position to understand the part that speech plays in literature and what writers are doing when they represent speech within certain types of text, such as dramatic works and interchanges between characters in novels – the two literary genres available to you to study in this specification at AS level.

For the purposes of both AS and A2 study, you must also be able to recognize, deconstruct and comment upon spontaneous speech or natural conversation. Your ability to do this, by examining different types of speech acts and the constituent parts of these acts, will enable you to analyse and, ultimately, compare the ways writers adapt or choose to represent speech in their works.

The differences between speech and writing

While this chapter is specifically about the differences between different representations of speech (which will all be written, as that is how they will appear on the examination paper), it is necessary to first look at the differences between speech and writing itself. Rather than confuse you by only examining the differences between speech and writing at A2 level, where it will be examined in Unit 3, it is more complete and more logical to examine those differences here so that you have a complete picture for both AS and A2.

The first section of this chapter therefore helps you contextualize those differences and you will probably want to make reference to it at A2 level; discussions of the language of spontaneous speech and the representation of speech come after this and will be of specific relevance to AS study. You will then need to carry these ideas forward when you come to compare speech with other written modes at A2 level.

Linguistically, there are many differences between speech and writing and we must take a number of factors into account when studying the differences between the two. These two types of communication are often distinguished by use of the term **mode**.

> **Mode**
>
> The modes are the two methodologies that we choose between when we communicate with each other; that is, we either use the **spoken mode** (speech) or produce the **written mode** (writing).

When a speaker or writer chooses a particular mode, he or she has often made intuitive (if sometimes unconscious) decisions as to why speech or writing should be adopted as a means or mode of communication. Before we look at some of the reasons why we choose a certain mode, let us examine two pieces of language that highlight some of the differences between speech and writing. The following two extracts show that the writers have explicit purposes and audiences in mind, by virtue of the mode they choose and what they do with their language within that mode.

Activity

Look closely at the following two pieces of language. The first extract is from the opening pages of a novel and the second is from a recording of a student speaking. Both pieces have a similar purpose, in that they are introductions to the speaker/writer.

- What differences can you see between the two pieces?
- For what reasons are these particular modes adopted?
- Who do you think is the target audience for each piece?

For each question, use textual evidence to support your answer.

Skin

I have very pale skin, very red lips. The lips are a fleshy cushion of pink, but I colour them dark scarlet. The skin is naturally pale, that prized magnolia of lovers, the skin of fairy tales and calves, and it is dusted with Shiseido, a white powder. The journalists have always talked about my skin.

Today I'm walking through the Jardin du Luxembourg on my own. It's April, there's a sore yellow light teasing the shadows between the trees, and the young English nannies push babies along the paths and stop at the sandpit.

The shaded section soothes me. I must protect my face from the divings of sunlight because I am using Retin-A, a vitamin A based cream that sheds layers of skin like sheaves of paper. If the sun reaches my face, it will burn. So I use sun block all over, that gives me a greased sheen when I first step out, but which is later absorbed, and will protect me from second degree burning. I am Adele Meier, something of a celebrity, and I must protect my skin.

Joanna Briscoe

Joanne

Key

(.)	micropause
(1.0)	pause in seconds
::	elongation of sound
[*italics*]	non-verbal sounds

My name's Joanne (0.5) I'm eighteen years old (1.0) an' I live in a small village (0.5) called Castleton (0.5) near Whitby (.) on in the middle o'the North Yorkshire Moors (0.5) with m'mum 'n dad (1.0) an' ma brother Simon (0.5) who's twenty-three a:::nd (0.5) erm (0.5) ma sister Emma (1.0) who's (1.0) fourteen (1.0) thirteen (1.0) fourteen (1.5) er (0.5) fourteen (0.5) [*laughs*] also and erm (0.5) I'm at (0.5) studyin' at the moment (1.0) I'm at uni Leeds University (0.5) erm (0.5) which I'm enjoyin' very much (1.0) I've made some really good fr (.) I've bin there since September (0.5) an' I've made some really good friends (.) and (0.5) having a bri::lliant time (0.5) erm (1.0) I'm quite small (3.0) errr (1.0) I like to think I'm quite thin (0.5) but er (0.5) I'm not sure if (0.5) if that's the case at the moment (2.5) um (1.0) I've got long blonde hair (1.0) blue eyes (1.5) a::nd (1.0) big feet (1.0) er:: (1.0) er I've bin home fer a coupla weeks (1.0) an' I went out with ma cousins ter do (.) at a party at a nearby pub (1.0) where we dressed up (0.5) as Reservoir Dogs (1.0) [*quietly laughs*] an' then this mornin' (1.5) I didn't feel too good [*laughs*]

- -

There are many differences between speech and writing, and you will have only touched the tip of the iceberg by focusing on the two passages above. Let us look at some of these differences in much more detail. We can best see the main differences between modes through the following distinctions:

1 the differences of **channel** or the way in which each mode is transmitted

2 the different **uses** of each mode, including the kinds of message each sends and the situations or contexts where each is used

3 the differences in **form**; this is the section that will outline the major characteristics of speech and will provide the basis of your understanding of how spontaneous speech operates.

Channel differences

The most obvious differences between speech and writing arise through the way each mode is produced; speech is formed through sound waves, from the mouth and voice box, and is transmitted to the ears. There are also usually other people present when we talk, but not always. Writing, on the other hand, is produced manually and is read, usually by eye, but in the case of blind people by touch. Writing is often undertaken for other people who are not present at the time of writing. These fairly transparent differences lead to another major distinguishing feature between the two: that is, speech, because it is transmitted orally at a certain point in time, is bound by time, whereas writing is produced for readers who are not present and is as such space-bound or spatial. This also results in the fact that the former is essentially temporary (although it can be given permanency through recording) and the latter is more permanent.

When considering channel, it is necessary to consider how the **forms** of each mode supplement the linguistic content, although the specific linguistic forms will be dealt with in much more detail later in the chapter.

In brief, speech includes what are known as **paralinguistic features**, those characteristics that transcend the language. These include:

- intonation, pitch and stress
- volume
- pace and rhythm
- pauses, gaps and silences
- laughter, coughing and other non-verbal sounds
- quality of voice.

On the other hand, the paralinguistic features of writing include:

- paragraphing
- punctuation including the spacing between words
- capitalization.

A sub-set of paralinguistic features is **kinesics**, which can be applied only to speech as it includes all those bodily features that go towards helping us communicate meaning. These include:

- body language, such as use of the hands (pointing) and head (nodding)
- facial expression including use of the eyes, the mouth (smiling) and the forehead (frowning).

If there is an equivalent of kinesics in writing, it is **graphology**, which would include:

- the design of specific graphemes (individual letters) or the font
- the point size in lettering
- use of colour
- use of white space and margins
- use of illustrations, pictures and other images
- use of columns and layout.

All of the above are, in many ways, incidental differences, but they do help to underpin your understanding of the more concrete differences between speech and writing. Therefore, your understanding of why communicators choose a certain mode, and by implication a certain channel with all its attendant characteristics, should be heightened, especially when in the next section we consider the uses or functions of each mode. Below is a table showing the differences we have considered so far.

Channel characteristics: permanent, dynamic and temporal differences

	Speech	Writing
1	When people speak to each other, they do so in the knowledge that there will be no record of the conversation (except in their minds or memories) and that when the conversation ends it ceases to exist. When they speak they use sounds to communicate.	When people write, they do so to make a record of their thoughts or ideas and they know that their writing will be permanent (as long as the text is kept). When people write, they use handwriting or some mechanical means to represent writing.
E.g.	*a conversation between two sixth-form students on the way to their next lesson*	hand-written (not permanent): *a shopping list* hand-written (permanent): *lecture notes* printed: *a novel or play-script*
2	Speech is most often an interactive process, where there are one or more other persons present. Thus, it can be seen as an active or dynamic process.	Writing is an activity where the audience is distant and very often not known. Thus, writing can be seen as a non-dynamic process.
E.g.	*any face-to-face conversation between two or more people*	audience unknown: *a magazine article* audience known: *a letter to a friend*

3	Speech is bound by time in that it is produced during a certain finite period of time where the participants are present during the interaction. Thus it is temporally bound.	Writing is bound by space as it is produced for readers who are not present at the time of writing; only the writer is usually present at the time of production, although there are exceptions. Thus it is spatially bound.
E.g.	*any verbal interaction that takes place*	space bound: *an essay for a teacher* space bound with participants: *minutes of a meeting*
4	Paralinguistic features and kinesics supplement meaning within speech.	Graphological features supplement the appearance of writing. Conventions of writing aid our understanding of its meaning.
E.g.	*someone telling a dramatic story using intonation and the hands to add to the effect he or she intends*	*the use of capitalization, sentence boundary markers, headlines, columns and photographs in a newspaper article*

Differences in mode usage

Speech

In the previous section on channel characteristics, we discovered that speech has the unique quality of being dynamic and that it is often temporary, in that it is 'lost' as soon as it has been said. However, speech can be made permanent through recording, transcription or a combination of the two. **Transcriptions** enable us to study various speech acts and events in this book, and it is the method you will become most familiar with when you study speech in an examination situation.

> **Transcription**
>
> A method of writing down exactly what is said in a systematic way. The style of transcription used in the English Language and Literature specification is **phonemic**, with additional symbols to aid understanding of what is said. This style of transcription is sometimes called an **impressionistic** transcription. A second style of transcription is **phonetic**, which uses symbols for sounds, the most widely known symbols being the International Phonetic Alphabet.

Speech can be seen as falling into the following categories, depending upon the intended degree of permanency:

- face-to-face interaction such as conversations or interviews
- non face-to-face interactions such as telephone conversations
- broadcast materials such as live radio or television programmes
- recordings such as audio books or 'teach yourself' tapes.

Even though speech in all of the above situations can be either temporary or permanent, it does have the unique quality of being 'live' in all of them because, as listeners, we hear the voices of the speakers, whether they are recorded or not, and the voice has the ability, through the paralinguistic features we have already outlined, to convey a unique personality which makes the communication more special.

Beyond the categories listed above, speech covers a range of specific functions that are dependent upon the situation, or are bound by the context.

> **Context**
>
> The social circumstances and situation in which speech takes place; the context influences the nature of what is said and how it is communicated. External contexts must be considered and commented upon when you analyse any speech act.

The definition given above is to draw your attention to the importance of context in speech, which is slightly different from the contexts we have examined so far. To highlight its importance, the following activity focuses solely on context.

Activity

Look closely at the following examples of speech from a range of situations. The context is vital for our understanding of each speech act, but can be guessed from these particular examples.

- What is the context for each of the following pieces of speech?
- What information can you give about each of the people speaking?
- What function does each piece of speech have?

1 **Young girl:** Can you tell me the way to the bus station, please?

     Man: Take the next right and follow the road for about half a mile and it's on your left. You can't miss it.

2   **George:** How are yer Fred?

    Fred: Mustn't grumble y'know, although t'missus in't too well.

3 So what yer need ter do (.) er is (0.5) er click on the bl (.) the tab (.) which says blank publications an' (0.5) er find cust (.) erm (1.0) the custom page button.

4 What a great song that is. Well, it's almost half past eight and it's time for our regular look at the papers. Hmm. Some interesting stories to catch the eye this morning.

5 Today we meet in the aftermath of the Falklands Battle. Our country has won a great victory and we are entitled to be proud. This nation had the resolution to do what it knew had to be done – to do what it knew was right.

These examples all show that the context or situation in which speech has been produced is integral to our understanding of what is being said. We can now look at the range of situations where speech is used.

The functions of speech

The situation or context of speech helps us to understand its function more clearly and to distinguish the nuances of certain speech acts. The functions of speech are as follows, starting with the most obvious and most common.

Conversation

This includes any spoken situation where speech is exchanged between participants, although they are not necessarily face-to-face. For instance, we often have telephone conversations without looking at the person we are talking to (with the advent of videophones and video conferencing, this is now not always the case). We can say that conversation is **interactional** in that it involves two or more participants. However, utterances within conversations have a number of sub-functions, which are outlined below:

- Making propositions. When we make conversation, we establish relationships with others, we co-operate and we keep channels open for further conversations. In order to facilitate these, we make propositions to each other where the things we talk about and discuss are linked to real or possible events in our own world, and where what we say can be either true or false. These are called **constative** (or **representative**) **utterances** since they are capable of being analysed as to their veracity or truthfulness. All of the following are examples of constative utterances:

  A: I've had a terrible day at school, Mum.

  B: It was lovely on Saturday.

  C: Coronation Street's on!

- Exchanging pleasantries. When we engage people in conversation, we do not launch straight into what we have to say without signalling that we want to open up a route of communication. These indicators, such as 'Excuse me' or 'Hello' are called **phatic utterances**, and usually precede the content of our conversations. We may also engage in phatic communication when it is not what is said that is important, more the fact that we are talking. When we meet one another and comment on the weather or ask how the other person is, it could be viewed as an exchange of simple pleasantries and nothing more; in other words, it is linguistically vacuous and serves only a social function.

- Expressing feelings. Another function of speech is to convey our feelings and emotions. Obviously, this depends upon how comfortable we feel about articulating our feelings and how confident we are as people. However, with people we know or are close to, we often use **expressive utterances** to transmit our innermost feelings.

  A: I feel awful about it.
  B: I really hate Pete Doherty.
  C: Oh, I love you so much!

- Doing something. There are certain times where we want someone to do something for us, so we will order, suggest or request a particular thing. This kind of utterance is a **directive**.

  A: A pint of beer and give me a bag of crisps, too.
  B: Shut the window for me, will you?
  C: Don't speak with your mouth full.

Pedagogic talk

It is sometimes difficult to draw the line between conversation and the kind of talk that takes place in the classroom. It is often said that educational talk is not only interactional but also **transactional**, since its function is to get something done.

The formality of the classroom has, to some extent, disappeared as teachers embrace the advantages of learning through informal means and differing teaching styles. Nonetheless, the classroom does not always allow the same degree of feedback in exchanges as everyday conversation, and the teacher often controls who can feed back. Similarly, when parents are talking to their children about appropriate behaviour, they adopt a position akin to a teacher and control the number of turns and amount of feedback from the child they are addressing.

Sub-functions of pedagogic talk are as follows:

- Conveying information. Speech is frequently used to communicate information and facts, as teachers do in many different ways. The talk is often informal, participatory and includes turn-taking and feedback. However, some aspects of conversational 'rules' are flagrantly ignored in teaching - this will be addressed later in this section. This type of conversation or speech produces **referential utterances** having factual information as their basis; they can also be constative or representative in their nature, since they are based on truth.

    A: England won the World Cup in 1966.
    B: There are a number of different types of noun: common, proper, abstract, collective and so on.
    C: Copenhagen is the capital of Denmark.

- Ethical transmission. There is also an aspect of teaching and parenting that embraces the transmission of morality and ethics. This results in **ethical propositions**, that is behavioural guides that usually embed values or moral codes within their main content. These types of utterance often have their foundation in civil law.

    A: You should not kill other people.
    B: Nice girls don't swear.
    C: Do not urinate in public places.

Accompanying performance

When people accompany certain actions in the real world with speech, a unique type of speech act takes place: the **performative** (or **declarational**) **utterance**. This includes ceremonies where certain procedures are followed, and formalized events that require certain accompanying actions. Events such as religious observances, marriage ceremonies and legal procedures can all be included here.

A: By the power invested in me in this court, I sentence you to sixty days of community service.
B: I take this woman to be my lawful wedded wife.
C: I name this ship the Bonnie Lassie.

This type of speech could also include those speech acts that require the speaker to undertake some future action. These are known as **commissive utterances** and include threats, promises, pledges and refusals.

A: I promise to meet you next week.
B: I'll come right back.
C: We will not be going to the shops today.

Entertainment

This includes talk on television, radio and the stage. These media all use speech in quite special ways. For instance, television and radio can include spontaneous, unscripted speech, as seen in interviews and chat shows, although these will usually have some kind of agenda or topic to guide the discussion. Obviously, the talk on television is supplemented by visual elements, but both television and radio base much of what is seen or heard on speech.

Scripted speech plays a massive part in such programmes as news bulletins (through the use of autocues), soap operas and documentaries. Scripted speech as seen in dramas and theatrical productions is another area that deserves separate consideration.

Rhetorical speech

Again this is a unique type of speech in that it is (usually) scripted and relies, to a great extent, on the use of rhetorical and persuasive devices, in order to influence listeners. Politicians are very adept at using rhetoric; advertisers often use persuasive techniques to boost sales of their products. Rhetoric and scripted speech will be examined later in this chapter.

Egocentric speech

When we are alone we sometimes talk to ourselves, children more so than adults perhaps. The purpose of this is unclear: are we articulating our thoughts, and if we are, then aren't thoughts a kind of silent speech in themselves? Whatever the purpose, we are certainly able to talk to ourselves and many of us do it, even if we might not admit it! Perhaps we should view egocentric speech as a kind of personal monologue for our own benefit.

Activity

Using a table set out like the one below, collect examples of your own that show:

- different usages of the range of utterances listed
- the context of each utterance.

Utterance type	Your example	Context
Constative utterance Phatic utterance Expressive utterance Referential utterance Directive utterance Commissive utterance Ethical proposition Performative utterance		

Writing

We noted at the start of this section that modern technology allows us to make speech permanent through recordings. Writing has always had the quality of permanency, as seen in the vast corpus of printed matter. So much printed matter is produced today that much of it is in fact disposed of as soon as (or even before) it is read: good examples of this are the tabloid culture or the plethora of junk mail everyone receives! It is an interesting fact that the amount of printed matter in just one copy of today's *Sunday Times* would represent the average reading for a year of an educated person in the seventeenth century. This is a good indicator of how adept we have become at coping with printed matter as well as revealing our reliance upon it in day-to-day life.

Until very recently, it was difficult to keep or store such vast amounts of literature. The advent of microfiche, CD ROMs, the Internet and the size of hard drives on computers has aided the process enormously and has certainly helped those people whose occupation requires access to large amounts of material on a regular basis for reference purposes.

To illustrate the variety of different materials we read on a daily basis, complete the following activity.

Activity

Use a table like the one below to collect names and details for the reading you do in a week. You could also collect examples of different types of writing to keep as a selection of different styles: this will help you to appreciate the range of materials a course such as this will draw on. Add to the table further ideas of your own on written materials which are not listed.

Type of written material	Name or title	Details e.g. genre, whether printed, handwritten, permanent, bought, etc.
Newspapers Magazines Periodicals Leaflets Literature Comics Catalogues Advertisements Application forms Manuals or instructions Menus or recipes Reference materials Computer materials Televisual materials E-mails and other correspondence		

The functions of writing

Having examined the variety and range of written matter that is available to us, let us briefly examine the different functions of writing. This will allow you to see some of the more obvious differences between the two modes, before we look at details of the characteristics of speech.

Cultural transmission

Writing allows us the opportunity to accumulate a huge amount of information and to pass it on generation after generation. This is how our greatest literature has been passed down to us. We must also remember that the written mode allows one person to communicate with potentially millions of other people, thus allowing the sharing of experience. It is this aspect of the written mode that makes it so culturally important. In direct contrast to the oral tradition, writing helps to preserve historical details that can be referred to at a later date. This definition accounts for such written material as novels, newspapers, magazines and other non-literary forms.

Reference and lists

This function is a direct result of cultural transmission, in that it is possible for the brain to store only a finite amount of factual information, and we need to access reference material fairly often. The existence of written lists allows our brains to be engaged in more important activities, and we can refer back when necessary to something that is written down; how many of us have forgotten to buy a vital item when we have not made a shopping list! It is also a reflection of the nature of our lives today that many electronic personal organizers have a list function as part of their software... and that many people rely on them massively.

Prose forms

Because of the difficulty in remembering long tracts of language, written prose has developed as the major literary form, used in the widest sense of the word. Fictional stories, biographies, news stories, history and religion all use the prose medium for recording details that could not be stored in the memory or transmitted orally with accuracy.

Dictionaries and thesauri

The dictionary developed out of the opulence of the language associated with literature and prose writing, and allows a formalized recording of the lexicon with an alphabetical, defined list. A thesaurus groups sets of words according to their meaning.

Legal documentation

Writing has given society the ability to record laws and thus promote consistency of interpretation and application. Consider the difference between slander and libel, for instance, and the difficulty of proving the former.

Education

Books and written material are vital in terms of our education. They supplement and verify the information passed on through educators and teachers, and in theory allow everyone (who can read) access to information that at one time was the privilege of a tiny proportion of the population.

Cognitive development

Written material and the vast amount of printed matter has, again theoretically, enabled the human race to become more educated. In other words, our cognitive skills have become more highly developed and consequently so has our intelligence. This would certainly account for the rapid expansion of technology during the past century.

Exploration of theories and views

The written word often formalizes theories and ideas that have developed through discussion and informal debate. Once they are written down, a more formal debate can occur, with a theory being either propounded or disputed. This is very important in the development of science and medicine as well as other fields such as philosophy.

Differences in function

The above divisions of the functions of writing are in many ways artificial, since they overlap with each other; and certainly more areas could be considered, such as advertising, which has a unique and vital place in contemporary culture. However, the purpose of this section is to underline the differences between the functions of the two modes – speech and writing – so let us finish by summarizing these in a table.

	Speech	**Writing**
1	Speech is essentially a social activity. We use it for many different ends, from passing the time of day to the more formalized rituals of ceremony.	Writing is more suited to the recording of factual material, giving an accurate account of what has happened in printed form.
E.g.	*talking to a friend about what we did last night*	*an account of what happened at a political summit in the newspaper*
2	Speech is suited to the 'here and now', where we do not need to make records. It is more immediate and temporary.	Writing allows us to record more facts and material than we could remember for future reference. It is less immediate but has the advantage of permanency.
E.g.	*any conversation which is purely informal and not recorded in any way*	*a diary that is written every day over a sustained period of time*
3	Speech allows us to tell someone how we feel, how to behave or what should be done in certain situations. We can access these perceptions instantly.	Writing tends to give us the opportunity to explore the possibilities of ideas and theories. It also records laws formally, rather than suggesting codes of behaviour.
E.g.	*telling someone what you believe they should do, after they have asked you for advice*	*scientific theories as seen in periodicals; written local by-laws*
4	Since the brain allows retention of only a certain number of facts, speech allows us to verbalize only what we can recall; it can therefore be subject to inaccuracy.	Writing allows us access to reference material when we do not know something or are uncertain of facts. It often allows us to ascertain the truth about matters.
E.g.	*retelling a story where certain facts are misreported or muddled up*	*any reference book, e.g. an encyclopaedia or dictionary*

Differences of form

Speech

Some of the major characteristics of speech arise out of the fact that much speech is **unplanned** or **spontaneous**. Because a lot of speech is not thought out before its expression, we find that a number of unique features occur that give spontaneous speech its special quality.

One of the characteristics we have already noted is that we do not speak in the carefully constructed, standard sentences which make up the prose of written English; we speak in non-sentences or **utterances**. This word is a much more accurate way to describe units of speech, since it reflects what we utter or say, and it would be quite misleading to say we speak in sentences. Indeed, if we did speak in sentences, we would find conversation boring and a trial to listen to and take part in. It is the fact that we use non-sentences, part-sentences, paralinguistics and kinesics that gives speech its distinctiveness and makes it such a useful tool in everyday life.

When we examine the form of spoken language, it is helpful to break down the component parts of the speech act itself: the relationship of the speakers, the manner of the speech, the topic or subject matter and, finally, the structure of the conversation. Many of the examples of spontaneous speech you have looked at so far in this book have been self-contained speeches (such as Joanne's piece of speech at the start of this section) or snippets of longer conversations where the full effect of the whole conversation cannot be seen. In practice, you will rarely have to work on full conversations, since they are often very lengthy and it can be difficult to determine where one conversation ends and another begins.

Examine carefully the following piece of spontaneous speech, which occurred at the start of a conversation between four young people having a break at college: Sarah (S), Kris (K), Hannah (H), and Will (W).

Key

(.) micropause
(1.0) pause in seconds
<u>underlining</u> particular emphasis of a word
[overlap
:: elongation of sound

S: will you get us a coffee Kris
K: yea:::::h (0.5) okay *(goes to coffee bar)*
S: what've yer just 'ad
H: further maths (.) I <u>rea:::lly</u> wish I hadner taken it
S: why
H: it's <u>solid</u> (.) <u>absolutely</u> rock hard
S: I feel the same about film (.) there's so much a <u>analytical</u> stuff (.) as well as all the (.) the <u>theory</u> an' all that (0.5) hiya *(Will sits down)*
W: hi
H: hiya
S: how was English
W: s'allright (.) our teacher's a right sarky git though (.) he had a go about me teeshirt (.) then me hair (.) and <u>then</u> he made me read (.) <u>bastard</u> *(laughs)*
S: who is it
W: Rob Myers
H: oh I've got him as well (.) seems okay <u>actually</u>

W: yeah (.) well (.) 'f 'e says any thing else I'll be *(inaudible)*
S: so (.) we goin' out on Friday or what
H: could do (.) I'll've been paid by then (.) you up for it Will
W: suppose so (.) don't <u>think</u> I'm doin' anything else
                                    [
H: great
                                    [
W: where's Kris
S: gone to get me a coffee
W: I'll go an' see if he'll get me one too
S: so (.) where shall we go then
H: the Piper

- -

This is a typical example of an exchange that youngsters have, where they are known to one another, where they see each other on a regular basis and where certain aspects of their life are very important to them at this time. Let us look at some of the evidence that helps us to see this.

1 **Relationship:** We can see immediately that the participants in the conversation are known to each other:

- the participants rarely use each other's names, certainly not when they are greeting each other
- the girls decide to discuss plans for Friday night
- they have common reference points (the teacher, the name of the club).

2 **Formality:** The conversation is quite informal, despite having a structure to it:

- the participants use many contracted forms (''f 'e' for 'if he')
- they also employ terms which are fairly exclusive to their peer group ('solid' and 'up for it')
- there are very few external constraints in terms of context, and it is obviously possible for others to join in (Will joins the conversation without any apparent difficulty and then leaves it to go and join Kris).

3 **Topicality:** Since this is part of a conversation that takes place during a break, a range of topics might come up:

- the need for a coffee; Sarah expresses this and Kris accepts the task of going to get one
- the way that their lessons are progressing
- their reaction to a member of staff
- the initial plans for a night out.

Once a topic has been exhausted, a new topic can be introduced and explored (Will does this by giving his opinion on a teacher); if a new topic is introduced before the present topic has worked out its natural course, then the new topic may be rejected or picked up later. A **topic shift** is when a new topic is taken up and is explored by the participants; we see this when Sarah asks if they are going out on Friday.

4 **Structure:** It is often easy to pick up the thread of what is happening in a conversation and discover what the participants are talking about if there are clues to help us. Sometimes the topic is the route into a conversation; here

we have a number of references to lessons and teaching as well as socializing, which help us to work out the way in which the conversation develops. But it can sometimes be difficult to tune into a conversation when it is in full flow, as you have no doubt experienced yourself when you have come into a room where the participants are completely immersed in their talk. It takes a little while to work out what the parameters of the conversation are and what subject is being discussed; sometimes we pick up the wrong subject, and this can result in misunderstandings or confusions.

Let us look in more detail at some of the strategies we use to make conversations progress, through the piece of conversation we have examined above.

Adjacency pairs

One vital organizational device we employ all the time in conversation, whether it be formal or informal, is the adjacency pair. This is where one type of utterance leads to another, always with a distinctive pattern that we have intuitively come to recognize through conversational practice. Adjacency pairs:

- are spoken by different people
- always have a rational link
- are characterized by the second utterance following on from the first utterance.

Adjacency pairs allow conversation to progress in a structured, if unplanned way. They are unplanned in the sense that we don't know what is going to be said next, even though the topicality has already been decided upon. Adjacency pairings can include the following, although this is not an exhaustive list:

- greeting and returned greeting
- question and answer
- request and acceptance or refusal
- statement and corroboration
- compliment and reply (not necessarily accepted)
- complaint and apology
- leave-taking and farewell.

We can see that there is a structure to the conversation by examining the way that the pairings are linked. The first section of the conversation is broken down for you below, to show how some of the adjacency pairs work:

S: will you get us a coffee Kris
K: yea:::::h (0.5) okay

- -

This is a request, where Sarah asks Kris to get a drink for her using an interrogative; he accepts the request, although his extended 'yea:::::h' indicates that he might not be too happy to begin with, especially since he seems to clarify his acceptance by confirming it through 'okay'.

S: what've yer just 'ad
H: further maths

- -

This is another question and answer adjacency pair, where Sarah simply asks for some information which is given by Hannah. She uses an interrogative utterance 'what've yer just 'ad' to elicit this information from her friend; Hannah gives a simple reply in the form of 'further maths'. However, the next adjacency pair starts with an opinion in the form of an expressive utterance where her feelings are shown by the extended and emphasized intensifier 'rea:::lly':

H: I <u>rea:::lly</u> wish I hadner taken it
S: why
H: it's <u>solid</u> (.) <u>absolutely</u> rock hard

- -

Here, Sarah asks Hannah to elucidate by use of the simple interrogative 'why', and Hannah gives her reply that the subject is '<u>solid</u>', which she then builds on with the adjectival phrase '<u>absolutely</u> rock hard'. This section can also be seen as a three-part exchange. This is where a particular section of conversation requires three distinct, ordered sections:

- an initiation or beginning utterance
- a reply
- a response to the reply or feedback.

> **Feedback**
>
> The process of receiving a reply to a piece of speech, which shows that the listener has understood the nature of the message sent by the speaker; a tool to show that the effectiveness of a piece of communication can be verified.

This applies to the part of the conversation we have just examined:

- the initial point about the difficulty of the subject: 'I <u>rea:::lly</u> wish I hadner taken it'
- Sarah's reply: 'why'
- and Hannah's response and feedback to the reply: 'it's <u>solid</u> (.) <u>absolutely</u> rock hard'.

The conversation continues with another adjacency pair, which chains from the last part of the three-part exchange:

H: it's <u>solid</u> (.) <u>absolutely</u> rock hard
S: I feel the same about film (.) there's so much a <u>analytical</u> stuff (.) as well as all the (.) the <u>theory</u> an' all that (0.5)

- -

Here Sarah seems to sympathize with Hannah's feelings about her problems with a new subject as she responds with one of her own, 'film [studies]'. We have here an example of a statement followed by a corroboration and example from Sarah, which is then exemplified through comment on the parts of the subject which are '<u>analytical</u>'. There is some general and imprecise use of language, often a characteristic of young people, when she uses the noun 'stuff' and the rather general noun phrase 'the <u>theory</u> an' all that'.

The next part is purely phatic as Will enters and she greets him, which he then replies to:

S: hiya
W: hi

- -

Hannah also indulges in phatic communication as she takes Will's greeting to be a signal to reply herself, as the second part of an adjacency pair:

W: hi
H: hiya

- -

The linking of some of these adjacency pairs is called **chaining**, since each pair is attached to the previous one, usually in a linear fashion and rather like the links in a chain. This enables the participants to explore topics and work them out to their natural conclusion. As you can see from the example you have just looked at, we are fairly dependent on the notion of conversational chaining through adjacency pairs, as they allow conversation to flow unimpeded. When we violate the unspoken rules of adjacency pairing, conversation tends to break down. For instance, if we persistently fail to respond to a question we have been asked, then the questioner will assume that something is wrong and will either ask what is the matter or end the conversation.

> ### Activity
>
> Break down the remainder of the conversation on pages 109–10 into its component adjacency pairs and comment on what is happening in each utterance of each adjacency pair, formulating your answer in the way that has been shown above with the first section. You will notice that each of the points made is supported by a comment and use of the relevant terminology.

Turn-taking

One of the skills we possess as conversational participants is taking turns when we talk. We 'pass' the conversation over to other group members, and it is taken up or refused by other participants as they see fit. Conversations are characterized by the fact that only one person speaks at a time: each is taking a turn, as it were. However, that turn may be relinquished, may be passed on to someone else or may even be 'stolen', especially if one speaker is monopolizing the conversation. As participants in a conversation, we are fairly certain that we will get a turn to say something at some point. But how do we know when a turn is 'up for grabs', or whether a certain person will speak as opposed to someone else? A number of signals occur in utterances to help us here. They include the following:

- The speaker **elongates** or **stresses** the final word of the utterance; there is a good example of this in the conversation above, where Hannah says she feels that the teacher is 'okay <u>actually</u>', the stress on the adverb signalling the end of her utterance. Because this is the part of the utterance that she wants to stress, she does so by placing the adverb at the end of her utterance.

- The speaker may also indicate that his or her turn is ending by dropping the sound level, coupled with less emphasis. A good example of this in the conversation is where Sarah says she is also finding aspects of Film Studies difficult: 'the <u>theory</u> an' all that'. We can see that the three words after the stress on the noun 'theory' are much less important and almost seem throwaway. The fact that it also includes a clipped form of the connective 'and' probably indicates that it is less important too.

- Phrases such as 'you know', 'like' and 'or something' can sometimes indicate the end of a turn as these words are being used like fillers, thus showing that the speaker is running out of steam and it is time for someone else to take up the turn.

- Speakers may designate that their turn is over by making their utterance complete grammatically and syntactically. Questions are good examples of this, although the fact that they require an answer makes it doubly obvious that the turn is being handed over. Completed statements such as 'And that's the end of it' or 'That's all I have to say on the matter' are examples of syntactically complete utterances which show the speaker has finished.

- Finally, there are those signals that cannot be seen on the page, which are paralinguistic in nature: eye contact with another listener, sitting back in a chair or another similar relaxation of the posture, and use of the hands or head (nodding) could all signal it is another person's turn to speak.

Turn-taking is a vital part of conversational management and, in conjunction with adjacency pairings, it is one of the two major structures of spoken interaction. There are other features that are less frequent, but nonetheless important.

Insertion and side sequences

Once a conversation has been initiated, there can be interruptions from unexpected sources. People can come into the room or something might happen that requires the speaker's immediate attention, such as a knock at the door or a telephone ringing. The consequence of this is a **conversational insertion** or **insertion sequence**, where the original conversation is suspended and then resumes once the interruption has been dealt with. An example might look something like this:

X: so there we were an' then

              [

Z: 'scuse me (.) d'you want me to type that up for you ⎫ Insertion sequence
X: oh yes please (.) thanks   ⎬
Y: so what happened   ⎭
X: right (.) there we were an' the whole thing just (.) <u>exploded</u>

- -

Z's interruption is obviously important and so it takes precedence over the original utterance, where a story is being told. The insertion sequence is dealt with and then the original topic is returned to.

Side sequences, however, are much more obvious and sometimes last for a number of utterances. They act as an elucidation or explanation of something that has previously been uttered:

X: Let's go to the pub.
Y: Will Mike be there? ⎫
X: Nah.   ⎪
Y: What about Alan?   ⎬ Side sequence
X: Don't think so.   ⎪
Y: Oh all right then. ⎭

- -

In the snippet of conversation given above, we see that Y wants clarification of who will be in the pub before giving his affirmation in the final utterance that he will go; note that the first and last utterances form an adjacency pairing within which the side sequence is embedded.

Closing sequences

When we draw towards the end of a conversation, especially if we are standing talking in the street or some other public place, we signal that we wish the conversation to come to an end by a variety of methods. This is another form of conversational management; it can often take a number of utterances to achieve, and repetition is frequently used to sum up and then close the exchange. Look at this example, taken from the end of the conversation between the four students to whom you were introduced earlier:

S: so I'll see you at lunch then
K: yeah
S: are we goin' down town
K: yeah (.) see yer then
S: okay (.) see yer later Will
W: bye
H: bye
W: bye

- -

This sequence has a number of distinctive features to it, including pre-closing signals which tell other people in the group that the closing ritual is about to commence ('so I'll see you at lunch then') and then some phatic utterances ('bye') which keep the channels open for further talk, at lunchtime presumably. In much the same way that phatic utterances signal the opening of a conversation and open up avenues for discourse, closing sequences round off a conversation in a co-operative manner, and also allow those conversational avenues to be re-opened at a later date. This is the basis for co-operative discourse and we use it all the time.

Some other features of conversation
Elision, ellipsis and other shortened forms

Because speech is often quick and characterized by informality among friends, **elision** often occurs. Elision is a characteristic of connected speech and often occurs when we put certain words together to make well-used phrases. A good example would be *fish 'n chips*, where the 'and' is contracted to 'n and the whole phrase sounds like one word. An example from the conversation we studied earlier is ''sallright', which is a **contraction** of 'it's all right'; there is also the phrase ''f 'e', which is an elided form of 'if he'. This last phrase also highlights some people's predilection for dropping the 'h' sound in speech, often through speed or laziness.

Whereas elision refers to the omission of certain letters in words and phrases, **ellipsis** refers to missing whole words, which are generally understood from the context of the speech. This can take a variety of forms:

- pronouns: Hope you can come   *for*   I hope you can come
- verb phrases: Wanna coffee?   *for*   Do you wanna coffee?
- full phrase: Q: Where are you off to? A: To town.   *for*   I am off to town

In the conversation above, a good example of an elliptical sentence is Hannah's utterance: 'could do (.) I'll've been paid by then (.) you up for it Will'.

In this utterance there are two elliptical sections. First, 'could do' is missing the personal pronoun 'I' as it isn't really needed; the original question has been directed at her only. Secondly, the question at the end of the utterance 'you up for it Will' has the verb 'are' missing from it, probably because of speed and the informality of the whole exchange.

Other contractions include shortened versions of such things as:

- names: shortening of names is often seen as an indicator of informality, for example Peter becomes Pete or Sarah becomes Sal
- verbs: in speech we often shorten negated verbs, so 'cannot' becomes 'can't', 'shall not' becomes 'shan't' and 'is not' becomes 'isn't'
- pronouns and verbs: as with the forms we have seen above, when some verbs are placed with pronouns, contraction occurs in speech: 'I will' becomes 'I'll', 'you will' becomes 'you'll' and so on.

Liaison

Liaison is another feature of speech that occurs when two words are spoken at speed and the running together or **liaison** of these two words produces a new sound. For instance, when a word starts with a vowel, there is sometimes a carry-over sound, from a previous word ending in a consonant.

'There is someone over there' might be heard as 'There ris someone', where the 'r' is sounded at the start of the verb 'is', resulting in a word that sounds like 'ris'.

Juncture

As we have already seen, when we speak we can meld words together so they become virtually indistinguishable. **Juncture** is the almost imperceptible gap that appears between words so we can distinguish them; it is most often characterized by silence, but it is not always clear in spontaneous speech. This can result in some interesting, and occasionally amusing, misunderstandings, which *The Two Ronnies* used in a famous sketch set in a hardware shop. A man enters the shop and asks for various items but the shopkeeper misinterprets his request, simply because of the juncture (or lack of it) between the shopper's words. For instance the shopper asks for 'fork 'andles' (his accent drops the 'h' at the start of the word 'handles') and the shopkeeper returns to the counter with four candles, as the lack of juncture between the shopper's words (as well as his accent) allows for this misinterpretation.

Non-standard forms and slang

The standard forms that are used in writing are often flouted in speech; no doubt those of you who use non-standard forms will have had some of your written English corrected before now! In the conversation we have been examining, a couple of non-standard forms are used: Will says, 'our teacher's a right sarky git though (.) he had a go about me teeshirt'. Here Will uses the non-standard intensifier 'right' for 'very' and then replaces the first-person possessive pronoun 'my' with 'me', which is technically not possessive at all. It can also be noted that the adjective 'sarky' is a non-standard, informal version of 'sarcastic'. Finally, the mildly derogatory term 'git' is certainly a feature of spontaneous speech, where slang, swearing and demotic forms often pepper informal conversations.

Informal speech is also characterized by use of slang terms, words that are acceptable in casual speech and understood by everyone; in writing, they would often be deemed inappropriate unless they were part of reported speech. Slang terms are often short-lived and sometimes recognizable only to the peer group who use them. An example within the conversation we have studied is 'solid' meaning 'difficult' or 'hard'.

Non-verbal aspects

We have already mentioned, and seen in the transcriptions, **overlaps** where two people speak at once; this is marked by a [in transcriptions, with the overlapping speech being printed in alignment. Overlaps occur for various reasons: an end of turn may have been misjudged, someone may be keen to add to a point and wish to steal a turn, or there may be many participants who all hold equal status within the conversational group.

Pauses are self-explanatory: they indicate a gap in something said, and are marked by a parenthesis with a number inside, to indicate the number of seconds of time that elapsed between speech: (1.5) would indicate a pause of one-and-a-half seconds. Pauses allow thinking time, obviously quite important in spontaneous speech. Micropauses (.) are sometimes seen as the punctuation of speech, as they can indicate the boundaries of clauses and unitary pieces of information; at other times, they exist solely to allow the speaker the opportunity of taking a breath or considering the next part of the utterance.

Voice-filled pauses are gaps that are filled. Examples of voice-filled pauses are 'erm', 'er', 'um' and 'ah' – you will see these all the time in spontaneous speech. They help to indicate that the speaker's turn is not over yet and so prevent interruption as well as indicating that some thought process is taking place; there is also a school of thought that says that they show our mouths do not move as quickly as our minds, so we get these little hiccups in speech.

If they are words in their own right but carry no apparent meaning, they are called **fillers**, because they fill a gap. Frequently used fillers include:

- you know
- sort of
- you see
- I mean
- kind of
- well.

Repetitions or **stuttering** can often be found in conversations: it is as if the speaker is searching for the right word and is unsure as to whether he or she has found it. It may be only a letter that is repeated, as in the conversation reported above, when Sarah says: 'there's so much a <u>analytical</u> stuff', where she is obviously searching for the correct word and makes a repair within her utterance.

False starts also occur periodically, especially if the speaker becomes muddled or has so much to say that he or she loses track of speech constructions. Sometimes, if we start an utterance and realize we have made a mistake and need to correct ourselves, we use a conversational **repair**, which can often be prefaced or coupled with the filler 'I mean'.

Remember that girl (.) er Stacey (.) er no (0.5) Tracy I mean

- -

Hedging is a feature that occurs when you don't necessarily want to make your feelings known or you are keen to fence-sit so as not to give your position away, often for fear of offending. An example of this kind of speech is the following:

X: what d'you think then
Z: we::::ll (.) I'm not sure really

- -

Here Z is hedging by using the interjection 'well' as a signal of hesitation, through the elongation of the word, and finally by directly stating uncertainty.

Discourse markers are words which often mark that a speaker is about to take a turn or establish some sort of position in the conversation. Words such as 'right' or 'so' or 'okay then' as initial words in utterances are good examples of this. They have the effect of saying, 'I'm going to speak now. I want you to listen to me.'

Markers of sympathetic circularity and **backchannel behaviour** are 'words' often heard when someone is in full flow and the listener feeds back by making noises to indicate that he or she is listening to what is being said. Examples of this would be 'uh uh', 'yeah', 'I see', 'mm' and so on. Often these are delivered while the other speaker is speaking, so they often involve examples of simultaneous speech.

> ### Activity
>
> Read the following transcript carefully. Here a 16-year-old talks with his mum and dad about what he wants to do after he has left school.
>
> Examine the ways that each speaker conveys his or her feelings, highlighting any speech features that help to deliver these opinions.

Tom: anyway (.) I've had a <u>fantastic</u> week (.) s'been <u>really</u> (.) <u>really</u> (.) good (3.0) an' an' (.) an' I'm not really sure (1.0) er (0.5) that I want to go to college <u>now</u>

Dad: what's been so good about it then Tom

Tom: we::::ll (1.0) I've been given some (1.0) re <u>responsibility</u> (.) an' (.) an' I've been doin' stuff which I kinda (.) <u>really</u> enjoy (.) an' that's <u>dead</u> important (.) to <u>me</u> anyway (1.0) an' I wanna (.)
　　　　[

Mum: 　so you thin (.) sorry (.) go on

Tom: right (.) all I wanna do is mountain bikin' (1.0) either in a shop (.) or try to do something with it (.) y'know (.) erm (1.0) <u>professionally</u> (0.5) or or (.) do a qualification in engineering or whatever

Mum: but you'd need to continue at school for that

Tom: no no (.) no you don't (.) the lads at Bike Scene (.) they're doin' erm (.) NVQs in Bike Maintenance (.) they're the first in the <u>country</u> to do it (.) I could train on the job (.) they told me that durin' me work experience

Dad: so can we get this straight then (.) y'you (.) you've decided that yer wanna leave school next year (.) an get a job (.) <u>preferably</u> something to do with mountain bikin'

Tom: well (0.5) yeah::::: (.) that's what I've been sayin'

Dad: I suppose that's what work experience is all about (.) findin' out what you want to do

Mum: what about sixth form though

Tom: well (1.0) at the moment (.) this is what <u>I::</u> want to do

- -

Writing

This chapter concentrates on the features of speech and we have now examined its major characteristics, so we need not go into great detail about writing, as many of the differences are obvious. However, a brief outline of some of the features of writing will help you to understand speech more fully.

When we write, we have the opportunity to develop and organize our work, making amendments and revisions as necessary. We also have the ability to plan out documents prior to writing them; this enables us to use complex sentence structures, with subordination and intricacy of syntax. In speech, especially spontaneous unplanned speech, we do not often use intricacy and we tend to keep our utterances syntactically and grammatically simple.

Similarly, because writing does not have the visual clues that speech often does, the former tends to use unambiguous expressions and descriptions and avoid **deixis**, that is the use of terms and expressions that rely on the context to give their meaning, such as 'that one', 'over there' and 'here'.

When we study literature, as you have already found in the earlier chapters in this book, we often see sophisticated patterning and elaborate use of literary techniques; these are, in many ways, characteristic of the written mode and allow the reader to reflect upon how construction and meaning both contribute to the overall effect intended by the writer. In speech, we are rarely faced with such complexity and we often find speech is shot through with vagueness and ambiguity.

Certain words, phrases and sentences are hardly ever spoken. For instance, the language of the legal system requires such precision and organization that sentences alone often run to hundreds of words. Other words that are rarely spoken are full names: we seldom, when we speak to each other, use full names, preferring instead to use one name, which is frequently contracted, such as Michael into Mike or Elizabeth into Lizzie. However, we often have occasion to write down our full names, when we are filling out official forms, for instance. Similarly, scientists would never refer in speech to some chemicals by their full name, preferring to use the chemical symbol, a more common name, or a contraction or abbreviation:

HCl	for	hydrochloric acid
Vinegar	for	acetic acid
Salt	for	sodium chloride
TNT	for	trinitrotoluene
HMD	for	hexamethylenediamine

However, in a paper for a scientific journal or periodical, the full name of the chemical would more likely be used, especially if it was obscure.

As we have already seen, speech is immediate and unplanned, and it can be quite difficult to recall the exact nature of what has been said, especially as time goes by. However, writing allows us to keep a record of events or data, if needed, and then we have the opportunity to refer back to it at a later date. Similarly, it is easy and more convenient to keep records through writing, rather than committing them to memory. It is also much less demanding to read text at your own speed, when it comes to learning something, than being told or taught something by another person through the mode of speech, where you have to follow at the speaker's pace, which is dictated by the speed of speech and delivery.

Mistakes, revisions, and shortfalls in writing can all be rectified or removed, either immediately or at a later time; in the intervening period, no one need see the document, so once the mistakes have been corrected, only the writer is aware that they were present in the first instance. In speech, however, once a mistake is made it cannot be undone.

Finally, writing does not share the prosodic or auditory properties of speech; intonation, pace, rhythm and volume are all characteristics of spoken discourse and will be discussed in the next section on rhetoric and the art of planned speech. Perhaps the only features writing does have that relate to prosody are elements such as emboldening or underlining for emphasis, and exclamation or question marks to indicate degrees of astonishment or inquiry.

Differences in form and features

As with the other sections in this chapter, we will end by summarizing the differences between speech and writing in a table.

	Speech	Writing
1	Speech is usually unplanned, with much repetition, hesitation and non-standard forms.	Writing can be planned and revised, and conform to Standard English usage.
2	Pauses, fillers and simple syntactical constructions often mark out where utterances begin and end. However, this still does not ensure that all boundaries are clear.	Sentence boundaries are marked by the conventions of punctuation. Sentences often vary in their simplicity and complexity in a way that speech utterances do not.
3	Speech is more immediate and quicker, but it is less easy to learn through listening to someone else talking to you, since you need to work at the speaker's speed.	Writing is less immediate and has to be searched out, and is slower to access than speech, but it does allow the reader to work at his or her own pace.
4	Once a mistake in speech is uttered it cannot be erased or withdrawn, although it can be qualified — but the audience may well be suspicious of these qualifications.	Mistakes in writing can be altered at the writer's own convenience prior to the written matter being seen by its audience.
5	Speech relies heavily on deictic expressions and the knowledge of immediate context.	Writing can often be free of context and needs to use detail and subordination for the sake of clarity.
6	Speech is enhanced by our ability to manipulate speed, volume and stress in what we say to facilitate meaning; this is difficult to replicate in the written mode.	In writing, if we wish to include prosodic features we need to resort to complex description or use punctuation to help us. This is not very efficient and can be cumbersome.
7	Speech is not conducive to recording and it is usually a matter of memory as to what has occurred in a conversation; it is therefore not a useful reference tool.	Writing allows easy and accurate reference to be made; it also allows easy recording of facts and data to enable us to have access to them at a later date; we do not need to rely on our own memory.

Different representations of speech

We now turn our attention to the different types of speech representation that you may be faced with. You will be asked to compare a particular speech representation with some spontaneous speech in the examination. Obviously, both of these will be written representations of speech, including the spontaneous speech.

A good place to start is with planned speech, that is, speech that is meant to be heard as speech but has been composed beforehand for rhetorical purposes. Obviously, political speeches are a very rich seam to mine here, and you can gather many examples from the Internet to help you see some of the techniques used by politicians to influence their audience.

However, there are other valuable areas to examine. As you have no doubt already seen, both the prose and dramatic works that you have studied will provide you with evidence of speech representation. Also, there are semi-scripted situations on the television, with interviews and chat shows being the most common. There is also speech representation in the media world, with radio and television scripts in soap operas and situation comedies, for example. There are printed versions of speech in non-fiction sources such as magazine interviews, newspapers and comics. Finally, a new area which is very prevalent in modern life is electronic communication that emulates speech in e-mails, text messages and chat rooms.

The language and features of planned speech

Planned speech differs from spontaneous speech, in that it is thought out, considered, and perhaps scripted in some form prior to its delivery. We hear many examples of this on a daily basis, ranging from the broadly planned but unscripted delivery of a teacher or lecturer, to the formulaic rhetoric of political speeches.

> **Rhetoric**
>
> The art of speech making, with the express purpose of altering or affecting the listener's emotions, by conveying the individual viewpoint of the speaker and/or the speaker's logic or reasoning.

In planned speech, the speaker often makes use of an assortment of devices that are specifically intended to convey his or her message. In many instances, this is inextricably linked to the purpose of persuading the audience to adopt, or at least consider, the speaker's point of view. The devices are often supplemented by skilful use of phonological features such as sound and rhythm, thus enhancing the impact of what is articulated. It can be quite difficult to represent such features on the page, although we will make brief reference to these in this section as they play such a vital part in the art of rhetoric.

Look closely at the following piece of rhetoric. Gordon Brown made this speech when he was appointed as the next prime minister in June 2007, at a special Labour Party conference. The following extract allows us to examine the use of a number of rhetorical devices at first hand.

And I've learned something else about how we can change our country – how we can build a progressive consensus.

In the last ten years, from Make Poverty History to campaigns on disability, gay rights and the environment, Britain has changed for the better, not just because of government, but because of movements that have gone beyond traditional parties, captured people's imaginations and transformed people's lives.

As a party we have always known that we succeed best when we reach out to and engage the whole community. So here I stand proud of our Labour party but determined that we reach out to all people who can be persuaded to share our values and who would like to be part of building a more just society.

So my message today is also to people who want to change from the old politics, who yearn for a public life founded on values, who are inspired by what we as a nation can now achieve together – join us. Join us in building the Britain we believe in.

And don't let anyone tell you the choice at the next election will be change with other parties and no change with Labour. Because when I take office on Wednesday I will, as our party has always done, heed and lead the call of change.

So for young people wanting the first step on the housing ladder to their first home, we will meet the challenge of change.

For families wanting their sons and daughters to get the chance of college or university, we will meet the challenge of change.

For parents wanting affordable child care, we will meet the challenge of change.

For families and pensioners who want an NHS there when they need it, we will meet the challenge of change.

For people wanting a stronger democracy, we will meet the challenge of change.

And we will govern for all the people of our country.

This week marks a new start.

A chance to renew.

And I say to the people of Britain:

The new government I will lead belongs to you.

I will work hard for you.

I shall always try my utmost.

I am ready to serve.

- -

There is no doubt that this piece of speech tells us much about the speaker's views and his reasoning: he constantly refers to the 'challenge of change' (the content that precedes this outlines the changes he wants for the country), and he underpins this by the use of the first-person singular pronominative form, 'I', and continues by including the audience in what he asserts, with a shift to the first-person plural pronominative form, 'we'. There is also little doubt that there is an appeal to the emotions of those listening. It is here that we can begin to examine specific rhetorical features.

Emotive language

Rhetorical speech-making uses emotive language to appeal to the audience. Gordon Brown uses strong verbs in his powerful closing section:

- build
- change
- transform
- capture

- stand
- persuade.

He supplements these by careful adjectival choice:

- traditional
- proud
- just
- stronger.

There are also many abstract nouns, which makes the speech much more theoretical as it moves towards its conclusion:

- consensus
- environment
- imagination
- challenge.

As well as the linguistic evidence, Brown also uses the following techniques.

Giving opinions

Brown offers his opinion on the position of the Labour party at the moment he is speaking:

> So here I stand proud of our Labour party but determined that we reach out to all people who can be persuaded to share our values and who would like to be part of building a more just society.

His use of the adjective 'proud' is foregrounded in the sentence, and he emphasizes common values by using the first-person plural possessive pronoun 'our', finally finishing his sentence with a reference to a 'just society', the implication being that his party have been instrumental in making society just as well as continuing to promote this goal.

Using exclamations

While Brown does not overtly use exclamatives in the speech, there is an exclamatory quality to the final section where he couples repetition with exclamation to finish each section with the same words: 'we will meet the challenge of change'. In particular, the following sentence has an exclamatory feel about it:

> And don't let anyone tell you the choice at the next election will be change with other parties and no change with Labour.

It indirectly criticizes other political parties as well as claiming that the Labour party will be at the cutting edge of change and that it would be a complete surprise it if wasn't; hence its exclamatory sense.

Exaggeration or understatement (respectively, **hyperbole** and **litotes**) may also be used to help add vigour to exclamatory statements.

Giving personal guarantees and surety

> So my message today is also to people who want to change from the old politics, who yearn for a public life founded on values, who are inspired by what we as a nation can now achieve together – join us. Join us in building the Britain we believe in.

Brown here emphasizes his political assurance by the foregrounding of 'my message' and then using the first-person plural pronoun 'us' to add further power to his personal guarantee.

Use of summary

In rhetoric, one of the most effective devices is the use of a conclusive sentence that draws the whole of the speech together, while also leaving the listener with something memorable to take away, ponder on and digest. A famous example is by Winston Churchill:

> Let us therefore brace ourselves to our duties and so bear ourselves that, if the British Empire and its Commonwealth last for a thousand years, men will still say, 'This was their finest hour'.

Gordon Brown's ending to his speech is strong as it has a certain conclusiveness about it; he moves from the collective, through use of the pronoun 'we', to the personal 'I' and the use of the modal verbs of certainty 'will' and 'shall':

> And we will govern for all the people of our country.
>
> This week marks a new start.
>
> A chance to renew.
>
> And I say to the people of Britain:
>
> The new government I will lead belongs to you.
>
> I will work hard for you.
>
> I shall always try my utmost.
>
> I am ready to serve.

Notice that some of his sentences are in very fragmentary form, and that this adds to the increasing pace of the piece; his final sentences are very similar syntactically and there is a simplicity and strength about his final utterance, with the infinitive verb 'to serve' having all kinds of historical resonances.

Some of the emotive devices that Brown does not use in this speech are as follows. The speech would probably lose some of its strength if *all* these devices were used.

Threatening disaster

This is a tool often used in planned speeches, akin to saying, 'if you don't do this then something earth-shattering will happen that will have dreadful consequences for all!' Brown hints at this with the following reference to the economy, and there is a suggestion of potential disaster in the use of the verb 'safeguarding' as well as the negative adjective 'vulnerable':

> I believe in a British economy founded on dynamic, flexible markets and open competition. But for workers undercut by employers in this country who break the law by paying less than the minimum wage we will act – new protection for vulnerable workers. That's what I mean by safeguarding and advancing the British way of life.

Mocking opponents

Disparaging one's opponents is something that comes very readily to politicians. In one of his first speeches as prime minister, Gordon Brown's predecessor Tony Blair poked fun at the Conservative party by making a comparison between the new Tory leadership and the fictional family of monsters, the Addams family:

> The only party that spent two years in hibernation in search of a new image and came back as the Addams family.

> Under John Major, it was weak, weak, weak! Under William Hague, it's weird, weird, weird! Far right, far out!

This evokes an image of, among other things:

- their grotesqueness
- their dysfunctional nature
- the artificial nature of their relationships
- the comical way that they behave
- the reaction of horror they provoke in some people.

Along with the opinions given earlier in the speech, this helps to disparage and belittle the Tory party, which is all part of Blair's agenda in this particular address.

Structural techniques

You have already seen the importance of structure in the way that pieces of writing are put together. Structure also plays an important role in planned speech. Some of these structural techniques are described below.

Patterning

Various types of pattern are often employed during planned speech. In the speech of Gordon Brown, we can see a very common technique: **patterns of three**. There is a certain cohesion to ideas packaged in threes, and the rhythm and completeness of the ordering can be clearly seen.

> campaigns on disability [1], gay rights [2] and the environment [3]

The three nouns or noun phrases give the sentence clear cohesive qualities, which help to communicate the attitude of the speaker and suggest comprehensiveness in the way that Britain has embraced change. This is then further emphasized by the second part of the sentence, which has another three parts or sections, thus mirroring the first part:

> ... because of movements that have gone beyond traditional parties [1], captured people's imaginations [2] and transformed people's lives [3].

Repetition

Any repetition of words or phrases can highlight the central ideas of a speech, and has the cumulative effect of driving home the message. Many orators use this technique simply to emphasize a point; Brown does this effectively at the end of five sections of his speech where he finishes each section with the phrase 'the challenge of change,' the key topic of his whole address.

At the end of the speech, he uses a similar method, this time repeating the second person pronoun 'you' at the end of two sentences while starting three of them with the first person pronoun 'I'. Once more, this helps the overall cohesive effect.

The new government I will lead belongs to you.

I will work hard for you.

I shall always try my utmost.

I am ready to serve.

Lists

The effect of listing is similar to that of using repetition, as the message is further emphasized simply through the accumulation of the list of words.

In the middle of this speech, Brown says:

> That's why I want a new constitutional settlement for Britain. And the principles of my reforms are these: government giving more power to Parliament; both government and Parliament giving more power to the people; Parliament voting on all the major issues of our time including peace and war; civil liberties safeguarded and enhanced; devolution within a Union of nations: England, Scotland, Wales and Northern Ireland – a Union that I believe in and will defend; local government strengthened with new powers – local communities empowered to hold those who make the decisions to account; and with community ownership of assets – greater power for more people to control their lives.

This type of listing, which makes use of commas or semi-colons to link the ideas together, is called **asyndetic listing**. It has the effect of allowing idea after idea to pile on top of one another, here showing the extent to which government will change. Sometimes, conjunctions such as 'and' are used to link ideas into lists, again having a cumulative effect. This technique is called **syndetic listing**.

Questions

The use of rhetorical questions, those that do not require an answer or where the answer is obvious from the context, is another feature of planned speech. It has the effect of adding weight to the point being made, by implicitly providing an answer, but it can also help to move an argument on. In Brown's speech, he does not use questions, which indicates that he is certain and wants to show that his speech is not about asking questions, rather to give solutions and answers.

Opposites

Use of antithesis, or balancing of opposite ideas, can also have a powerful effect when coupled with other devices. Again Brown does not use it in this speech but you will find plenty of examples in the activity that follows on page 128.

Literary techniques

Metaphor (and imagery and simile) are terms you will be familiar with from your literary studies, and they need no glossing here. Earlier in the speech we have been examining, Brown says:

> Because we all want to address the roots of injustice, I can tell you today that we will strengthen and enhance the work of the Department of International Development and align aid, debt relief and trade policies to wage an unremitting battle against the poverty, illiteracy, disease and environmental degradation that it has fallen to our generation to eradicate.

The noun phrase 'the roots of injustice' is both interesting and clever: it is possibly a gardening metaphor where Brown wants to pull up weeds by the roots and address such issues as poverty. He then talks of 'wag(ing) an unremitting battle' against a variety of things: the metaphor of conflict is again powerful, indicating he is ready for a fight. The use of the premodifying adjective 'unremitting' shows he will maintain this fight.

Similes gain their effects by comparing one thing to another. Brown steers away from these in his speech, in order to keep his examples rooted in the factual.

There may also be examples of **personification**, **symbolism** and **irony** in planned speech, all terms you have already been introduced to in your literary studies. Any effect they have will be largely similar to the effect gained when used in literature.

Phonological techniques

Phonological techniques use the sound qualities of language to enhance its effects.

Alliteration and assonance

These are literary devices that you will have already come across: **alliteration**, the repeated use of the same consonant sounds, and **assonance**, the repeated use of the same vowel sounds. An example of alliteration is the 'ch' sound in 'the challenge of change'. Both techniques have the effect of making the words and phrases stand out and consequently help us to remember them later, something that Brown wants us to do with this speech, especially as the key idea in the speech is his appetite to embrace 'change'. Naturally, these techniques are often used in advertising and other forms of persuasive writing too.

Consonance

This technique is perhaps one that is often overlooked in planned speech but has, when used, a similar strength to alliteration and assonance – it helps us to remember a phrase, because of a consonant repetition in the middle or at the end of words, as in a phrase by Tony Blair in the speech quoted earlier: 'the uneata<u>ble</u>, the unspeaka<u>ble</u> and the unelecta<u>ble</u>'. This is a type of repetition, but it has the added effect of drawing attention to the words through the repeated sound.

Rhyme

This is a subject you will study in Chapter 6, Studying Poetry. As with all other phonological techniques, the use of rhyme enhances the sound of the words and adds to the structural cohesion of the speech, particularly at the end of phrases or sentences. A good example of this in Brown's speech is:

> I will, as our party has always done, <u>heed</u> and <u>lead</u> the call of change.

The two underlined verbs help to emphasize Brown's actions.

Intonation and stress

The way in which words are intoned and the stress they are given can often help to convey the attitude of the speaker. It is often difficult to see this when the speech is printed on the page but there are often syntactic clues as to which words are important. In the final line, for instance, we can imagine that the adjective and verb are the stressed words here as they carry the real sense and power of the line:

> I am <u>ready</u> to <u>serve</u>.

Sometimes words are elongated to accentuate their importance; you have already seen examples of this in the section on unplanned speech.

Volume and speed

Changes in volume can have a radical effect on any speech, whether planned or unplanned. The effect of raising one's voice is obvious: it carries with it associations of power, commitment, certainty, passion and possibly anger. It can also be used for dramatic effect, especially after a period of quiet and calm speech. This can help shock the audience and have the effect of waking them up to listen more intently to the speaker.

Putting theory into practice

Now that we have examined some of the different features of planned speech, here is a short political speech where you can see some of the features being used for a particular purpose.

The speech below was given by US President John F. Kennedy in his inaugural address on 20 January 1961. It is often seen as a turning point in American politics.

Activity

What purposes does this piece of speech have, and how does Kennedy convey his ideas to his audience? In your answer you should comment on:

- the choice of vocabulary
- the use of speech features
- the use of grammatical features
- the ways in which attitudes and values are conveyed.

So let us begin anew – remembering on both sides that civility is not a sign of weakness, and sincerity is always subject to proof. Let us never negotiate out of fear, but let us never fear to negotiate.

Let both sides explore what problems unite us instead of belabouring those problems which divide us.

Let both sides, for the first time, formulate serious and precise proposals for the inspection and control of arms, and bring the absolute power to destroy other nations under the absolute control of all nations.

Let both sides seek to invoke the wonders of science instead of its terrors. Together let us explore the stars, conquer the deserts, eradicate disease, tap the ocean depths, and encourage the arts and commerce.

Let both sides unite to heed, in all corners of the earth, the command of Isaiah – to 'undo the heavy burdens, and [to] let the oppressed go free.'

And, if a beachhead of cooperation may push back the jungle of suspicion, let both sides join in creating a new endeavour – not a new balance of power, but a new world of law – where the strong are just, and the weak secure, and the peace preserved.

All this will not be finished in the first one hundred days. Nor will it be finished in the first one thousand days; nor in the life of this Administration; nor even perhaps in our lifetime on this planet. But let us begin.

In your hands, my fellow citizens, more than mine, will rest the final success or failure of our course. Since this country was founded, each generation of Americans has been summoned to give testimony to its national loyalty. The graves of young Americans who answered the call to service surround the globe.

Now the trumpet summons us again – not as a call to bear arms, though arms we need – not as a call to battle, though embattled we are – but a call to bear the burden of a long twilight struggle, year in and year out, 'rejoicing in hope; patient in tribulation,' a struggle against the common enemies of man: tyranny, poverty, disease, and war itself.

Can we forge against these enemies a grand and global alliance, North and South, East and West, that can assure a more fruitful life for all mankind? Will you join in that historic effort?

In the long history of the world, only a few generations have been granted the role of defending freedom in its hour of maximum danger. I do not shrink from this responsibility – I welcome it. I do not believe that any of us would exchange places with any other people or any other generation. The energy, the faith, the devotion which we bring to this endeavour will light our country and all who serve it. And the glow from that fire can truly light the world.

And so, my fellow Americans, ask not what your country can do for you; ask what you can do for your country.

My fellow citizens of the world, ask not what America will do for you, but what together we can do for the freedom of man.

Finally, whether you are citizens of America or citizens of the world, ask of us here the same high standards of strength and sacrifice which we ask of you. With a good conscience our only sure reward, with history the final judge of our deeds, let us go forth to lead the land we love, asking His blessing and His help, but knowing that here on earth God's work must truly be our own.

Speech in the broadcast media

In the media, speech is often very like spontaneous speech but it has an agenda. A topic will have been decided beforehand, especially if it is some kind of interview or chat show, as shown below.

In the following piece of conversation, which is part of a longer interview that was conducted on television by Michael Parkinson (P), with the Scottish comedian, Billy Connolly (C), Parkinson appears to be simply chatting with Connolly. However, there is careful use of the following:

- topic management by the interviewer
- evidence of research having been done beforehand
- opportunities taken by the interviewee to seize the turn and say something funny.

Nonetheless, it still has the look of spontaneous speech as Connolly probably doesn't know the questions that will arise.

Activity

Examine this interview transcript closely and pick out the features that suggest:

- the spontaneous nature of the conversation
- that specific exchanges have been selected beforehand to be used in the interview.

P: There's a there's a (.) kind of sense of vocation isn't there in a comic (.) I think I mean (.) you are driven to it aren't you

　　　[

C: 　　　It's vocational

P: It not (0.5) er really

　　　[

C: Witho::ut (.) question

P: It has to be doesn't it

C: Aye (1.5) an' I think most k (.) things are (0.5) yours is vocational obviously (.) you've a great love of what you do (0.5) I have a love of what I do (.) an' we're very lucky because you find it (0.5) I think it's a question of bein' (0.5) try to be honest with yourself (0.5) what you a:ctually want to be (1.0) an be (.) eve even if it's embarrassin' (.) like yer wanna be a comedian (.) an' you say to yer dad (.) I'd like to be a comedian an' he goes (.) you're no funny (0.5) you're no very funny (0.5) w w what t d'y'wanna be a comedian for (0.5) are you daft (1.5) an' I became (0.5) a welder to escape the worst excesses of homosexuality actually (1.0) I

P: Wha'

C: I wanted (.) ter go to drama school (0.5) an' an' ma father said (.) O:::::h they're all homosexuals (.) you don't wanna go there (1.0) an' I said I'd like to be in the merchant navy (1.0) O:::::h for God's sake (1.0) they're all homosexuals (2.0) so I I became (.) this this welder guy

P: And this

C: an' it haunted me you know (1.0) u until (.) I er got

P: What what (.) er haunted you

C: Bein' bein' (.) what I thought I should be

P: Yes

Speech representation in prose fiction

As you will have already read in Chapter 3, Analysing Prose Fiction, there are a number of methods that the writer uses to help convey a particular style within prose when representing speech. Refer to pages 39–44 in Chapter 3 to remind yourself of the details.

Look at the following extract, taken from the novel *Eden Close* by Anita Shreve. In this particular section, the main character's mother and a neighbour, Edith, look at a baby who has been left outside Edith's house; her husband Jim is away on business.

'Jesus God,' said his mother, stepping back quickly as if she'd seen something deformed.

The two women stood looking at each other for a moment and didn't speak.

'What is it?' his mother asked finally.

The other woman didn't understand the question. 'What is it...?'

'A boy or a girl?'

Edith looked momentarily stunned. Then she tilted her head back and closed her eyes. 'Oh God, I wish Jim were here,' she suddenly cried. 'I don't know. I don't know.' She looked as though she were about to fall, with the bundle in her arms.

'We'll go inside,' said his mother quickly, clicking into gear in that way she had when there was a crisis or when he had fallen and hurt himself.

This section is typical of the way that speech is represented in prose fiction, with the following features being evident:

1 Separate speakers are given separate lines to indicate who is talking.

'What is it?' his mother asked finally.

The other woman didn't understand the question. 'What is it...?'

- -

The first speaker is the main character's mother, and the neighbour's reply to the initial interrogative 'What is it?' is met with another question, to indicate her flustered nature as well as her misunderstanding of the original question's purpose.

2 Use of speech marks around what is said to indicate the actual speech.

'Jesus God,' said his mother.

- -

The mother's involuntary outburst, in the form of a mild blasphemy, is shown with speech marks before and after it.

3 Use of punctuation to convey the particular utterance type, such as an exclamatory or interrogative utterance. In the following example, an interrogative is indicated by the question mark at the end of the utterance:

'A boy or a girl?'

- -

4 Use of reporting clauses to help indicate who the speaker is, especially when there are multiple characters within a particular scene.

'Oh God, I wish Jim were here,' she suddenly cried.

- -

In this example the reporting clause 'she cried' is qualified by the use of the adverb 'suddenly'.

Because there are only two characters, it is also possible to leave out reporting clauses as the turn-taking is indicated by the use of separate lines.

5 Use of adverbs, adverbial clauses or subordinating clauses attached to the reporting clause to help convey the way that the speaker delivers the lines:

'We'll go inside,' said his mother quickly, clicking into gear in that way she had when there was a crisis...

- -

Here the use of the adverb 'quickly' shows that the mother takes charge of the situation, followed by the subordinating clause 'clicking into gear in that way she had when there was a crisis...' to convey that this character is used to dealing with tricky situations, perhaps because she is a parent herself while Edith is not.

Activity

Read the following section taken from *Great Expectations* by Charles Dickens. How does Dickens convey the attitude of both Mrs Joe Gargery and Pip in this exchange?

'Where have you been, you young monkey?' said Mrs Joe, stamping her foot. 'Tell me directly what you've been doing to wear me away with fret and fright and worrit, or I'd have you out of that corner if you was fifty Pips, and he was five hundred Gargerys.'

'I have only been to the churchyard,' said I, from my stool, crying and rubbing myself.

'Churchyard!' repeated my sister. 'If it warn't for me you'd have been to the churchyard long ago, and stayed there. Who brought you up by hand?'

'You did,' said I.

'And why did I do it, I should like to know!' exclaimed my sister.

I whimpered, 'I don't know.'

'*I* don't!' said my sister. 'I'd never do it again! I know that. I may truly say I've never had this apron of mine off, since born you were. It's bad enough to be a blacksmith's wife (and him a Gargery) without being your mother.'

- -

Quite often, when there are only two characters, the speech can have more of a realistic feel to it since reporting clauses are missed out. When this occurs, there is more of a focus on the words that are spoken rather than the writer's interpretation through reporting clauses and subordination.

Activity

Read the following exchange. It is the opening section of Iain Banks's novel *The Business*. Since it is the opening of the novel, Banks has had no opportunity to introduce or develop his characters. In other words, he leaves us to make up our own minds about the characters through what they say.

How does Banks make it clear that the two characters are different? What speech features does he use to help him to convey the attitude of both Mike and Kate? How does he use speech to help establish some key plot lines from the start?

'Hello?'

'Kate?'

'Yes.'

'Itsh Mike.'

'Mike?'

'Mike! Mike Danielsh! Chrisht, Kate, don't –'

'Mike, it's... it's four thirty-seven.'

'I know what time it ish!'

'Mike, I'd really like to get back to sleep.'

'I'm shorry, but it'sh fucking important!'

'You should get some sleep too, maybe whatever it is won't seem so important after you've slept. And sobered up.'

'I'm not drunk! Will you jusht lishten?'

'I am. I'm lishtening to a drunk man. Go to sleep, Mike. Hold on, aren't you due in Tokyo today?'

'Yesh!'

'Right. So get some sleep. I'm going to switch the phone off now, Mike. I didn't mean to leave it on in the first –'

'No! That'sh what I'm calling about! Tokyo!'

'What? What about Tokyo?'

'I can't go!'

'What do you mean? Why not? You have to go.'

'But I *can't*!'

'Calm down.'

'How can I be fucking *calm*? Shome fuckersh taken out half my teesh!'

'Say that again?'

'I shaid shome fuckersh taken out half my fucking teesh!'

'Is this some sort of joke? Who the hell is this?'

'It'sh me, for Chrisht'sh shake! It'sh Mike Danielsh!'

'It doesn't sound like the Mike Daniels I know.'

'Of courshe not! I've had half my teesh taken out!'

- -

Very occasionally, novelists will go against convention and not use the accepted forms of delineation of speech between characters, and instead use other methods to make speech different from the prose narrative. In the following extract, taken from *The Heart of It* by Barry Hines, the main character Cal is talking to his mother (who calls him Karl) about his life and his girlfriend.

Because Hines uses no speech marks, the reader has to concentrate very hard to work out the following:

- what is speech
- what is thought
- who is speaking
- which parts are narration.

Activity

What is the overall effect that Hines is looking for in this extract, do you think?

You're spoiling that cat. You'll never get rid of it now, you know.

Didn't you ever fancy having a family, Karl?

Cal stalled for a few moments by watching television and he was still looking at the screen when he answered her. Not really. I've moved round a lot. There's been one or two women along the way, but children never came into it.

What about Hélène?

What about her?

You've known her a long time.

Cal worked it out. Five, six years. Yes, I suppose that is a long time. For me.

Isn't she interested in children?

Hélène! His exclamation was loud enough to wake up the cat. No way. She's too interested in her career. Oh, by the way, I've got a little surprise for you tonight.

What is it?

Wait and see. If I tell you now it won't be a surprise, will it?

Why don't you stop for your tea then?

Cal tried to think of an excuse, but he couldn't come up with anything convincing. Yes. All right then. That'll be nice.

- -

In the novel *A Prayer For Owen Meany* by John Irving, the narrator, Johnny Wheelwright, puts all that Owen Meany says in capital letters. This has the effect of emphasizing everything that Owen says; coupled with the fact that he is very small for his age, yet is very wise and ends up being a Christ-like figure, this helps to make Owen's words almost inspirational:

'YOU SEE WHAT A LITTLE FAITH CAN DO?' said Owen Meany. The brain-damaged janitor was applauding. 'SET THE CLOCK TO *THREE* SECONDS!' Owen told him.

'Jesus Christ!' I said.

'IF WE CAN DO IT IN UNDER FOUR SECONDS, WE CAN DO IT IN UNDER THREE,' he said. 'IT JUST TAKES A LITTLE MORE FAITH.'

'It takes more practice,' I told him irritably.

'FAITH TAKES PRACTICE,' said Owen Meany.

- -

These are just two examples of the creative ways that some authors present speech in prose.

Speech representation in drama

As you will already have read in Chapter 4, Analysing Drama, playwrights use a variety of methods to help to convey their characters' speech. Refer to Chapter 4 to remind yourself of these particular stylistic details.

However, it is worth briefly outlining here some of the essential characteristics of layout and presentation which would help you identify a piece of dramatic writing. Look at the following extract from *The Caretaker* by Harold Pinter.

Aston: (*attending to the toaster*). Would... would you like to sleep here?
Davies: Here?
Aston: You can sleep here if you like.
Davies: Here? Oh, I don't know about that. (*Pause.*) How long for?
Aston: Till you... get yourself fixed up.
Davies: (*sitting*). Ay well, that...
Aston: Get yourself sorted out. ...
Davies: Oh, I'll be fixed up... pretty soon now... (*Pause.*) Where would I sleep?
Aston: Here. The other rooms would... would be no good to you.

Davies: (*rising, looking about*). Here? Where?

Aston: (*rising, pointing upstage right*).There's a bed behind all that.

Davies: Oh, I see. Well, that's handy. Well, that's... I tell you what, I might do that... just till I get myself sorted out. You got enough furniture here.

Aston: I picked it up. Just keeping it here for the time being. Thought it might come in handy.

This extract shows a number of features which you would commonly find in dramatic representation of speech. The names of the speakers are on the left side of the page (occasionally in the middle of the page), usually with a colon or a full stop after the name. Speech is correctly punctuated, with a capital letter at the start of the sentence and a full stop at the end (or a question mark or exclamation mark as appropriate).

The use of stage directions (shown in the extract above in brackets and in italics) helps to illustrate:

* action
* speech and the way it is delivered
* the mood of a particular character.

Activity

What features of speech does Pinter also use in this section to help the conversation between Davies and Aston progress?

Drama plays a very important role in our lives, even though we may not often go to the theatre; every day, we see or hear many variations of drama and dramatic scripts representing speech. Some of these are:

* radio scripts and plays, e.g. *The Archers*
* soap operas, e.g. *EastEnders*, *Coronation Street*
* scripts for television and radio adverts
* situation comedies.

Activity

Look at the extract printed below. It is taken from the first series of *The Office*, a situation comedy with a difference, in that it purported to be a documentary series about an office but in reality was a comedy without the canned laughter.

In what ways do the writers Ricky Gervais and Stephen Merchant convey the characters of Tim and Gareth here through their interaction with each other, as well as with Dawn?

Dawn: You're so lovely.

Tim: No, I'm not lovely.

Dawn: You are.

Tim: No, you are.

Dawn: I'm snotty.

Tim: You're snotty and lovely. I'd marry your snot. I'd wed your...

(**Dawn** *is laughing, spirits lifted.* **Gareth** *appears.*)

Gareth: Alright?

Tim: Alright, mate.

Gareth: What's going on?

Tim: Nothing. It's fine.

Gareth: Are you upset... about Lee, is it? Hey, don't worry, right? 'Cos, you know 'Monkey' Alan, down in the warehouse? He fancies you even if no one does, so...

(*The mere mention of Monkey Alan reduces* **Dawn** *to tears again. She hurries off, upset.*)

Tim: What was that?

Gareth: You just can't say anything when they're like that, can you?

Tim: No *you* can't, *you* can't. I was doing okay. What you doing with the Monkey Alan business?

Gareth: He fancies her. I'm just saying...

Tim: Yeah, she doesn't need to know that mate. It's Monkey Alan! Do you know what I mean? Even the name... I don't even know who Monkey Alan is. You know what, I'm betting that Monkey Alan...

Gareth: You do, he's a little bloke...

Tim: No, I don't need to know it. No, it's not... Go away, please. Go over there.

Speech representation in non-fiction

Speech is often quoted in magazines, newspapers and comics; in some cases, this is to give them a sense of 'real life', but also possibly to make them more informal or chatty. Look at any magazine or newspaper and you will find quotations aplenty as well as interviews conducted in a number of ways.

Here is an example of one way an interview can be represented in a magazine. In this article, printed in *Books Quarterly*, 'Louise Candlish chats to three female fiction superstars about chick lit.' The three writers are Sophie Kinsella, Wendy Holden and Jill Mansell.

Louise Candlish: Do you actually describe your writing as 'chick lit'?

Sophie Kinsella: I usually say I write contemporary romantic comedies. Readers don't think of it that way, they don't think, 'Oh, I'll read some chick lit today'.

Wendy Holden: I do think the term needs updating. I think we should call ourselves 'novelistas': much more fun.

SK: In the States, I've seen my books displayed under 'wit lit'. I thought 'Yes!'

Jill Mansell: When I started writing there was 'Riders' and 'Rivals', all the glitzy fiction, and my publishers called me 'cosy glitz' because I wasn't as outrageous as that.

LC: And was there ever a moment when someone rang you up and said, 'You're not cosy glitz any more, Jill, you're young and sassy chick lit'?

JM: No, I just read that I was!

LC: I recently stood behind a woman in the queue at Waterstone's who was buying *Jonathan Strange and Mr Norrell* and a *Shopaholic* book and she said to her friend, 'When I buy books I always get one I ought to read and then one I want to read.' I thought that was very defining.

SK: What I find interesting about that is that clearly she feels a bit guilty, like chick lit is a guilty pleasure. But she shouldn't. Reading is for enjoyment.

- -

In this interview you can see that there are similarities to the way that a drama script might be presented, with the names printed down the left side, with utterances formulated into sentences, and so on. This helps the reader to focus on what the speakers are saying and it also relies on the interviewer to ask questions which are both penetrating and help the fluency of the conversation.

In newspapers too, speech is seen in a number of forms, either a development on the way it is presented in prose fiction or similar to the extract from the interview above. Below is an article from the *Mirror* where the actress Jane Asher is interviewed and speaks about her complexion.

ASHER: PEOPLE THINK I'M DEAD!

She dated a Beatle and her porcelain skin makes her look 20 years younger. But will actress and baking goddess Jane Asher tell us her secrets? JANE ODDY finds out... .

She may look fantastic for her age, but don't even think of asking Jane Asher if she's had surgery. 'I've always said that beauty secrets should remain secret because I'm sure there will be a time, like anybody, when I would consider it,' she says.

'Mystery is much better. It's like marriage, the less you say about it, the more likely it is that it'll work in your own life.'

Still boasting the flawless, English rose complexion that she had in the 60s, it's hard to believe that Jane is a pensioner. So how does she do it?

Reluctantly, the 61-year-old actress agrees to share her secret formula. 'I never sunbathe,' she reveals. 'I loathed being a redhead when I was younger because it meant I couldn't go in the sun – now I realise I was lucky. I tried and tried, but melanin doesn't exist in my skin. I never got that tanned look.'

- -

Perhaps one of the most interesting representations of speech is in comics for children where the language has to be both understandable and accessible for the audience reading the comic. Some of the techniques that are used are as follows:

- the simplification of language
- simple, accessible lexis
- simple sentences, usually with only one verb or verb clause
- the use of phonological representation to indicate non-verbal aspects of speech
- elliptical utterances
- the use of puns and word-play
- speech presented as an explanation of or a complement to the drawing it is a part of.

Activity

Read the following comic strip, Roger the Dodger. Using the list above, what methods can you see the writer using to represent speech aimed at a younger audience? To what extent is the speech realistic?

Speech representation through electronic media

The recent explosion of electronic communication has led to some very interesting representations of speech. Text messages (SMS) are used by the majority of people today as a quick and efficient method of getting in touch with one other. People have become adept at writing and sending them quickly, expecting fairly instant replies. These messages are distinctly speech-like, especially when they are used as a speedy communication method.

Text messages are characterized by:

- their brevity
- their innovative use of abbreviation and shortened forms
- their use of **emoticons** (symbols intended to indicate the sender's feelings or emotions)
- their informality
- their shared understanding of topicality.

Activity

Read the following text message between two friends. In the message, the person mentioned, Lorna, has just had an operation. Her daughter is Heather.

Thanx. Hve text heathr already so knw lorna hd hd it dun. Hpe all ok wth u.X

In what ways is the message like speech? In what ways does it differ and rely on knowledge about the written word?

E-mails are another well-used communicative tool with speech-like features. Again, we use these because of their speed, but we do not always write them like text messages, so they can often appear to be more formal.

Activity

In the one printed below, a friend is writing to someone he meets on a fairly irregular basis. Read the e-mail and pick out its speech-like qualities.

Now then Mr M,

I've been hibernating for a few weeks and months, trying to work a few things out I s'pose. Career plan still ongoing. I'm off to Miniature G's school soon to see what's what. I'm thinking about sodding off round the world for bit too, and as I've just got a pay-rise at work, I can clear my debts and naff off next August time without too many troubles, and think of a new settling down plan when I get back.

I have heard of this Fischer gentleman. He's very good at whistling and has a hairy back. He'll go far with the right management. I would've headed across there yesterday but I was up in Newcastle for the weekend, which was really good. Got a bit tiddly and dancing like an uncoordinated ice-skating octopus, but I didn't injure anyone so it was ok.

Shack

Another electronic version of speech is the typed talk that is used by people when they communicate with each other through on-line messaging. An example of two people talking (one called Private healthcare..yippee and the other named Vince Noir) is printed below for you to read.

Vince Noir says:

>   hey mate

Private healthcare..yippee says:

>   hello tom

Vince Noir says:

>   how you doin

Private healthcare..yippee says:

>   not too bad

Private healthcare..yippee says:

>   think the pills are finally kicking in

Vince Noir says:

>   ah good

Private healthcare..yippee says:

>   have u been anywhere on ya own yet?

Vince Noir says:

>   yeh yeh

Vince Noir says:

>   me mate was over from whitby last night

Vince Noir says:

>   so i drove him back

Private healthcare..yippee says:

>   that the 1st time

Vince Noir says:

>   by myself?

Vince Noir says:

>   or goin to whitby

Private healthcare..yippee says:

>   on ya own

Vince Noir says:

>   no no

Private healthcare..yippee says:

> are u enjoying this freedom

Vince Noir says:

> its ok yeh

Private healthcare..yippee says:

> lol

Private healthcare..yippee says:

> u been racing with si yet?

Vince Noir says:

> yeh i creamed him

Vince Noir says:

> 0-60 in 2.32 seconds the c2 does

Activity

In what ways does on-line messaging resemble conversation? Use examples from the exchange above to answer the question.

How to tackle the speech comparison

When you come to write about speech, you will be expected to compare spontaneous speech with another representation of speech. It is essential therefore to use a framework around which to build your answer. This will help ensure that you have covered all the required areas and that you have commented on the effects of the type of speech you are analysing and comparing.

Here is one framework for approaching speech questions:

- Opening paragraph (a brief opening which addresses some or all of the following if appropriate)
- What types of speech are you presented with?
- What are the linguistic determiners for:
  audience (who?)
  purpose (what?)
  context (where produced? situation of use?)
  level of formality of each piece
- Main comparison (compare aspects of the two pieces by picking out individual examples and using the three-point critical sentence for each point made)
- Topicality and subject matter
- Structural features
  phatic communication
  turn-taking and adjacency pairs
  chaining
  other speech features

- Grammatical features
  lexis and words
  grammar and grammatical features
  clause and sentence structure
  cohesion
- Phonological features
  rhetorical features
  patterning
  prosodic features
  literary features
- Graphological features
  layout differences
- How meaning and effect are conveyed (if you have not already covered this)
- How speakers' values and attitudes are shown

Try applying this framework to the two different comparisons printed below. You are reminded that you will have about 50 minutes in the examination room to complete these types of comparison.

Activity

Read the transcript (Extract A) and the scripted speech (Extract B) printed below.

A is an extract from an exchange between a teacher and student, discussing a recent written assignment, handed in late by the student.

B is a speech made by Hollywood actor Tom Hanks at the fund-raising TV show 'America: A Tribute to Heroes', broadcast across America, as well as in other countries worldwide, shortly after the attacks on the World Trade Centre in New York and The Pentagon in Washington on 11 September 2001. It was the opening address for the show.

Compare how the speakers' feelings and attitudes are revealed in these two texts.

In your answer you should comment on:

- the choice of vocabulary and of grammatical, stylistic and speech features
- the influence of context on the ways in which the speakers convey their ideas and feelings.

Extract A

Key

(.) micropause
(1.0) pause in seconds
underlining particular emphasis of a word
[overlap
X student's name

Teacher: and I don't think that h (.) this particular piece of work (.) if you can call it work (.) <u>represents</u> the best that you you (.) you can do (.) d'you X

Student: erm (.) suppose not no (3.0) but I

[

Teacher: have y (1.0) sorry go on (1.0)

Student: sorry (.) but I have to say that I I (.) didn't really understand what I (.) er (.) <u>we</u> (.) had to do (1.0) I mean if I had known I'd'a given it a real good go

Teacher: and you didn't think to ask me for any help with it (3.0) mm (1.5)

Student: suppose not (2.0)

Teacher: well I have ter say that you haven't made a very (.) <u>auspicious</u> start to the course X (1.0) 'n furthermore you're not showin' any signs of wantin' to to (.) to be actually <u>on</u> this course (0.5) what wi' the lateness an' the (.) the lack of quality in your work (.) which is to be frank pretty poor to say the very least (.) I (1.0)

Student: well I'm gettin' good marks with Alan (.) he seems to feel that I'm doin' ok

Teacher: hang on (1.5) we're not talking about how you're doin' with other members of staff (.) we're talking about how you're performin' in <u>my</u> lessons (.) that's where the problems are X (.) and what I wanna know is what you intend to do about (.) these (.) er (.) problems (1.0) an' don't try to <u>divert</u> me (.) by bringin' in another member of staff (.) okay

Extract B

Tom Hanks: (*directly to camera*) We're going to do something.

That was the message sent by some very American heroes, with names like Sandra Bradshaw, Jeremy Glick, Mark Bingham, Todd Beamer and Thomas Burnett. They found themselves aboard the hijacked flight 93 that went down in Somerset County, Pennsylvania on September 11th 2001. They witnessed the brutality on board and somehow summoned the strength to warn us and take action.

United they stood and likely saved our world from an even darker day of perhaps even more unthinkable horror. And since that day millions of us everywhere of all ages, races, creeds have asked ourselves, 'What are we doing?' In their heroic undying spirit we all feel the need to do something, however small, symbolic, to honour the remarkable heroes among us, those who have fallen and those still standing, united.

Those of us here tonight are not heroes. We are not healers nor protectors of this great nation. We are merely artists and entertainers here to raise spirits and, we hope, a great deal of money. We appear tonight as a simple show of unity to honour the real heroes and to do whatever we can to ensure that their families are supported by our larger American family.

This is a moment to pause and reflect, to heal and to rededicate ourselves to the American spirit of one nation indivisible.

Activity

Read the transcript (Extract A) and the printed interview (Extract B) below.

A is an extract from a transcription of spoken English. It is taken from a local radio news programme. The presenter, Mark Turnbull, is talking to a police officer, Ian Garrett.

B is an extract from a magazine called *What Mountain Bike.* This is a regular interview feature called '5 Minutes of Your Time'. In this particular article, Ned Overend, a former World Champion cyclist, is interviewed.

Compare how the speakers convey their feelings and how they give information in these two texts.

In your answer you should comment on:

- the choice of vocabulary and of grammatical, stylistic and speech features
- the influence of context on the ways in which the speakers convey their ideas and feelings.

Extract A

Key

(.) micropause
(1.0) pause in seconds
<u>underlining</u> particular emphasis of a word
:: elongation of sound

Turnbull: over twelve thousand pounds' worth of (.) heroin have been found at a house in er (.) <u>Billingham</u> (1.0) it's er the latest raid on er (.) houses er (.) by Stockton (.) Drugs Unit and the (.) district (.) support teams (1.0) 'n I'm <u>delighted</u> to say er <u>Inspector</u> Ian Garrett from Cleveland Police joins me on the phone (.) so er twelve thousand pounds' (.) worth ey er (0.5) Mr Garrett

Garrett: yes it's very good (.) an' it's all part of our continuin' action against drugs in the Stockton area (0.5) can I jussay that (.) I'll give you an example of how well we've bin doin' but also shows just how much drugs are out there (.) that (.) you've mentioned the twelve (.) and a <u>half</u> thousand pounds' worth of drugs (.) there was also two thousand pounds of <u>cash</u> (1.0) earlier in the week we also recovered a further <u>eight</u> thousand pounds' worth of heroin from a (.) house in Stockton town centre (.) a::nd in the middle of December we recovered heroin with a street value of <u>one hundred and twenty-five</u> thousand pounds <u>and</u> (.) one hundred thousand pound in cash (.) considerable recoveries

Turnbull: g give give us some of details of this raid then

Garrett: is this the latest one y'mean

Turnbull: absolutely

Garrett: yeh (1.0) well we've bin gatherin' intelligence for <u>some time</u> (.) we don't just jump <u>willy-nilly</u> into these things (0.5) a::nd we receive information from a number of sources (.) we're very grateful (.) an' we always ask the public to tell us if they think there's anything suspicious in the area (.) as I say the intelligence came from a number of sources to this one (1.0) we watch (0.5) we wait (0.5) an' we attack when it's right (0.5) an' as you've already mentioned it was good work by the District Support Unit (0.5) who carried out the searches on three houses (.) a::nd the District Drugs Unit (.) which co-ordinated everything an' dealt with the prisoners

Turnbull: how many houses did y'say

Garrett: three houses in Billingham

Turnbull: and er did you succeed in each house

Garrett: no:: we succeeded in two (.) but there w there was certainly a link between the three which is what our intelligence an' our watchin' had shown us

Extract B

What gets you up in the morning?

I drive my son to school in the morning. If he gets his act together and gets better grades, I'll get him a car and then I will sleep in.

What's been the biggest highlight of last year for you?

Competition wise, I beat (long-time rival) Travis Brown to win the Mountain States Cup event at Telluride, Colorado. Travis and I had some epic battles last summer. On the road I was second to Scott Moninger at the Mount Evans Hillclimb but I only lost by a few seconds.

Where do you see the MTB going?

I see product development continuing to go in the direction of lighter, more efficient full suspension systems. I think the racing scene is healthy with a lot of participation in a variety of events. Unfortunately there's not a lot of salary or prize money for pros and I don't see that improving anytime soon.

How much do you get to ride?

I ride 5-6 days a week about 2 hours a day. It's a mixture of road and off-road. The days off are usually due to travel.

What would you be doing if you weren't doing this?

I have a background in motorcycle mechanics, so I'd be involved in high-performance tuning for road bikes and riding motos on pavement and dirt.

...

Full suspension or hardtail?

I have a hardtail – it's called a road bike! My job is to help Specialized create full suspension cross country bikes that outperform hardtails on everything but the smoothest trails, so I'm a little biased.

6 Studying Poetry

You will study poetry for Unit 4 – Comparative Analysis through Independent Study. For that unit you will study two texts (at least one of which must be poetry) from the set texts offered by the specification, and produce a comparative study. Exactly what you need to do for this will be covered in the next chapter. You may also encounter poetry in the comparative analysis section of Unit 3, in which you will need to analyse and compare unseen texts.

This chapter will focus on the ways in which language is used in poetry texts. At the centre of this study will be the choices that poets make in terms of language, form and structure in order to achieve the effects that they want. In your Language and Literature course, the study of poetry texts will involve looking at both linguistic and literary issues in the texts and understanding the ways that poets use language to achieve and enhance literary effects.

The nature of poetry

Like prose, poetry cannot be neatly categorized, and the question of what exactly poetry is – what it is that marks it out as being different from prose – is a question that has tested writers, critics, philosophers and all concerned with literature for centuries. Certainly poets can choose from a whole range of different forms, structures, techniques and styles when writing their poetry. They can play with language and manipulate it, even invent a 'new' language to express their feelings, ideas and themselves.

Because, generally, the ideas in poems are expressed in fewer words than are used in prose, the messages or ideas expressed in a poem are sometimes more difficult to understand than if they were expressed in prose. Also, the poet may be expressing himself or herself in a unique way – it is more acceptable for the language of poetry to deviate from generally observed rules. This 'poetic licence' allows poets to experiment with language, perhaps playing around with word order, or using dialectal forms, or using lexical or syntactical patterning to create or reinforce meaning. Of course, prose writers can use these techniques too, but they will be much more frequently found in the language of poetry.

> **Activity**
>
> Throughout your life you will probably have encountered various kinds of poetry, at school, college, in reading for pleasure, on the radio, television, etc. Based on your experience, write down all the features you can think of that make poetry different from other kinds of writing.

Features of poetry

Poetry is an extremely varied genre in every respect – in content, structure, style, intention and every other way. Some poems present narratives that tell stories; some are written to be performed; some explore philosophical, emotional, or spiritual concepts and ideas; some are amusing, some are sad. In fact, it is probably safe to say that in one way or another poetry covers the whole range of human experience and the features that it possesses can be many and varied. Poems can rhyme or not, they can use figurative language or not, they can be organized in stanzas or not, they can be written in conventional English or they can break all the rules of grammar. In other words, every poem is an individual piece of work with a range of features peculiar to itself. When you are reading a poem for the first time, therefore, it is important to establish what the poet is saying to the reader – in other words, what the **purpose** of the poem is. Having identified that, you can then go on to examine how the poet says whatever it is that he or she wishes to say.

The purpose of poetry

In poetry, language is used in both poetic and expressive ways to convey meaning to the reader, and the purpose of the poem could be to serve any one of a wide range of functions. For example, a poem could:

- entertain
- describe
- appeal to the emotions
- tell a story
- provoke thought
- inform
- console
- celebrate
- express grief

or any combination of these things.

Of course the vocabulary, style, form and other linguistic choices that a poet makes are closely linked to the purpose and effect the poet wants the poem to achieve.

In order to understand fully any message that a poem might carry for us, it is important to look at the linguistic and stylistic features of the poem. Poets can draw upon many varied linguistic features and it is not possible to consider them all in detail here. However, there are certain devices, features and forms that are well worth examining and we will look at some of them now.

Level of formality

The first thing to consider when encountering a poem for the first time is to establish the **manner** in which it is written. Basically the manner can be either formal or informal, depending on the kind of relationship the poet wants to establish with the reader. Of course, there can be different levels of formality or informality. Poetry is often associated with a heightened use of language – the poet generally uses fewer words than the prose writer and therefore the language is in a more concentrated form. Not all poems work on a 'heightened' level, however. Some poets use poetry to mirror the language of everyday speech to create a particular tone.

Tone, mood and atmosphere

The overall effect that a poem creates in the mind of the reader is very closely linked to the mood and tone that it creates. The 'voice' of the poem can create a certain **tone** that conveys to the reader certain messages about the poem itself. Obviously there are many different kinds of tone.

Activity

Think of as many words as you can to describe tone.

Tone can be difficult to define exactly, but there are many words that can be used to describe it. This is not an exhaustive list – add any more you have on your own list. It may help you when you are uncertain as to how to describe a particular tone. (Make sure you know what all the words mean.)

Playful	Ironic	Assertive	Frivolous	Gloomy
Humorous	Sarcastic	Cynical	Calm	Heavy
Melancholy	Sardonic	Serious	Personal	Mocking
Light-hearted	Dramatic	Impersonal	Angry	Sad
Philosophical	Intimate	Solemn	Religious	

Just as you might pick up clues as to how a friend feels through the tone of voice that he or she uses, so you can pick up clues from the 'voice' of the poem.

The **mood** of the poem, although closely linked to the tone, is a slightly different thing – it refers to the atmosphere or feeling that the poem creates. Very often tone and mood are closely linked and a certain tone produces a certain mood. For example, if a poet uses a lively, humorous tone it is far more likely to produce a light atmosphere than a melancholy one. In your Language and Literature course you will not only need to recognize the tone, mood and atmosphere of poems but you will also need to examine the ways in which poets use language to create their tones, moods and atmosphere.

Activity

Read the following poems carefully and think about the **manner** in which they are written. What kind of relationship do you think each poet wishes to establish with the reader? Comment on the tone, mood and atmosphere created in each poem and the ways in which the poets use language to create it.

Hey There Now!

(For Lesley)

Hey there now
my brownwater flower
      my sunchild branching
from my mountain river
          hey there now!
my young stream
      headlong
          rushing
I love to watch you
     when you're
         sleeping
          blushing

Grace Nichols

Advent

Earth grown old, yet still so green,
   Deep beneath her crust of cold
Nurses fire unfelt, unseen;
   Earth grown old.

   We who live are quickly told;
Millions more lie hid between
   Inner swathings of her fold.

When will fire break up her screen?
   When will life burst through her mould?
Earth, earth, earth, thy cold is keen.
   Earth grown old.

Christina Rossetti

I Say I Say I Say

Anyone here had a go at themselves
for a laugh? Anyone opened their wrists
with a blade in the bath? Those in the dark
at the back, listen hard. Those at the front
in the know, those of us who have, hands up,
let's show that inch of lacerated skin
between the forearm and the fist. Let's tell it
like it is: strong drink, a crimson tidemark
round the tub, a yard of lint, white towels
washed a dozen times, still pink. Tough luck.
A passion then for watches, bangles, cuffs.
A likely story: you were lashed by brambles
picking berries from the woods. Come clean, come good,
repeat with me the punch line 'Just like blood'
when those at the back rush forward to say
how a little love goes a long long long way.

Simon Armitage

- -

One student had clear ideas about what the poems meant to her. Read her responses through carefully. How close are her responses to your own thoughts on these poems? Remember, responses to poetry can be very individual.

Grace Nichols appears to have written the poem 'Hey There Now!', in celebration of someone she loves very dearly. Writing in an informal manner, she appears to invite the reader into sharing in this celebration. The poem has a loving tone which Nichols has created through the sentiments she expresses and which is enhanced by her use of language. For example, Nichols repeats the personal pronoun 'my' when referring to the subject of the poem, emphasizing ownership of the subject. In addition, the subject is described in affectionate terms, 'my sunchild', 'my brownwater flower'. The vitality of her love for the subject is complemented by Nichols's use of natural imagery which also adds to the celebratory mood. 'Flower', 'stream', 'river' and 'mountain' are all natural images included in the poem and they present the idea of a 'forever' love which is natural and pure. The sense of 'forever', as in an unending love, is further enhanced by the use of present continuous verb forms: 'branching', 'rushing', 'sleeping', 'blushing'. These verb endings give the poem 'movement' and add to the lively tone. The repetition of the exclamatory phrase, 'Hey there now!' also adds to the lively tone enhancing the celebratory mood of the poem as a whole.

Although natural imagery is contained in Christina Rossetti's poem, 'Advent', the mood of the poem is somewhat sorrowful. Writing in a formal manner, the poet adopts a melancholy tone in her presentation of 'Earth grown old'. The language that Rossetti uses helps to create a mood of sadness. For instance, the earth is described as 'cold', 'earth, earth, thy cold is keen', which suggests that it is an unwelcoming, uncomfortable place to be. The formal manner in which the poem is written further enhances the detachment from her surroundings that the poet feels. Rather than seeing Advent as a time which precedes the warmth of Spring, Rossetti presents the near-end of the year as a time of unfulfilment and decay and this is evident in the poem's vocabulary: 'unseen', 'unfelt', 'mould'. The hope of Spring, a 'better' time, is questionable and uncertain in this poem: 'When will fire break up her screen?' adding to the melancholy tone by creating a sense of despair. The unyielding nature of the earth, as seen by the poet, is expressed and enhanced by the apparent rigidity and restrictiveness of the rhyme sequence.

The disturbing content of the poem, 'I Say I Say I Say' is made more so as it is places us in a context in which we would expect to be in a 'happy' environment. As readers, we are placed in the audience of the poet as a 'stand-up' comedian. Using informal words and phrases we would expect to hear light-hearted humour from the comedian on stage: 'Anyone here had a go at themselves/ for a laugh?', 'Those in the dark/ at the back', 'Those at the front'. However, the poet shocks the audience with his subject of attempted suicide. An uncomfortable atmosphere is therefore created as a sad, solitary act, an attempted suicide, is given centre stage, the poem acting as an exposé, 'Let's tell it/ like it is'. However, the poet expresses the difficulty of 'telling it like it is' through various means and use of language in the poem. For instance, he describes how one would cover up the marks on the wrists left after a suicide attempt by developing a 'passion then for watches, bangles, cuffs'. In addition, he includes a 'cover story', a 'likely story' in which 'you were lashed by brambles/ picking berries from the woods'. Indeed, the whole poem avoids 'telling it like it is' as it fronts the disturbing act of attempted suicide with a light-hearted, comical approach: 'I Say I Say I Say'. Individual phrases in the poem are also seen to avoid directness. For instance, by writing, 'between the forearm and the fist', which almost sounds like a comical attempt at Cockney rhyming slang, the poet avoids using the word 'wrist'. When people are faced with uncomfortable situations, it is often difficult to know what to say and they often resort to using clichés. Consequently, Armitage concludes the poem with a clichéd response from 'those at the back', those who are not 'in the know'. This clichéd response confirms and enhances the uncomfortable, disturbing mood of the poem, 'a little love goes a long long long way'. The unsuitability of this expected response is further stressed as an extra 'long' has been inserted into this well-known cliché.

Examiner's comments

This is a mature and perceptive response to these poems, in which the student shows a close focus on the poets' use of language and the effects created through tone, mood and atmosphere. The student is greatly advantaged in expressing her ideas on these poems by her knowledge of both literary and linguistic terminology, which makes the expression of ideas much more straightforward than it would be if basic vocabulary were missing. For example, being able to identify 'my' as a personal pronoun and see its repetition as emphasizing a kind of 'ownership' is a point well made. So is the point about verb endings giving a sense of 'movement', thereby adding 'to the lively tone' and 'enhancing the celebratory mood of the poem as a whole'.

Her appreciation of the effects of imagery is also a great merit here, and once again the close focus on language and the use of specific examples from the texts is extremely helpful. With the Armitage poem the student also shows an awareness of the effects of juxtaposing the stand-up comedian's 'I say I say I say' with the disturbing theme of attempted suicide. Overall, a sophisticated response.

Form and structure

Form and structure can also tell the reader something about the poet's intentions. The way that the language of the poem is laid out will have been carefully chosen by the poet to enhance or reflect the meaning of the poem. There are many different ways in which poems can be structured, and in looking at the structure of a particular poem we must ask ourselves why the poet has chosen to use a particular form.

Form can refer to the way that the poem is actually written on the page, or the way that the lines are organized or grouped. Basically, poetry can be divided into general categories. First there is the kind where the lines follow on from each other continuously without breaks. Long narrative poems such as *The Wife of Bath's Tale* often take this form, and poems such as Wordsworth's *The Prelude*, Sylvia Plath's *Getting There* or Robert Frost's *The Census Taker*. The technical term for this kind of poetic form is **stichic** poetry.

The other kind of poetry is that where the lines are arranged in groups, which are sometimes incorrectly called 'verses'. The correct term for these groups of lines is **stanzas**. This kind of poetic form is called **strophic** poetry and examples of its use are in poems such as Philip Larkin's *An Arundel Tomb* or Seamus Heaney's *Follower*.

Stanzas can be organized in many different ways. Here are some examples.

The sonnet

The sonnet is a very popular form in English poetry, and one that poets have used for centuries. Basically a sonnet consists of 14 lines with a structured rhyme scheme and a definite rhythm pattern (usually **iambic pentameter**, see page 159). There are two main kinds of sonnet, the first being the Petrarchan or Italian sonnet (so called because it is named after the medieval Italian writer, Petrarch). The Petrarchan sonnet divides the 14 lines into an octave (eight lines) and a sestet (six lines). The rhyme scheme (see page 172) can vary but generally the pattern is *abbaabba cdecde* or *abbaabba cdcdcd*. The octave sets out the theme or key idea of the poem and the sestet provides some kind of response to it.

The other main kind of sonnet is the Shakespearean or English sonnet. In this kind of sonnet the lines are divided into three quatrains (of four lines each) and end with a couplet (two lines). The rhyme scheme in this kind of sonnet generally follows the pattern of *abab cdcd efef gg*. The theme or idea is developed through the quatrains.

Now read the following two sonnets. In the first two the poets follow a more conventional sonnet format, but in the third poem Larkin uses his own variation on the form.

'The world is too much with us'

The world is too much with us; late and soon,
Getting and spending, we lay waste our powers:
Little we see in nature that is ours;
We have given our hearts away, a sordid boon!
This Sea that bares her bosom to the moon;
The Winds that will be howling at all hours
And are up-gathered now like sleeping flowers;
For this, for every thing, we are out of tune;
It moves us not – Great God! I'd rather be
A Pagan suckled in a creed outworn;
So might I, standing on this pleasant lea,

Have glimpses that would make me less forlorn;
Have sight of Proteus coming from the sea;
Or hear old Triton blow his wreathed horn.

William Wordsworth

An Evil Spirit

An evil spirit, your beauty haunts me still,
Wherewith, alas, I have been long possessed,
Which ceaseth not to tempt me to each ill,
Nor gives me once but one poor minute's rest;

In me it speaks, whether I sleep or wake,
And when by means to drive it out I try,
With greater torments then it me doth take,
And tortures me in most extremity;

Before my face it lays down my despairs,
And hastes me on unto a sudden death,
Now tempting me to drown myself in tears,
And then in sighing to give up my breath.

> Thus am I still provoked to every evil
> By this good wicked spirit, sweet angel-devil.

Michael Drayton

First Sight

Lambs that learn to walk in snow
When their bleating clouds the air
Meet a vast unwelcome, know
Nothing but a sunless glare.
Newly stumbling to and fro
All they find, outside the fold,
Is a wretched width of cold.

As they wait beside the ewe,
Her fleeces wetly caked, there lies
Hidden round them, waiting too,
Earth's immeasurable surprise.
They could not grasp it if they knew,
What so soon will wake and grow
Utterly unlike the snow.

Philip Larkin

Activity

1 Examine the form each sonnet is written in and the rhyme scheme each poet has employed.
2 What are the key ideas each sonnet deals with? Examine the language each poet has used to express his ideas.
3 How does the language combine with the structure of each sonnet to fulfil the poets' intentions?

Other forms which you may come across in your studies include the following.

Ballads

Ballads date back to the oral tradition of the late Middle Ages and originally were often set to music. They are poems that tell a story, and therefore the focus tends to be on action and dialogue rather than the contemplative exploration of some kind of theme. The structure of the ballad normally consists of rhyming quatrains, sometimes using dialect forms or repetition to create effects.

Odes

Odes are lyrical poems, often elaborate, addressed to a particular person or thing or an abstract idea. They can present straightforward praise or they can develop complex philosophical ideas, and they can focus on positive or negative feelings with, perhaps, involved arguments. They are complex poems – the language often reflects the complexity of the content and many images may be contained within the poem. Odes are generally organized into fairly long stanzas.

Here is Wordsworth's *Ode to Duty*. Read it through carefully.

Ode to Duty

Stern Daughter of the Voice of God!
O Duty! if that name thou love
Who art a light to guide, a rod
To check the erring, and reprove;
Thou, who art victory and law
When empty terrors overawe;
From vain temptations dost set free;
And calm'st the weary strife of frail humanity!

There are who ask not if thine eye
Be on them; who, in love and truth,
Where no misgiving is, rely
Upon the genial sense of youth:
Glad Hearts! without reproach or blot;
Who do thy work, and know it not:
Oh! if through confidence misplaced
They fail, thy saving arms, dread Power! around them cast.

Serene will be our days and bright,
And happy will our nature be,
When love is an unerring light,
And joy its own security.
And they a blissful course may hold
Even now, who, not unwisely bold,
Live in the spirit of this creed;
Yet seek thy firm support, according to their need.

I, loving freedom, and untried;
No sport of every random gust,
Yet being to myself a guide,
Too blindly have reposed my trust:
And oft, when in my heart was heard
Thy timely mandate, I deferred

The task, in smoother walks to stray;
But thee I now would serve more strictly, if I may.

Through no disturbance of my soul,
Or strong compunction in me wrought,
I supplicate for thy control;
But in the quietness of thought:
Me this unchartered freedom tires;
I feel the weight of chance-desires:
My hopes no more must change their name,
I long for a repose that ever is the same.

Stern Lawgiver! yet thou dost wear
The Godhead's most benignant grace;
Nor know we anything so fair
As is the smile upon thy face:
Flowers laugh before thee on their beds
And fragrance in thy footing treads;
Thou dost preserve the stars from wrong;
And the most ancient heavens, through Thee, are fresh and strong.

To humbler functions, awful Power!
I call thee: I myself commend
Unto thy guidance from this hour;
Oh, let my weakness have an end!
Give unto me, made lowly wise,
The spirit of self-sacrifice;
The confidence of reason give;
And in the light of truth thy Bondman let me live!

William Wordsworth

Activity

1 Examine this ode and draw a diagram to show how Wordsworth develops his thoughts throughout the poem.

2 How does this development of ideas relate to the form of the poem?

3 What have you noted about Wordsworth's use of language in this poem?

Free verse

A final form of verse that we should mention at this point is free verse. Although modern poets also write in forms which adhere to strict patterns and forms, some of which we have already looked at, it is true that in the twentieth century there was a move towards poetry that does not have constraints of form, structure, rhyme or rhythm. Sometimes this type of verse does not even have regular lines, and the flexibility of free verse allows poets to use language in whatever ways seem appropriate to their purpose, and to create the effects they desire in their work.

Here is a poem written in free verse. Read it carefully.

To Women, As Far As I'm Concerned

The feelings I don't have I don't have.
The feelings I don't have I won't say I have.
The feelings you say you have, you don't have.

The feelings you would like us both to have, we neither of us have.
The feelings people ought to have, they never have.
If people say they've got feelings, you may be pretty sure
      They haven't got them.
So if you want either of us to feel anything at all
You'd better abandon all ideas of feelings altogether.

D.H. Lawrence

Activity

1 From the evidence of the way Lawrence uses language here, what do you think are the main features of free verse?

2 How do you think it differs from most other kinds of poetry?

You might have noted some of the following:

- Free verse does not follow any regular syllabic, metrical or rhyming pattern.
- It tends to follow speech rhythms of language.
- The line is the basic unit of rhythm.
- Spaces on the page can indicate pauses in the movement of the poem.

Poetic devices

There are a range of poetic devices and techniques of language use that poets can draw upon in writing their poetry. For the most part these techniques, like the use of imagery for example, are common to all kinds of literary writing. However, some devices are found only in poetry. Here are some of the main ones.

Enjambment

Enjambment is the term used to describe an instance where, because of its grammatical structure, verse runs on from one line to another. This can sometimes take the reader by surprise, as the meaning is not complete at the end of the line. Often, punctuation elsewhere in the line reinforces the need to run on at the end of the line.

End stop

End stop, in contrast, describes an instance where the grammatical break coincides with the end of a line. The break is often marked by a punctuation mark, and the meaning of the line is complete in itself.

Caesura

A caesura is simply a break or a pause in a line of verse, but it can be very important in influencing the rhythm of the poem. The example below is from *Letter in November* by Sylvia Plath:

This little black
Circle, with its tall silk grasses – babies' hair

Now read *At a Potato Digging* by Seamus Heaney.

I
A mechanical digger wrecks the drill,
Spins up a dark shower of roots and mould.

Labourers swarm in behind, stoop to fill
Wicker creels. Fingers go dead in the cold.

Like crows attacking crow-black fields, they stretch
A higgledy line from hedge to headland;
Some pairs keep breaking ragged ranks to fetch
A full creel to the pit and straighten, stand

Tall for a moment but soon stumble back
To fish a new load from the crumbled surf.
Heads bow, trunks bend, hands fumble towards the black
Mother. Processional stooping through the turf

Recurs mindlessly as autumn. Centuries
Of fear and homage to the famine god
Toughen the muscles behind their humbled knees,
Make a seasonal altar of the sod.

II

Flint-white, purple. They lie scattered
like inflated pebbles. Native
to the black hutch of clay
where the halved seed shot and clotted
these knobbed and slit-eyed tubers seem
the petrified hearts of drills. Split
by the spade, they show white as cream.

Good smells exude from crumbled earth.
The rough bark of humus erupts
knots of potatoes (a clean birth)
whose solid feel, whose wet inside
promises taste of ground and root.
To be piled in pits; live skulls, blind-eyed.

III

Live skulls, blind-eyed, balanced on
wild higgledy skeletons
scoured the land in 'forty-five,
wolfed the blighted root and died.

The new potato, sound as stone,
putrefied when it had lain
three days in the long clay pit.
Millions rotted along with it.

Mouths tightened in, eyes died hard,
faces chilled to a plucked bird.
In a million wicker huts
beaks of famine snipped at guts.

A people hungering from birth,
grubbing, like plants, in the bitch earth,
were grafted with a great sorrow.
Hope rotted like a marrow.

Stinking potatoes fouled the land,
pits turned pus into filthy mounds:
and where potato diggers are
you still smell the running sore.

IV
Under a gay flotilla of gulls
The rhythm deadens, the workers stop.
Brown bread and tea in bright canfuls
Are served for lunch. Dead-beat, they flop

Down in the ditch and take their fill,
Thankfully breaking timeless fasts;
Then, stretched on the faithless ground, spill
Libations of cold tea, scatter crumbs.

Activity

1   Look at the poem carefully and make a note of where lines are end-stopped and where Heaney uses enjambment.

2   Notice how Heaney's punctuation often forces you to pause in the middle of a line rather than at the end. What effect do you think this has?

Rhythm

Rhythm can be an important element in poetry and some of the earliest poems you remember, nursery rhymes such as *Hickory, Dickory Dock* or *Humpty Dumpty Sat on a Wall*, have very strong rhythms. It is these strong rhythms, along with the sounds of the words themselves and the rhymes, that give them such appeal to young children.

However, the influence of rhythm is not something exclusively reserved for nursery rhymes – a sense of rhythm can exert a profound influence on the overall effect of any poem. The rhythm can help to create mood and influence the tone and atmosphere of a poem. It is this rhythm that can give a poem its feeling of 'movement' and life, and the poet can use rhythm to create a whole variety of effects within the poem.

Syllable stress

Poets can create rhythms in poetry in various ways. Language has natural rhythms built into it, which we use automatically every time we pronounce words. For example, with the word 'randomly', we naturally stress the first syllable and not the second. If we did not do this, the word would sound rather strange. Poets, then, use these natural stresses and in-built rhythm patterns to contribute to the overall rhythmic effect.

Emphatic stress

Poets often deliberately place the emphasis on a particular word or part of the word in order to achieve a particular effect. The stress could be shifted to emphasize a particular meaning or reinforce a point, or even change meaning.

Phrasing and punctuation

The rhythm of poetry, along with other kinds of writing, can be influenced by factors such as word order, length of phrases or the choice of punctuation marks, line and stanza breaks and use of repetition.

Metre

Poetic metre is the pattern of stressed and unstressed syllables in a line of poetry, and as such is very closely linked to the idea of rhythm. The concept originated from the principles of classical Greek and Latin verse and was adopted by English poets from early times. These principles stated that each line of verse should follow a precise and regular pattern in terms of how many syllables it contained and the stress pattern used. These regular patterns of stressed and unstressed syllables are called **metres.** By analysing the metre, the reader can see how the poet is using the stress patterns within the language as one of the ways by which the meaning of the poem is conveyed. Variations in the pattern could mark changes in mood or tone, or signify a change of direction in the movement of the poem.

In identifying the metre of a poem, the first thing to do is to establish how the rhythm pattern is created. To help do this, the syllables are divided up into groups of two or three (depending on the particular pattern). Each of these groups is called a **foot.** The number of feet in a line can vary.

Here are the main patterns:

One foot	monometer
Two feet	dimeter
Three feet	trimeter
Four feet	tetrameter
Five feet	pentameter
Six feet	hexameter
Seven feet	heptameter
Eight feet	octameter

The process of identifying the metre is called scansion. Stressed syllables are marked / while unstressed syllables are marked ˘ and the feet are divided up using vertical lines |. A double vertical line ‖ indicates a caesura.

There are five basic patterns of stress. These are:

- Iambic: (iamb) — one unstressed syllable followed by a stressed one.

  When I | have fears | that I | may cease | to be

  Before | my pen | hath glean'd | my teem | ing brain,
  Keats

- Trochaic: (trochee) — one stressed syllable followed by one unstressed.

  Tyger! | Tyger! | Burning | bright

  In the | forests | of the | night.
  Blake

- Dactylic: one stressed syllable followed by two unstressed syllables.
  (dactyl)

  Half a league, | half a league,

  Half a league | onward.

  Tennyson

- Anapaestic: two unstressed syllables followed by one stressed syllable.
  (anapaest)

  Will's | at the dance | in the Club | –room below,

  Where | the tall liqu | or cups foam;

  Hardy

- Spondaic: two stressed syllables.
  (spondee)

  One, two

  Buckle my shoe.

  Anon.

For example, look at these lines from Keats's *When I have Fears*.

When I have fears that I may cease to be
    Before my pen hath glean'd my teeming brain,
Before high-piled books, in charact'ry,
    Hold like rich garners the full-ripen'd grain:
When I behold, upon the night's starr'd face,
    Huge cloudy symbols of a high romance,
And think that I may never live to trace
    Their shadows, with the magic hand of chance;
And when I feel, fair creature of an hour!
    That I shall never look upon thee more,
Never have relish in the faery power
    Of unreflecting love! – then on the shore
Of the wide world I stand alone, and think
    Till love and fame to nothingness do sink.

John Keats

Activity

The first two lines were scanned for you on page 159. Now scan the remainder of the poem. How many metrical feet are there per line? What is the metrical pattern? Look at the poem again. What effect does the metrical pattern have on the overall effect of the poem?

Lexical choice

The lexical choice (sometimes referred to as **diction**) is the decisions about language that a poet has made when writing his or her poem. The choices that are made will inevitably be influenced by the complex relationship between the reader and the poet. They will depend on the level of formality or informality of the poem, the poet's intentions and the effect that the piece is intended to have on the reader. Abstract or concrete nouns can be chosen depending on the subject matter of the poem, and modifiers can be used to add detail to descriptions of people or places, to create atmosphere, arouse emotions or express opinions and judgements. Verbs will be selected to express actions of various kinds, as well as adding to the message that the poet wishes to convey to the reader.

Of the various aspects considered in lexical choice, probably the most important is a word's **connotations**, or the associations suggested by a word. This is quite separate from its **denotation**, or dictionary definition. Words can carry with them many connotations that might bring suggested meanings quite different from the dictionary definition of the word. Connotations are acquired by words depending on how they have been used in the past.

Activity

Look at the following list of words. Although they share a common basic meaning, they have very different connotations. Use each of the words in a sentence, to show the difference in connotation between them.

cunning; sly; devious; crafty; wily; artful; shifty; subtle; guileful.

There are occasions when writers choose words which have the clearest meaning or denotation, without complicating connotations. It all depends on the effects that the writer wishes to achieve – words are chosen to suit the audience and purpose. Sometimes a writer or poet might choose words that are particularly colloquial or particularly formal, according to context. Sometimes archaisms are used to give a sense of the past or add a sense of dignity and solemnity to the language, or dialect words may be used to create a certain social or regional atmosphere – for example, as in this poem by Simon Armitage, written in the Yorkshire dialect:

On an Owd Piktcha

(from tjerman)

Int swelterin eet, mongst birds n tbeez,
side cool watter n rushes n reeds,
tChrahst Chahld sithee, born bath taint,
laikin arahnd on tVirgin's knee.

N poorakin its nooas aht o tleaves n tmoss,
already green, tTree o tCross.

Activity

Read Armitage's poem carefully.

1 Try writing a 'Standard English' version of it.

2 What are the differences between the two versions?

3 Why do you think Armitage chose to write this in dialect form?

Poets can make their lexis very modern by using **neologisms** (invented words), which can add a sense of individuality to the poem. Sometimes a word may be chosen because it is incongruous and doesn't fit in with the other lexis. It may jar or shock the reader, or defy the reader's expectations.

Activity

Look at the following extracts from various poems.

Fill each blank with one word from the selection, and explain why you have made your choice.

1   __a__ the spring onions,
    She made this mental note:
    You can tell it's love, the real thing,
    When you __b__ of slitting his throat.
                    Wendy Cope

    a   slicing, decapitating, washing.
    b   think, talk, dream.

2   Closed like __a__ , they thread
    __b__ noons of cities, giving back
    None of the __c__ they absorb.
    Light __d__ grey, arms on a plaque
    They come to __e__ at any kerb:
    All streets in __f__ are visited.
                    Philip Larkin

    a   boxes, confessionals, graves
    b   bright, busy, loud
    c   stares, glances, looks
    d   glossy, dirty, pale
    e   a stop, visit, rest
    f   the town, time, turn

3   It is a beauteous evening, __a__ and free;
    The holy time is quiet as a Nun
    Breathless with __b__ ; the broad sun
    Is sinking down in its __c__ .
                    William Wordsworth

    a   calm, still, fine
    b   prayer, devotion, adoration
    c   close, tranquillity, stillness

Now let's have a look at a complete poem. This is by Dylan Thomas.

Do not go gentle into that good night

Do not go gentle into that good night,
Old age should burn and rave at close of day;
Rage, rage against the dying of the light.

Though wise men at their end know dark is right,
Because their words had forked no lightning they
Do not go gentle into that good night.

Good men, the last wave by, crying how bright
Their frail deeds might have danced in a green bay
Rage, rage against the dying of the light.

Wild men who caught and sang the sun in flight,
And learn, too late, they grieved it on its way,
Do not go gentle into that good night.

Grave men, near death, who see with blinding sigh
Blind eyes could blaze like meteors and be gay,
Rage, rage against the dying of the light.

And you, my father, there on the sad height,
Curse, bless, me now with your fierce tears, I pray.
Do not go gentle into that good night.
Rage, rage against the dying of the light.

Dylan Thomas

Activity

Read the poem carefully.

1 What effect is created by the opening stanza?
2 What effects does Thomas create through his choice of lexis (vocabulary)?
3 Pick out any words or phrases that you find particularly striking. What effects do these create?
4 What overall effect does Thomas create in his poem?

Grammar

Many poets use standard forms of grammar, although sometimes the language can be manipulated to fit the restrictions of a particular poetic form.

In the following example, Byron uses standard forms of grammar to create a logical progression that forms the structure of the poem.

So We'll Go No More A-Roving

So we'll go no more a-roving
    So late into the night,
Though the heart be still as loving,
    And the moon be still as bright.

For the sword outwears its sheath,
    And the soul wears out the breast,
And the heart must pause to breathe,
    And love itself have rest.

Though the night was made for loving,
    And the day returns too soon,
Yet we'll go no more a-roving
    By the light of the moon.

Lord Byron

In terms of Byron's use of grammar in this poem, here are some points you might note:

- the relationship between 'So', at the beginning the poem and 'Yet', which begins the closing sequence – these signal the movement of thought through the poem
- the words that create a link with the 'So' and 'Yet' of the opening and closing – 'So' (line 2), 'Though' (line 3) and the repeated 'still' (lines 3 and 4)
- the unspoken question suggested here: though the heart is still as loving, though the moon is still as bright, the roving will stop – why?
- the second stanza provides the answer through four examples ('the sword...', 'the soul...', 'the heart...', 'And love...'), suggesting that age or physical fatigue rather than the loss of love has brought an end to the 'roving'
- the final stanza completes the grammatical and the narrative sequence, repeating the key phrases and expanding the central idea.

Descriptive analysis

Grammatical analysis of a poem can help to shed light on how the text of the poem works. In order to look at the grammar of poetry it is useful to be aware of the various word classes or **parts of speech**, as they are sometimes called. Here is a list of the key ones to be aware of, although it is not exhaustive. They can be used to describe how the language is working and are sometimes referred to as **units of structure**.

Word class	Examples
Verb	ran, said, eat, served, made, went
Noun	table, window, book, beauty, planet, daughter
Adjective	happy, small, clean, hard, metallic
Adverb	swiftly, harshly, probably, soothingly
Personal pronoun	he, she, they, it, theirs, his, hers
Indefinite pronoun	anyone, someone, everyone, everybody, anything
Preposition	in, on, up, beside, after, at, underneath, towards
Article	the, a, an
Demonstrative	this, that, those, these
Modal	should, could, must, might, can, shall, would
Degree modifier	how, very, rather, quite
Quantifier	some, every, all

Thinking about what poets are doing with language through describing its grammatical make-up can help you understand just how a particular poem is working.

Some poets might deliberately disrupt our expectations to create their effects, and sometimes they go further still in breaking the conventions of grammar. E.E. Cummings is well known for the unconventional ways in which he uses language in his poems. Here is the first stanza from one of his poems. Some of the words have been removed.

__a__ lived in a pretty __b__ town

(with __c__ so floating many bells __d__)

spring summer autumn winter

he sang his __e__ he danced his __f__ .

Activity

Fill in the blanks in this stanza, choosing words from the appropriate lists.

a	b	c	d	e	f
someone	small	light	din	song	jig
Bill	quiet	gleaming	down	didn't	round
She	how	up	bright	turn	dance
They	hot	down	clamour	notes	did
anyone	slow	chimes	clash	solo	favourite

Now check your version against the original. Here are the words Cummings used:

a anyone **b** how **c** up **d** down **e** didn't **f** did

You probably found some or all of these choices rather surprising – not least because they apparently produce lines that seem nonsensical. This is because Cummings breaks the grammatical rules for combining the parts of speech or units of structure together. In order to see exactly what Cummings has done it is useful to identify each of the parts of speech. In the first line of the poem this works out as –

pronoun	verb	preposition	article	adjective	degree modifier	noun
anyone	*lived*	*in*	*a*	*pretty*	*how*	*town*

However, it appears here that Cummings is using the some of these words in a different way grammatically. He seems to use them here as:

proper noun	verb	preposition	article	degree modifier	adjective	noun
anyone	lived	in	a	pretty	how	town

You might have noticed in this line the use of 'how' in an unexpected position. Here Cummings uses a degree modifier where we would expect to see another adjective. In fact that word order of article → adjective → degree modifier → noun is one that does not conform to the 'rules' of English grammar.

Apart from the use of the word 'how', the other problem with this opening line is the use of the word 'anyone'. In this context, 'anyone' is an indefinite pronoun. Some indefinite pronouns such as 'someone' or 'it' would fit here, and various personal pronouns such as 'he', 'she', 'they' would also make sense. Cummings, though, has clearly chosen to use a word that again does not conform to the rules of English grammar. The big question is, why? This is a question that you might be in a better position to answer after you have read the whole poem.

The other words missing from the first stanza pose similar problems. Neither 'up' nor 'down' seem to make sense in the positions they appear in. If you look carefully, though, at the words the poet uses you might begin to see that he is, in fact, working to a set of rules of his own making. It is just that they are not the normal rules of grammar that we recognize and understand.

Now have a look at the whole poem.

anyone lived in a pretty how town

anyone lived in a pretty how town
(with up so floating many bells down)
spring summer autumn winter
he sang his didn't he danced his did.

Women and men(both little and small)
cared for anyone not at all
they sowed their isn't they reaped their same
sun moon stars rain

children guessed(but only a few
and down they forgot as up they grew
autumn winter spring summer)
that noone loved him more by more

when by now and tree and leaf
she laughed his joy she cried his grief
bird by snow and stir by still
anyone's any was all to her

someones married their everyones
laughed their cryings and did their dance
(sleep wake hope and then)they
said their nevers they slept their dream

stars rain sun moon
(and only the snow can begin to explain
how children are apt to forget to remember
with up so floating many bells down)

one day anyone died i guess
(and noone stooped to kiss his face)
busy folk buried them side by side
little by little and was by was

all by all and deep by deep
and more by more they dream their sleep
noone and anyone earth by april
wish by spirit and if by yes.

Women and men(both dong and ding)
summer autumn winter spring
reaped their sowing and went their came
sun moon stars rain

E.E. Cummings

Activity

Now you have read the whole poem, answer the following questions:

1   Identify all the words that you think are used in the 'wrong' place.

2   Does the poet's use of the word 'anyone' mean more to you now in the context of the whole poem? How do you think we are meant to interpret 'anyone', 'noone' and 'someone'?

3   How does Cummings use pairings of words, such as 'up/down', 'did/didn't'? Have you found any more such pairings of opposites?

4   How does Cummings make use of repetition in the poem?

5   Now write a brief summary of what the poem is about.

6   The key question is why Cummings chooses to break the conventions of grammar and write his poem in this way. What effects do you think he achieves by this?

When dealing with poems such as this one where the meaning is not necessarily immediately apparent, your initial responses may well be quite tentative. Don't worry about this, and don't worry about putting things down on paper that you feel unsure about. It is all part of the process of unravelling meaning from the text.

Here are the initial, tentative responses of two students as they work towards finding their meaning of 'Anyone lived in a pretty how town.'

Student A

1   The word 'Anyone' is used to describe the people in the town. It also indicates that it is informal and impersonal, making the poem a story open to interpretation. A trivial tale about two or three people, yet the words indicate he's talking about mankind. 'Anyone' and 'Noone' are opposite words and the poet contrasts these types of words throughout the poem. They are meant to be interpreted as words which create a larger scale to the environment it is set in. The word 'Anyone' throws the poem open to a wider scale of people and 'Someone' is specific to one person. Anyone – male, Noone – female – gives it a universal theme.

2   He uses pairs of words such as 'did' and 'didn't', and 'up' and 'down', to describe how objects did things (in place of an adjective). Examples of pairing of words are:

did/didn't, down/up, joy/grief, sun/moon, rain/snow – gives a pattern to the words.

3   He uses repetition to emphasize his points, for example about sleep he says 'all by all' and 'more by more'. The repetition of the seasons indicates people moving on, living and then dying.

4   The poem describes what happens to anyone in a certain town. Through the seasons and through the weather how the men and women dance, sleep and live.

Student B

1   The poet uses the words 'Anyone' and 'Noone' throughout the poem. This could be to give the poem a more universal and wider meaning than would have been achieved if the characters had been named. 'Anyone' and 'Noone' could mean that the poem would be meant to apply to the reader. It stops stereotyping. Anyone is male + Noone is female.

2   Cummings uses pairings of words and opposites throughout the poem such as 'up/down', 'did/didn't', 'joy/grief', 'little/small', 'dong/ding'. This gives some degree of logic to often illogical sentences. It also means there is some rhyme in the verses. It leaves quite a lot open to interpretation.

3   Some words and lines are repeated throughout the poem. Although in a different order, 'spring, summer, autumn, winter' and 'reaped' and 'sowed' are repeated to show a sense of passing of time. There is also the sense of people moving on and a cyclical element – closely tied in with environment.

4   This poem seems to tell a life story of a person. The fact that there are no names or characters generalizes the story, so it could apply to anyone. The repetition of 'spring, summer, autumn, winter' suggests that life is the same every year. The inclusion of 'sun, moon, stars' and 'rain', especially at the end, shows that things go on and everybody is the same, as the sun, moon, stars and rain are a constant for everyone. It seems to trivialize life as everyone is there, they do their thing ('reaped their sowing and went their came') and then die, and it is no big deal.

Examiner's comments

Although these comments are initial and tentative, they are also exploratory. Both students have begun the process of coming to terms with a tricky brief through some of these comments. There are quite a number of points here that could be picked up and examined in more detail – some ideas are very perceptive, and already the students are beginning to identify the effects of such features as word pairings and repetition.

Metaphorical devices

Very often the language of poetry is made more intense through the use of metaphorical devices, which can add layers of meaning to a poem beyond the literal sense of the words on the page. You are likely to encounter several of these linguistic devices in the poetry you study. You may sometimes see these devices referred to as **figurative language** or see individual examples called **figures of speech**. These are blanket terms used to describe the individual features that we will now look at. This kind of language use, in which the words require an intellectual and/or emotional response beyond their literal meaning, is also called **representational language**.

In Old English poetry, poets often used a device using figurative language called the **kenning** which consisted of a word or phrase made up to identify a particular thing through its specific quality or characteristic, without actually naming it. They had a large selection of kennings for words that were commonly used. For example, the used the term 'mail-shirt' for armour; instead of 'ocean' they could say 'swan's road' or 'foaming field' or 'realm of monsters'; for 'ship' they might say 'sea goer' or 'sea wood', for a 'lord' a 'dispenser of rings' or 'treasure giver', for the 'sun', 'candle of the world' or 'Heaven's candle' or 'wind-eye' meaning window. Such was the importance of this kind of figurative language to Old English that it has been estimated that in one of the best-known poems written in Old English, *Beowulf*, as many as a third of the words are kennings.

Kennings are not just a feature of language use of the past, though. We still make up kennings today to describe features of modern life. For example, 'the beautiful game' – football, 'the Devil's dandruff' – cocaine, 'gas-guzzler' – a car that is heavy on petrol, 'wood-pusher' – skateboarder, 'sport of kings' – horse racing, 'cannon fodder' – soldier killed (often futilely) in war, 'pen-pusher' – office worker.

Activity

1 Make up ten kennings of your own.
2 Exchange these with a partner and try to identify the meaning of each other's kennings.

In their use of kennings, the Old English poets were using a kind of imagery to describe their particular subject. Images can work in several ways in the mind of the reader. For example, an image can be used literally to describe something, as in Wordsworth's description of taking a boat out on to the lake at night, as the boat moves forward:

> Leaving behind her still, on either side,
> Small circles glittering idly in the moon,
> Until they melted all into one track
> Of sparkling light...

Wordsworth, Prelude Book 1

This creates a **literal image** as we can picture the scene in our minds from the way in which Wordsworth describes it. Non-literal, figurative or representational images can be created when the thing being described is compared to something else. You will probably already be familiar with the **simile**, in which the comparison is made very clear by the poet using the words 'like' or 'as'. Often the elements being compared are essentially different in nature, but they come together in the poet's perception and ultimately in the reader's perception. Here are some examples of the simile in action:

> Her goodly eyes like Sapphires shining bright...
> Her cheeks like apples which the sun hath redded,
> Her lips like cherries charming men to bite.

Edmund Spenser

> My love is like a red, red rose
>   That's newly sprung in June:
> My love is like the melody
>   That's sweetly played in tune.

Robert Burns

The **metaphor** is another representational device that poets often use, and with which you are familiar. In some ways a metaphor is like a simile in that it too creates a comparison. However, the comparison is less direct than the simile in that it does not include the terms 'like' or 'as', but often describes the subject as *being* the thing to which it is compared. For example, in Simon Armitage's poem *The Anaesthetist*, he describes the anaesthetist entering the operating theatre:

> Hard to believe him when he trundles in,
> Scrubbed up and squeaky clean, manoeuvering
> A handcart of deep-sea diving gear.

Simon Armitage

Of course, Armitage does not literally mean that the anaesthetist enters pushing a cart piled high with deep-sea diving gear – it is meant metaphorically: the look of the anaesthetist's equipment reminds Armitage of deep-sea diving gear.

Another kind of representational device frequently used by poets is **personification**. This is really a kind of metaphor in which the attributes of a person are given to either abstract or non-human things. In this example from Wilfred Owen's poem *Futility*, the sun is personified:

Futility

Move him into the sun –
Gently its touch awoke him once,
At home, whispering of fields unsown.
Always it woke him, even in France,
Until this morning and this snow.
If anything might rouse him now
The kind old sun will know.

Wilfred Owen

Closely associated with the idea of personification is that of **apostrophe**. This term describes a feature where a personified thing is addressed directly as if it were animate, or the dead are addressed as if alive. In this example, John Donne uses apostrophe when he addresses Death as a person:

Death, be not proud, though some have called thee
Mighty and dreadful, for thou art not so

Two other representational features that you might encounter in your poetic studies are **metonymy** and **synecdoche**. Metonymy is the figure of speech where the term for one thing is substituted for the term for another thing with which it has become closely associated. For example, if we say 'The pen is mightier than the sword', then 'pen' and 'sword' are metonymies for written thoughts or ideas and military power, respectively. If we use the term 'the Crown' to mean royalty or the power invested in royalty we are similarly using a metonym. A synecdoche is a figure of speech in which part of something is used to represent the whole. For example, Shakespeare uses this device in the following line:

Nay, if you read this line, remember not
The hand that writ it

The 'hand' here means the whole person who wrote the line.

Another metaphorical device that poets often use is that of **symbolism**, sometimes drawing on commonly recognized symbols and sometimes inventing their own. In basic terms a symbol is simply a device whereby a word or phrase represents something else – for example the colour white could be used to represent peace. Symbolism in poetry can be very complex, with some poems operating on two levels, the literal and the symbolic. Sometimes in order to fully understand the significance of a poem it is necessary to understand the symbolic importance of some of the ideas or images used.

Now read Keats's *To Autumn*.

To Autumn

Season of mists and mellow fruitfulness,
    Close bosom-friend of the maturing sun;
Conspiring with him how to load and bless
    With fruit the vines that round the thatch-eves run;
To bend with apples the moss'd cottage-trees,
    And fill all fruit with ripeness to the core;

To swell the gourd, and plump the hazel shells
With a sweet kernel; to set budding more,
    And still more, later flowers for the bees,
    Until they think warm days will never cease,
    For Summer has o'er-brimm'd their clammy cells.

Who hath not seen thee oft amid thy store?
    Sometimes whoever seeks abroad may find
Thee sitting careless on a granary floor,
    Thy hair soft-lifted by the winnowing wind;
Or on a half-reap'd furrow sound asleep,
    Drows'd with the fume of poppies while thy hook
    Spares the next swath and all its twined flowers:
And sometimes like a gleaner thou dost keep
    Steady thy laden head across a brook;
    Or by a cyder-press, with patient look,
    Thou watchest the last oozings hours by hours.

Where are the songs of Spring? Ay, where are they?
    Think not of them, thou hast thy music too, –
While barred clouds bloom the soft-dying day,
    And touch the stubble-plains with rosy hue;
Then in a wailful choir the small gnats mourn
    Among the river sallows, borne aloft
    Or sinking as the light wind lives or dies;
And full-grown lambs loud bleat from hilly bourn;
    Hedge-crickets sing; and now with treble soft
    The red-breast whistles from a garden-croft;
    And gathering swallows twitter in the skies.

John Keats

Activity

Write a short essay (approximately 400–500 words) in which you examine the following aspects of *To Autumn*:

- the imagery
- the symbolism
- any other representational features

and comment on the effects that Keats achieves through their use.

Rhetorical techniques

Poets use rhetorical techniques to provide extra effects or meanings for their poems. These rhetorical techniques fall into two categories: **phonological patterning**, through such devices as **alliteration**, **onomatopoeia** and **rhyme**, and **structural patterning**, through the use of **parallelism**, **repetition**, **antithesis** and **listing**. Let us have a closer look at these features.

Phonological features

The term 'phonological' will probably have already told you that these kinds of features are to do with sound. Of course, the notion of sound and the repetition of sound is very important in poetry and contributes to what is sometimes called the 'music' of the words. Sometimes a sound or words might be repeated simply because the effect created is pleasing to the ear, but more often the repetition plays an integral part in supporting the sense and overall effect of the poem. Sometimes the repetition might be of a word, a phrase or a whole stanza, as in the case of a refrain, but there are many other smaller units of sound that can be repeated. Here are the key ones that you will come across in your studies.

Rhyme

Rhyme can make an important contribution to the 'musical quality' of a poem and, like rhythm, it affects the sound and the overall effectiveness. The system of rhyme within a poem, or **rhyme scheme**, can influence this effect in a variety of ways. The rhyme scheme could help to unify the poem and draw it together, it could give it an incantatory quality or add emphasis to particular elements of the lexis (vocabulary).

There are various kinds of rhymes and rhyme schemes. The most common rhymes work on the basis of a rhyme occurring at the end of a line and are called 'complete rhymes', as in 'free' rhyming with 'tree', or 'feel' with 'seal'. Sometimes rhymes occur within the line itself. These are called **internal rhymes**. Coleridge makes use of this kind of rhyme in *The Rime of the Ancient Mariner*:

> The fair breeze blew, the white foam flew,
> The furrow followed free;
> We were the first that ever burst
> Into that silent sea.

In this case, the rhyming of 'blew' and 'flew' stresses these words and adds emphasis to the image of the ship's speed and movement.

A rhyme may appear incomplete or inaccurate in various ways. The vowels may not be pronounced in the same way, for example 'love/ move' or 'plough/ rough'. These are called **eye rhymes** or **sight rhymes**. Some poets choose deliberately to weaken the force of the rhyme by making either the consonant or vowel different. Wilfred Owen frequently uses this technique, as here for example:

> Like twitching agonies of men among its brambles
> Northward, incessantly, the flickering gunnery rumbles

Or:

> We only know war lasts, rain soaks, and clouds sag stormy
> Dawn massing in the east her melancholy army
> Attacks once more in ranks on shivering ranks of gray,

This kind of rhyme is called **half rhyme**, **slant rhyme** or **para-rhyme**.

In the same way that the rhythm in a poem often follows a recognized pattern, so can rhyme. Working out the rhyme scheme is quite a straightforward business and is done by indicating lines that rhyme together through giving them the same letter of the alphabet. For example, look at the first stanza from Thomas Hardy's *The Darkling Thrush*:

I leant upon a coppice gate	**a**
When Frost was spectre-gray	**b**
And Winter's dregs made desolate	**a**
The weakening eye of day.	**b**
The tangled bine-stems scored the sky	**c**
Like strings of broken lyres	**d**
And all mankind that haunted nigh	**c**
Had sought their household fires	**d**

Here Hardy uses a straightforward *abab cdcd* rhyme scheme, where pairs of alternate lines rhyme within the stanza. Various rhyming patterns are described by particular terms. Here are the main ones.

- **Couplets or rhyming couplets:** Pairs of lines that rhyme together; pairs of lines that are written in iambic pentameter (see page 159) are called **heroic couplets**.

- **Quatrain:** A set of four rhyming lines, usually with a rhyme scheme *abab*, *abcb*, *aaaa*, or *abba*.

- **Sestet:** A six-line unit that can rhyme in a variety of ways, e.g. *ababcc*; this can also refer to the concluding part of an Italian sonnet.

- **Octave:** An eight-line unit which can be constructed in a number of ways. It can be formed by linking two quatrains together (as in Hardy's stanza above) or it can have a rhyme scheme which integrates all eight lines. It is also the name given to the first eight lines of an Italian sonnet.

The important thing in looking at the rhyme scheme of a poem, though, is not spotting the rhymes or working out the scheme but being able to identify what effect the rhyme scheme has on the poem. In other words you need to be able to explain why the poet has chosen to use language in this particular way, and what the overall effects of those language choices are. Here are some of the effects that the use of rhyme might have on a poem.

- It can make a poem sound musical and pleasing to the ear.
- It can create a jarring, discordant effect.
- It can add emphasis to certain words and give particular words an added prominence.
- It can act as a unifying influence on the poem, drawing it together through the rhyme patterns.
- It can give the poem a rhythmic, incantatory or ritualistic feel.
- It can influence the rhythm of the verse.
- It can provide a sense of finality – the rhyming couplet, for example, is often used to give a sense of 'ending'.
- It can exert a subconscious effect on the reader, drawing together certain words or images, affecting the sound, or adding emphasis in some way.

Alliteration

Another phonological feature often used by poets is **alliteration**. This involves the repetition of the same consonant sound, usually at the beginning of each word, over two or more words together, as in Shakespeare's lines from *The Tempest*:

Fall **f**athom **f**ive thy **f**ather lies,
Of his bones are coral made.

Assonance

Assonance is a feature similar to alliteration but instead of consonants involves the repetition of vowel sounds to achieve a particular effect. An example is the long, drawn-out 'o' sounds in the first line of Sylvia Plath's *Frog Autumn*:

> Summer gr**o**ws **o**ld, c**o**ld-bl**oo**ded m**o**ther

This creates an impression of lethargy and lack of life as summer passes and winter approaches.

Onomatopoeia

Onomatopoeia refers to words that, by their sound, reflect their meaning – 'bang' or 'ping' are simple examples that sound like the noises they describe. Here is a more sophisticated example, from Coleridge's *The Rime of the Ancient Mariner*.

> The ice was here, the ice was there,
> The ice was all around;
> It **cracked** and **growled**, and **roared** and **howled**,
> Like noises in a swound

The words 'cracked', 'growled', 'roared' and 'howled' suggest the sounds of the icebergs grinding around the ship, and therefore make the description more graphic in an aural as well as visual way. It is perhaps worth noting also that Coleridge makes use of repetition here, emphasizing the fact that ice was everywhere.

Structural features

Obviously, the way in which a poem is structured can play an important part in the overall effect it produces. The poet has several devices to draw on to create effects through a poem's structure.

Repetition and listing

The technique of repeating or listing several words with the same or similar meaning (sometimes called **cumulation**) is often used to add emphasis or a persuasive quality to the poem. Such repetition of a word or words can add force and power to the subject, or it can be used to work towards a dramatic climax. In Gerard Manley Hopkins's poem *God's Grandeur* the simple repetition reinforces the meaning of the line:

> Generations have trod, have trod, have trod

The repetition of 'look' at the opening of Hopkins's *The Starlight Night* creates a sense of excitement as the poet urges us to look at the stars:

> Look at the stars! look, look up at the skies!
> O look at all the fire-folk sitting in the air!

Parallelism

Parallelism is another form of repetition but involves the repetition of larger structural features. It could include the repetition of the same verse form using different words, mirroring the main theme of the poem, or the use of recurring motifs or symbols.

The difference between repetition and parallelism can be seen in these examples:

Repetition:

> Onward, onward rode the six hundred

Parallelism:

> Those that I fight I do not hate
> Those that I guard I do not love

Dorothy Parker uses a parallel structure in her poem *Resume*.

Resume

Razors pain you;
Rivers are damp;
Acid stains you;
And drugs cause cramp.
Guns aren't lawful;
Nooses give;
Gas smells awful;
You might as well live.

Dorothy Parker

Antithesis

Antithesis involves contrasting ideas or words balanced against one another. Usually there are two groups of words with a parallel syntax (or word order) but with a contrasting or opposite meaning, as for example in the phrase:

> to live a sinner or to die a saint

or in Alexander Pope's *Imitations of Horace*:

> 'Tis the first Virtue, Vices to abhor
> and the first Wisdom, to be a fool no more.

Now read *Inversnaid* by Gerard Manley Hopkins.

Inversnaid

This darksome burn, horseback brown,
His rollrock highroad roaring down,
In coop and in comb the fleece of his foam
Flutes and low to the lake falls home.

A windpuff-bonnet of fawn-froth
Turns and twindles over the broth
Of a pool so pitchblack, fell-frowning,
It rounds and rounds Despair to drowning.

Degged with dew, dappled with dew
Are the groins of the braes that the brook treads through,
Wiry heathpacks, flitches of fern,
And the beadbonny ash that sits over the burn.

What would the world be, once bereft
Of wet and of wildness? Let them be left,

O let them be left, wildness and wet;
Long live the weeds and the wilderness yet.

Gerard Manley Hopkins

Activity

Examine the ways in which Hopkins uses language to achieve his effects in *Inversnaid*. You should refer to specific details of language use including Hopkins's use of:

- imagery and other metaphorical features
- phonological features
- structural patterning.

Poetic intention

Poets, like other writers, use language to fulfil various intentions. In most poems, of course, there may be elements of a range of poetic intentions, each serving a particular purpose.

Creating character

Sometimes poems focus on the physical description of a character or characters, but sometimes the description moves beyond this surface level to tell you something about the inner person. Chaucer's description of the Wife of Bath tells us about the physical aspects of the character, but we also learn something about the kind of woman she is from the way in which Chaucer presents his portrait. Look at the following extract.

From *The General Prologue to the Canterbury Tales*

A good WIF was ther OF biside BATHE,
But she was somdel deef, and that was scathe.
Of clooth-makyng she hadde swich an haunt
She passed hem of Ypres and of Gaunt.
In al the parisshe wif ne was ther noon
That to the offrynge bifore hire sholde goon;
And if ther dide, certeyn so wrooth was she
That she was out of alle charitee.
Hir coverchiefs ful fyne weren of ground;
I dorste swere they weyeden ten pound
That on a Sonday weren upon hir heed.
Hir hosen weren of fyn scarlet reed,
Ful streite yteyd, and shoes ful moyste and newe.
Boold was hir face, and fair, and reed of hewe.
She was a worthy womman al hir lyve:
Housbondes at chirche dore she hadde fyve,
Withouten oother compaignye in youthe –
But thereof nedeth nat to speke as nowthe.
And thries hadde she been at Jerusalem;
She hadde passed many a straunge strem;
At Rome she hadde been, and at Boloigne,
In Galice at Seint-Jame, and at Coloigne.

She koude muchel of wandrynge by the weye.
Gat-tothed was she, soothly for to seye.
Upon an amblere esily she sat,
Ywympled wel, and on hir heed an hat
As brood as is a bokeler or a targe;
A foot-mantel aboute hir hipes large,
And on hir feet a paire of spores sharpe.
In felaweshipe wel koude she laughe and carpe.
Of remedies of love she knew per chaunce,
For she koude of that art the olde daunce.

Geoffrey Chaucer

Activity

How does Chaucer use language to:

1   tell you about the Wife's physical appearance?
2   tell you about her character?

Look particularly at Chaucer's choice of lexis, and the metaphorical and rhetorical features he uses.

Now compare this with *The Village Schoolmaster* by Oliver Goldsmith:

The Village Schoolmaster

Beside yon straggling fence that skirts the way,
With blossomed furze unprofitably gay,
There, in his noisy mansion, skilled to rule,
The village master taught his little school;
A man severe he was, and stern to view,
I knew him well, and every truant knew;
Well had the boding tremblers learned to trace
The day's disasters in his morning face;
Full well they laughed, with counterfeited glee,
At all his jokes, for many a joke had he:
Full well the busy whisper, circling round,
Conveyed the dismal tidings when he frowned;
Yet he was kind, or, if severe in aught,
The love he bore to learning was in fault;
The village all declared how much he knew;
'Twas certain he could write, and cipher too;
Lands he could measure, terms and tides presage,
And even the story ran that he could gauge.
In arguing, too, the parson owned his skill,
For, even though vanquished, he could argue still;
While words of learned length and thundering sound
Amazed the gazing rustics ranged around;
And still they gazed, and still the wonder grew
That one small head could carry all he knew.

Oliver Goldsmith

> ### Activity
>
> Write a comparison of about 300–400 words in which you compare Chaucer's and Goldsmith's presentation of a particular character.

Scene setting

Scene setting can also be an important element in poetry, particularly if the poem has a narrative quality to it or the setting is an important focus for the poet. The language of the poem may provide specific details about a particular place, or the setting could be created symbolically and changes in the description could signal changes in mood or tone.

Read *The Combe* by Edward Thomas.

The Combe

The combe* was ever dark, ancient and dark,
Its mouth is stopped with bramble, thorn, and briar;
And no one scrambles over the sliding chalk
By beech and yew and perishing juniper
Down the half precipices of its sides, with roots

And rabbit holes for steps. The sun of winter,
The moon of summer, and all the singing birds
Except the missel-thrush that loves juniper,
Are quite shut out. But far more ancient and dark
The combe looks since they killed the badger there,
Dug him out and gave him to the hounds,
That most ancient Briton of English beasts.

Edward Thomas

*A valley or hollow on the side of a hill.

> ### Activity
>
> The setting is an important element in this poem. Examine the ways in which Thomas uses the language here to set the scene and create a sense of place.

Creating mood or atmosphere

The creation of atmosphere can be a very important element in poetry. The atmosphere is often linked very closely to the mood and tone of the poem.

Read the poem *Discord in Childhood* by D.H. Lawrence.

Discord in Childhood

Outside the house an ash-tree hung its terrible whips,
And at night when the wind rose, the lash of the tree
Shrieked and slashed the wind, as a ship's
Weird rigging in a storm shrieks hideously.

Within the house two voices arose, a slender lash
Whistling she-delirious rage, and the dreadful sound
Of a male thong booming and bruising, until it had drowned
The other voice in a silence of blood, 'neath the noise of the ash.

D.H. Lawrence

Activity

Make notes on the ways in which Lawrence creates atmosphere in this poem. You should refer specifically to the following:

- physical description
- the use of connotations
- metaphorical language
- phonological and rhetorical patterning.

Experimenting with language

We have already looked at some of the ways in which poets can use language in all kinds of ways that deviate from normal usage. Poetry as a medium is very flexible, and poets can effectively convey their ideas in all sorts of ways using non-standard forms. Look at the following poem by Wendy Cope.

Strugnell in Liverpool

For Allan Ginsberg, Charlie Parker, T.S. Eliot,
Paul McCartney, Marcel Proust and all the
other great men who have influenced my writing

Waking early
listening to
birdsong watching
the curtains brighten
like a shirt
washed in Omo
feeling the empty
space beside me
thinking of you

crawling out of
bed searching
for my glasses
piles of clothing
on the carpet
none of it yours

alone in the toilet
with the Harpic
and the Andrex
thinking of you

eating my cornflakes
plastic flowers on
the windowsill green
formical table lovesong
on the radio bacteria
in the drainpipe
thinking of you

going
up
stairs
again
and
getting
dressed

think-
ing
of
you

thinking
of you your pink
nylon panties
and your blue bra
Body Mist
hairsmell of Silvikrin
shampoo and your white
nylon panties

thinking of you.

Wendy Cope

Activity

Why do you think Cope uses language in the way she does here? What effects do you think she wants to achieve, and how does she use language to achieve it? How successful do you find the poem?

Aspects of poetry

In this chapter we have discussed some aspects of the language of poetry and you have looked at these features through the examples you have worked on. It is important to remember, though, that simply identifying features is meaningless unless you link them to a wider explanation of the purpose of using language in a particular way to create specific effects.

In the next chapter we will go on to look in more detail at comparative literary study for Unit 4, and the importance of poetry in this part of your course.

7 Producing a Comparative Literary Study

For Unit 4 you will need to produce a comparative analysis of texts through independent study. In other words you will need to produce a piece of coursework in which you compare and analyse two texts.

The unit will test your ability to:

- use appropriate terminology in their analysis
- make comparisons by sustaining a particular line of thinking in relation to the two chosen texts
- produce accurate, fluent and coherent written work.

You will be required to answer one question on two set texts which you will choose from the list of set texts provided by the examination board. You will have a free choice of question on the two texts you have chosen to study, but your question must be approved by your teacher, tutor or lecturer.

Your coursework piece should be between 1500 and 2500 words in length and you will also need to show evidence of drafting, which means that you will need to submit a draft of your answer as well as the finished product.

The texts

One of the texts you choose must be poetry, but the other can be either more poetry or a text from a different genre.

The text choices are as follows. You must **either** choose both texts from list A **or** one text from list A and one text from list B.

List A (poetry)

Ariel: Sylvia Plath
The Whitsun Weddings: Philip Larkin
The Wife of Bath's Prologue and Tale: Geoffrey Chaucer
Selected Poems: D.H. Lawrence
Taking off Emily Dickinson's Clothes: Billy Collins
Selected Poems: Robert Frost
Songs of Innocence and of Experience: William Blake
Selected Poems 1965–75: Seamus Heaney
Selected Poems: William Wordsworth
Mean Time: Carol Ann Duffy
Selected Poems: Emily Dickinson
Selected Poems: Elizabeth Jennings

List B (other genres)

The Handmaid's Tale: Margaret Atwood
Hamlet: William Shakespeare
As You Like It: William Shakespeare
The Penguin Book of Modern Short Stories: ed. Malcolm Bradbury
Small Island: Andrea Levy
The Accidental Tourist: Anne Tyler
Waterland: Graham Swift
A Prayer for Owen Meany: John Irving
Dubliners: James Joyce
Hotel World: Ali Smith
Death of a Salesman: Arthur Miller
Translations: Brian Friel

Texts change from time to time, so consult the current specification.

The question

The question that you devise and that is approved by your teacher must focus on a close comparative analysis of the texts. A good coursework question will begin by pointing up the importance of comparison and will then indicate the area or theme of the comparison.

For example, here is a possible coursework question based on a comparison of *The Whitsun Weddings* by Philip Larkin and *Ariel* by Sylvia Plath:

Compare the ways in which Larkin and Plath present ideas about death in their poetry.

Here is a possible mixed-genre coursework question based on a comparison of *Mean Time* by Carol Ann Duffy and *Death of a Salesman* by Arthur Miller:

Compare the ways in which Duffy and Miller explore ideas about relationships in *Mean Time* and *Death of a Salesman*.

In producing your coursework you are encouraged to read widely. You should make appropriate references to the works you have read, where relevant, in the body of your work and include a bibliography at the end. However, it must be stressed that a personal response is what is needed, and not a list of critical references.

Do's and Don'ts when preparing your coursework

Do

- Think carefully about your question choice and discuss your ideas with your teacher or tutor. (It may be that your teacher sets your question for you.) Remember – if you have the opportunity to create your own question, your teacher must approve it.

- Make sure that your question is clear, straightforward and to the point.

- Make sure that your essay answers the question – plan carefully.

- Focus on **how** or **in what ways** writers use language in order to create their effects.

- If you are comparing poetry to a work of a different genre, explain the different effects of the different genre, but confine your remarks to specific points related to the texts you are studying.

- Refer to context if it is important in terms of analysing specific detail of the language use in the texts you are studying.
- Make sure that you present an integrated comparison where you move fluently from one text to the other and back again throughout your essay.
- Make sure that your work is technically accurate in all respects.
- Keep your earlier drafts. You will need to submit a draft together with your finished essay.
- Make sure that you include a bibliography which lists all the texts you have referred to in writing your essay.

Don't

When tackling your coursework do *not*:

- devise an overly complicated question (note the advice given earlier)
- describe what the text says or what it is about – remember – the examiner will be looking for analysis, not description
- become too involved with historical or social contextual factors, unless they are significant to the analysis of the texts in terms of their language and effects, and to your comparison
- become over-reliant on other sources – it is your ideas that count
- forget to acknowledge any sources that you use
- write broadly on general themes, ideas, characters etc. – remember, detailed analysis and comparison should be at the heart of your essay
- include biographical detail unless it is important in terms of your analysis of the texts
- write about the texts separately – remember, your objective is to produce a piece of **comparative analysis.**

Approaching the comparison

Before you can really get to grips with the comparison, of course, you must study each of your texts carefully, looking at all the relevant features that we have discussed in earlier chapters. However, when you have developed a sound knowledge of the two texts you are studying, you will need to begin to think carefully about them as a pair. Of course, as you have been reading and studying them it is likely that you will have been noting possible links, similarities or differences between them, but in order to fully compare them it is useful to have some kind of framework to help structure your thoughts and your work.

The following model is one way in which you could approach your comparative study.

Framework

- Identification of comparative areas and issues in the texts

Analysis and explanation

- Identification and exemplification of central features of the texts, using contextual and structural frameworks
- Description and comparison of the features of the text, e.g. exploration of ideas, themes, character, linguistic issues

- Consideration and comparison of meanings and effects created in each text
- Consideration of different levels of analysis

Evaluation

- Consideration and comparison of texts' success with reference to explanatory frameworks

Here is a possible framework you could use to approach your comparison.

Comparative areas and issues

- Characters/personas
- Themes and ideas
- Linguistic features
- Poetic/narrative techniques
- Historical context
- Social context.

Activity

Think about the pair of texts you are studying. Using the methods described above, draw up a plan of how to approach your comparative study of these texts. Make sure that you think about details such as which themes you are to deal with, the characters, the linguistic elements, etc.

The methods discussed above will give you a framework within which to plan your comparative study. We will now look at some specific comparisons between texts. These are not meant to replicate the kind of essay you will undertake for your coursework. The activities are to give you practice in comparing the ways that different writers use language to achieve their effects.

Activity

Read the following two texts carefully. Text A is a poem from *The Whitsun Weddings* by Philip Larkin called *First Sight*, which we discussed in Chapter 6. Text B is a poem from *Ariel* by Sylvia Plath called *Morning Song*.

Compare the ways in which Larkin and Plath use language to create effects in their poems. You may wish to consider such features as lexis, syntax and various aspects of descriptive language in your response, as well as any other features that strike you as effective.

First Sight

Lambs that learn to walk in snow
When their bleating clouds the air
Meet a vast unwelcome, know
Nothing but a sunless glare.
Newly stumbling to and fro
All they find, outside the fold,
Is a wretched width of cold.

As they wait beside the ewe,
Her fleeces wetly caked, there lies
Hidden round them, waiting too,
Earth's immeasurable surprise.
They could not grasp it if they knew,
What so soon will wake and grow
Utterly unlike the snow.

Philip Larkin

Morning Song

Love set you going like a fat gold watch.
The midwife slapped your footsoles, and your bald cry
Took its place among the elements.

Our voices echo, magnifying your arrival. New statue.
In a drafty museum, your nakedness
Shadows our safety. We stand round blankly as walls.

I'm no more your mother
Than the cloud that distils a mirror to reflect its own slow
Effacement at the wind's hand.

All night your moth-breath
Flickers among the flat pink roses. I wake to listen:
A far sea moves in my ear.

One cry, and I stumble from bed, cow-heavy and floral
In my Victorian nightgown.
Your mouth opens clean as a cat's. The window square

Whitens and swallows its dull stars. And now you try
Your handful of notes;
The clear vowels rise like balloons.

Sylvia Plath

Here is how one student responded to this task. Read the response through
carefully.

Student response

In these poems Larkin and Plath have numerous ways of conveying their ideas to the audience. 'First Sight' and 'Morning Song' have many things in common, such as the theme of new life and beginnings and the use of poetic devices such as assonance and alliteration. However, the poets do many things differently, such as Plath's abstract approach as opposed to Larkin's more literal way of describing things.

In both 'Morning Song' and 'First Sight', Larkin and Plath deal with the idea of new life and beginnings. The lexis that both poets use reflects this. For example, Plath starts 'Morning Song' with 'Love set you going like a fat gold watch'. Here, the adjectives 'fat' and 'gold' used in this simile give the image of something precious and beautiful. Similarly, Larkin uses the phrase 'Newly stumbling to and fro' to show the reader that new life is frail and delicate.

As well as this obvious theme, both poems also have hidden darker connotations. In Plath's poem this dark side is the sense of uncertainty and the poet's fear that she will not be a good mother. The phrase 'your nakedness/ Shadows our safety' indicates this fact, because the word 'shadows' suggests that the doubt never goes from the back of Plath's mind. The assonance of 'o' and 'a' give the lines a serious tone, although the sibilance of 'shadows our safety' counter-balances this by making the lines seem soft and tender. Another way that a dark side is shown in Plath's poem is by her simile 'rise like balloons'. Although on the surface this seems to be a simile linked to celebration, Plath often used the metaphor of balloons and saw them as a negative thing. This was because balloons eventually fly away or pop or shrivel, just like a life.

Like 'Morning Song', Larkin's poem seems to be happy because it presents a picturesque image to the reader of lambs learning to walk in snow. However, by choosing words such 'wretched', 'unwelcome' and 'cold', Larkin portrays the idea that the world is a harsh place for these lambs to be born into, and just like human children these lambs have to learn to fend for themselves.

As with Plath's balloons the image that Larkin creates of white lambs in white snow could be interpreted in different ways. One way is that the colour white has traditional connotations of innocence and purity, and so Larkin could be saying that new life is an innocent and beautiful thing. However, another way to look at this could be that white lambs are camouflaged in snow and so Larkin could be commenting on the insignificance of a single person in the world.

In 'First Sight', Larkin seems to be saying that beauty and innocence can never last because they have to learn to fend for themselves in the 'wretched width of cold', even though for the time being 'they wait beside the ewe'. Here, the ewe could signify a person's mother and the 'wretched width of cold' could be life. This can be compared to 'Morning Song' because the way Plath describes the baby makes it seem innocent and vulnerable. For example, the term 'moth-breath' gives a sense of delicacy and provokes a strong image in the reader's head of a baby breathing so delicately that it almost sounds like the flutter of a moth's wings.

One thing that Plath and Larkin do differently is that Larkin uses a distinct rhyming pattern, whereas Plath does not. The rhyme in Larkin's poem almost gives a sing-song tone which helps to add to the image of beauty and innocence that Larkin has created. On the other hand, because Plath's poem has no rhyme pattern, it means that the reader is inclined to read the poem in a 'prose-like' tone, as if they were reading a story. The punctuation in this poem adds to this sense, for example '...your bald cry/ Took its place among the elements'. The enjambment here ensures that the reader reads straight on without pausing. Larkin uses enjambment in 'First Sight' to quicken the pace of the poem and therefore this device almost gives the sense of things being new and scary for the lambs.

Another difference between the poems is that Plath's is more personal, because she is describing the birth of her daughter. There are many ways that Plath makes the poem personal, for example, by addressing the poem to her daughter. We know that this is the case because words such as 'you' and 'your' are used frequently. Another way is that Plath groups the stanzas into groups of three lines, which could represent the family group of mum, dad and baby. Larkin's poem on the other hand does not have the same personal feel because it does not describe one of his personal experiences.

A major difference between these two poems is that the style of Plath and Larkin's writing is very different. Plath's poem is full of more abstract and in some ways harder to comprehend metaphors, whereas in Larkin's poem his style is much more literal. He uses simple vocabulary to describe the settings, such as 'cold' and 'sunless', which quite clearly show the atmosphere to the reader. A key feature of 'First Sight' is that Larkin uses little imagery whereas in 'Morning Song' Plath uses a variety of similes and metaphors in order to achieve her effects.

Activity

Look carefully at the student response above. How closely does it agree with what you thought about the poems? Write down what you think are the strengths and weaknesses of the response.

Examiner's comments

The student begins with an introduction in which general comparisons are made relating to theme, ideas and techniques. Then the response goes on to compare the language which the two poets use to present their ideas and specific details from the poems are used to illustrate the points. Adjectival use and effect is discussed and further comparisons are drawn.

The student then gives a more detailed consideration of Plath's poem, examining the connotations of the language and the possible viewpoint of the poet. Again, ideas are supported by reference to specific details of language use. Phonological features are discussed, again with the use of examples, and then the student moves on to a discussion of the effect of the simile 'rise like balloons', and its symbolic significance. This is followed by a further discussion of the effects created through the poet's use of vocabulary.

The focus of the response moves back to the Larkin poem with a comparison and well-developed analysis of the ways in which imagery is used in *First Sight*, and its possible significance. Further comparisons are drawn with *Morning Song* and the effects of the rhyme and punctuation in each poem are discussed, together with mention of the use of enjambment. To conclude, further comparisons are made focusing on the general style of the poems.

Overall some relevant ideas are discussed and there is a strong sense of a personal response. The student adopts an integrated approach to comparison and moves effectively from one poem to the other and back again. There is also coverage of a number of key areas and some well-supported points are made. Analytical comment could more developed, however, as some sections of the response tend to be generalized.

Summary of examiner's advice

- Focus closely on the effects of individual words.
- Focus on the effects of imagery, etc.
- Be sensitive to atmosphere and tone.
- Be sensitive to the connotations of words, phrases, etc.
- Deal with the two texts fairly evenly – don't write mainly about one and then just give a brief examination of the other. Aim for balance.
- *Compare* the texts. Don't just write about them in isolation – draw comparisons.

Activity

The following texts are two poems from Carol Ann Duffy's collection *Mean Time* (*Welltread* and *Havisham*) and a section from *The Wife of Bath's Prologue and Tale* by Chaucer.

Compare these three texts focusing on how the writers create a sense of character. You should refer closely to the writers' use of language to create their effects, and describe the impact that each has on you, the reader.

Welltread

Welltread was Head and the Head's face was a fist. Yes,
I've got him. Spelling and Punishment. A big brass bell
dumb on his desk till only he shook it, and children
ran shrieking in the locked yard. Mr Welltread. Sir.

He meant well. They all did then. The loud, inarticulate dads,
the mothers who spat on hankies and rubbed you away.
But Welltread looked like a gangster. Welltread stalked
the forms, collecting thruppenny bits in a soft black hat.

We prayed for Aberfan, vaguely reprieved. My socks dissolved,
two grey pools at my ankles, at the shock of my name
called out. The memory brings me to my feet
as a foul would. The wrong child for a trite crime.

And all I could say was No. Welltread straightened my hand
as though he could read the future there, then hurt himself
more than he hurt me. There was no cause for complaint.
There was the burn of a cane in my palm, still smouldering.

Carol Ann Duffy

Havisham

Beloved sweetheart bastard. Not a day since then
I haven't wished him dead. Prayed for it
so hard I've dark green pebbles for eyes,
ropes on the back of my hands I could strangle with.

Spinster. I stink and remember. Whole days
in bed cawing Nooooo at the wall; the dress
yellowing, trembling if I open the wardrobe;
the slewed mirror, full-length, her, myself, who did this

to me? Puce curses that are sounds not words.
Some nights better, the lost body over me,
my fluent tongue in its mouth in its ear
then down till I suddenly bite awake. Love's

hate behind a white veil; a red balloon bursting
in my face. Bang. I stabbed at a wedding-cake.
Give me a male corpse for a long slow honeymoon.
Don't think it's only the heart that b-b-b-breaks.

Carol Ann Duffy

from The Wife of Bath's Prologue and Tale

Now, sire, now wol I telle forth my tale.
As evere moote I drynken wyn or ale,
I shal seye sooth; tho housbondes that I hadde,
As thre of hem were goode, and two were badde.
The thre were goode men, and riche, and olde;
Unnethe myghte they the statut holde
In which that they were bounden unto me.
Ye woot wel what I meene of this, pardee!
As help me God, I laughe whan I thynke
How pitously a-nyght I made hem swynke!
And, by my fey, I tolde of it no stoor.
They had me yeven hir lond and hir tresoor;
Me neded nat do lenger diligence
To wynne hir love, or doon hem reverence.
They loved me so wel, by God above,
That I ne tolde no deyntee of hir love!
A wys womman wol bisye hire evere in oon
To gete hire love, ye, ther as she hath noon.
But sith I hadde hem hoolly in myn hond,
And sith they hadde me yeven al hir lond,
What sholde I taken keep hem for to plese,
But it were for my profit and myn ese?
I sette hem so a-werke, by my fey,
That many a nyght they songen 'Weilawey!'
The bacon was nat fet for hem, I trowe,
That som men han in Essex at Dunmowe.
I governed hem so wel, after my lawe,
That ech of hem ful blisful was and fawe
To brynge me gaye thynges fro the fayre.
They were ful glad whan I spak to hem faire;
For, God it woot, I chidde hem spitously.

Now herkneth hou I baar me proprely,
Ye wise wyves, that kan understonde.
Thus shulde ye speke and bere hem wrong on honde,
For half so boldely kan ther no man
Swere and lyen, as a womman kan.
I sey nat this by wyves that been wyse,
But if it be whan they hem mysavyse.

A wys wyf, if that she kan hir good,
Shal beren hym on honde the cow is wood,
And take witnesse of hir owene mayde
Of hir assent. But herkneth how I sayde:

'Sire olde kaynard, is this thyn array?
Why is my neighbores wyf so gay?
She is honoured overal ther she gooth;
I sitte at hoom; I have no thrifty clooth.
What dostow at my neighebores hous?
Is she so fair? Artow so amorous?
What rowne ye with oure mayde? Benedicite!
Sire olde lecchour, lat thy japes be!
And if I have a gossib or a freend,
Withouten gilt, thou chidest as a feend,
If that I walke or pleye unto his hous!
Thou comest hoom as dronken as a mous,
And prechest on thy bench, with yvel preef!
Thou seist to me it is a greet meschief
To wedde a povre womman, for costage;
And if that she be riche, of heigh parage,
Thanne seistow that it is a tormentrie
To soffre hire pride and hire malencolie.
And if that she be fair, thou verray knave,
Thou seyst that every holour wol hire have;
She may no while in chastitee abyde,
That is assailled upon ech a syde.

'Thou eyst som folk desiren us for richesse,
Somme for oure shap, and somme for oure fairnesse,
And som for she kan outher synge or daunce,
And som for gentillesse and daliaunce;
Som for hir handes and hir armes smale;
Thus goth al to the devel, by thy tale.
Thou seyst men may nat kepe a castel wal,
It may so longe assailled been over al.

'And if that she be foul, thou seist that she
Coveiteth every man that she may se,
For as a spaynel she wol on hym lepe,
Til that she fynde som man hire to chepe.
Ne noon so grey goos gooth ther in the lake
As, sëistow, wol been withoute make.
And seyst it is an hard thyng for to welde
A thyng that no man wole, his thankes, helde.
Thus seistow, lorel, whan thow goost to bedde;
And that no wys man nedeth for to wedde,
Ne no man that entendeth unto hevene.
With wilde thonder-dynt and firy levene
Moote thy welked nekke be tobroke!

'Thow seyst that droppyng houses, and eek smoke,
And chidyng wyves maken men to flee

Out of hir owene houses; a, benedicitee!
What eyleth swich an old man for to chide?

'Thow seyst we wyves wol oure vices hide
Til we be fast, and thanne we wol hem shewe –
Wel may that be a proverbe of a shrewe!

'Thou seist that oxen, asses, hors, and houndes,
They been assayed at diverse stoundes;
Bacyns, lavours, er that men hem bye,
Spoones and stooles, and al swich housbondrye,
And so been pottes, clothes, and array;
But folk of wyves maken noon assay,
Til they be wedded – olde dotard shrewe! –
And thanne, seistow, we wol oure vices shewe.

'Thou seist also that it displeseth me
But if that thou wolt preyse my beautee,
And but thou poure alwey upon my face,
And clepe me "faire dame" in every place.
And but thou make a feeste on thilke day
That I was born, and make me fressh and gay;
And but thou do to my norice honour,
And to my chamberere withinne my bour,
And to my fadres folk and his allyes –
Thus seistow, olde barel-ful of lyes!

'And yet of oure apprentice Janekyn,
For his crispe heer, shynynge as gold so fyn,
And for he squiereth me bothe up and doun,
Yet hastow caught a fals suspecioun.
I wol hym noght, thogh thou were deed tomorwe!

'But tel me this: why hydestow, with sorwe,
The keyes of thy cheste awey fro me?
It is my good as wel as thyn, pardee!
What, wenestow make an ydiot of oure dame?
Now by that lord that called is Seint Jame,
Thou shalt nat bothe, thogh that thou were wood,
Be maister of my body and of my good;
That oon thou shalt forgo, maugree thyne yen.
What helpith it of me to enquere or spyen?
I trowe thou woldest loke me in thy chiste!
Thou sholdest seye, "Wyf, go wher thee liste;
Taak youre disport, I wol nat leve no talys.
I knowe yow for a trewe wyf, dame Alys."
We love no man that taketh kep or charge
Wher that we goon; we wol ben at oure large.

'Of alle men yblessed moot he be,
The wise astrologien, Daun Ptholome,
That seith this proverbe in his Almageste:
"Of alle men his wysdom is the hyeste
That rekketh nevere who hath the world in honde."
By this proverbe thou shalt understonde,

Have thou ynogh, what thar thee recche or care
How myrily that othere folkes fare?'

Geoffrey Chaucer

- -

The following texts are from the poems *Tintern Abbey* and *Resolution and Independence* by William Wordsworth, and the novel *Waterland* by Graham Swift.

Activity

Read the texts carefully. Compare the ways in which the writers present a sense of the natural world.

You should look carefully at the following:

- the use of vocabulary
- the use of imagery
- the sense of atmosphere created
- the use of other stylistic features.

---

from Tintern Abbey

Five years have passed; five summers, with the length
Of five long winters! and again I hear
These waters, rolling from their mountain-springs
With a sweet inland murmur. – Once again
Do I behold these steep and lofty cliffs,
Which on a wild secluded scene impress
Thoughts of more deep seclusion; and connect
The landscape with the quiet of the sky.
The day is come when I again repose
Here, under this dark sycamore, and view
These plots of cottage-ground, these orchard-tufts,
Which, at this season, with their unripe fruits,
Among the woods and copses lose themselves,
Nor, with their green and simple hue, disturb
The wild green landscape. Once again I see
These hedge-rows, hardly hedge-rows, little lines
Of sportive wood run wild; these pastoral farms
Green to the very door; and wreaths of smoke
Sent up, in silence, from among the trees,
With some uncertain notice, as might seem,
Of vagrant dwellers in the houseless woods,
Or of some hermit's cave, where by his fire
The hermit sits alone.

William Wordsworth

from Resolution and Independence

I

There was a roaring in the wind all night;
The rain came heavily and fell in floods;

But now the sun is rising calm and bright;
The birds are singing in the distant woods;
Over his own sweet voice the Stock-dove broods;
The Jay makes answer as the Magpie chatters;
And all the air is filled with pleasant noise of waters.

II

All things that love the sun are out of doors;
The sky rejoices in the morning's birth;
The grass is bright with rain-drops; on the moors
The Hare is running races in her mirth;
And with her feet she from the plashy earth
Raises a mist; which, glittering in the sun,
Runs with her all the way, wherever she doth run.

III

I was a Traveller then upon the moor;
I saw the Hare that raced about with joy;
I heard the woods and distant waters, roar;
Or heard them not, as happy as a Boy:
The pleasant season did my heart employ:
My old remembrances went from me wholly;
And all the ways of men, so vain and melancholy.

IV

But, as it sometimes chanceth, from the might
Of joy in minds that can no farther go,
As high as we have mounted in delight
In our dejection do we sink as low,
To me that morning did it happen so;
And fears, and fancies, thick upon me came;
Dim sadness, and blind thoughts I knew not nor could name.

V

I heard the Sky-lark singing in the sky;
And I bethought me of the playful Hare:
Even such a happy Child of earth am I;
Even as these blissful Creatures do I fare;
Far from the world I walk, and from all care;
But there may come another day to me,
Solitude, pain of heart, distress, and poverty.

William Wordsworth

About the Ouse (from Waterland)

The Great Ouse. Ouse. Say it. *Ouse*. Slowly. How else can you say it? A sound which
exudes slowness. A sound which suggests the slow, sluggish, forever oozing thing it is.
A sound which invokes quiet flux, minimum tempo; cool, impassive, unmoved motion. A
sound which will calm even the hot blood racing in your veins. Ouse, Ouse, Oooooouse...

Once upon a time there was a river which flowed into another river which one day men
would call the Rhine. But in those days there were no men, no names and no North
Sea and no island called Great Britain and the only beings who knew this river which
flowed into the nameless Rhine were the fishes which swam up and down it and the
giant creatures which browsed in its shallows and whose fantastic forms we might never

have guessed at were it not for the fact that now and then they lay down to die in circumstances that would preserve their fossilised bones and so, millions of years later, became a subject for human inquiry.

Then there was an ice age, or, to be precise, a series of glacial advances and withdrawals, during which time the sea interposed itself between the conjunctive Ouse and Rhine, and the land mass later known as Great Britain began to detach itself from the continent. And during this same lengthy period the first men, or their ape-like ancestors, coming from no one knows exactly where, perhaps from Africa, perhaps from China, or even, by way of an evolutionary detour, out of the sea, migrated across the continental shelf and began to inhabit this not yet severed peninsula, thus setting a precedent many times to be followed, but for the last time successfully in 1066.

What these first men and their waves of successors called the Ouse we have no idea, having no inkling of their language. But how the Ouse regarded (for let us adopt the notion of these primitive peoples who very probably thought of the Ouse as a God, a sentient Being) these two-legged intruders who by daring to transmute things into sound were unconsciously forging the phenomenon known as History, we can say readily: with indifference. For what did such a new-fangled invention matter to a river which flowed on, oozed on, just as before. What did the three Stone Ages, the Beaker Folk, the Bronze Age, Iron Age, the Belgic Tribes and all their flints, pots, axes, bangles, brooches and burial customs signify to a river which possessed as no man did, or does, the secret capacity to move yet remain?

Then the Romans came. What they called the Ouse we do not know either, but we know that they called the Wash 'Metaris'. And they were the first to impose their will on the sullen, disdainful Ouse. For they employed several miles of it in the construction of their great catchwater channel, the Car Dyke, which ran, and can still be traced, from the Cam to the Witham – from near Cambridge to near Lincoln – round the whole western flank of the Fens, thus providing yet another example of that Roman skill in engineering and dauntlessness before nature at which modern man still gasps in admiration.

But in those days the Ouse took a different course from that which it takes today. It is a feature of this footloose and obstinate river that it has several times during its brush with human history changed direction, taken short-cuts, long loops, usurped the course of other rivers, been coaxed into new channels and rearranged its meeting-place with the sea. All of which might be construed as a victory for history (for it is human ingenuity which in so many cases has effected these changes), yet which is more aptly to be interpreted as the continued contempt of the river for the efforts of men. Since without the old Ouse's perpetual if unhurried unruliness, without its ungovernable desire to flow at its own pace and in its own way, none of those cuts and channels and re-alignments, which are still being dug, and which enmesh the tortuous, reptilian Ouse in a net of minor waterways, would ever have been necessary.

In Roman times and in that period known as the Dark Ages but which, as many, notably Charles Kingsley, the Fenland fabulist, have opined, was for the Fens their most lustrous and legendary era – the Ouse flowed northwards, nearly to March, before meeting with the old River Cam. In that period in which Canute, who could no more stop rivers flowing than he could bid waves retreat, was mesmerised by the singing of the monks as he was rowed past Ely in his royal barge, the Ouse, giving a free ride to its brother Cam, met the sea at Wisbech (which is now ten miles from the coast).

But in the Middle Ages, under licence of great floods, the Ouse took it upon itself to flow eastwards to one of its own westward-flowing tributaries and by way of this channel to meet the Cam where it still meets it, some dozen miles downstream of Cambridge. At much the same time it abandoned its outfall at Wisbech to the encroachment of silt, and found a new exit at Lynn. Thus the old river became extinct and a new river, a great ragged bow thrown out to the east, was formed, much to the rejoicing of the people of Ely and the tiny community of Gildsey who now found themselves not only on the water-route between Lynn and Cambridge but also on that between Lynn and Huntingdon. And much to the disgruntlement of the corn merchants of Huntingdon, whose way to the sea was now extended by many miles.

Then, as we know, Vermuyden came, to put matters right, and dug the Bedford and New Bedford Rivers – straight strings to the bow of the rebellious river – to the glee of the men of Huntingdon who now had better access than ever to the coast, and the dismay of the men of Cambridgeshire whose three-centuries-old waterway was reduced to little more than a land drain. And thus the fate of that true and natural, if wayward, Ouse (and still called 'Great' despite the sapping of its waters along the Bedford Rivers) was to lie thenceforth (for we have now moved into a period which even historically speaking is recent and which in the limitless life of a river is but yesterday) in the hands of those local men of ambition so characteristic of this island which as a nation was approaching the peak of its world-wide ambitions – not least amongst whom were the Atkinsons of Norfolk and later of Gildsey.

Graham Swift

Activity

Having studied the extracts given here, think about the texts on which you are going to base your comparative study. Make a detailed plan of how you are going approach your coursework.

Bear in mind when planning and writing your assignment that in order to achieve a top grade you must show:

- the use of a clear analytical framework
- a clear overview and detailed understanding of your texts
- illuminating textual interpretation
- close engagement with your texts
- effective conceptualized analysis
- an integrated comparative framework
- clear, fluent and well-structured writing.

8 Extending Comparative Analysis

The first part of Unit 3 is a comparative analysis between three unseen texts. You will need to deal with the unseen material in a question on which you can spend 1½ hours. The question will always have the same format, an analytical comparison of three unseen texts which will consist of a speech text, a non-fiction text and a literary text.

The comparative element at A2 develops the skills you learned at AS level, where you compared two different types of speech text. The comparative question here is more demanding, in that you now need to compare three texts from different genres and not from the same mode.

This analytical question tests your ability to:

- compare different types of text, including those from literary and non-literary contexts as well as speech
- use appropriate terminology to support your analysis
- write fluently and coherently.

This unit is therefore testing your overall ability by drawing on the parts of the course that are the most important for an integrated study of language and literature. You should be using the terminology in a natural and unforced way by this point in the course, so that it facilitates your textual interpretation rather than being some kind of bolt-on exercise. Similarly, the practice you have had during the course should enable you to fuse technical vocabulary with an analytical framework that helps you deal with the texts in a logical fashion.

The analytical comparison

The three texts which you will deal with in the examination are all unseen and drawn from a range of sources. The group of texts will always have representatives of the following among them:

- a piece of literary writing
- a piece of non-literary writing
- a spontaneous unscripted extract of speech
- texts drawn from a range of historical periods.

Obviously, it is important that you are familiar with the form and nature of these types of texts before you begin the comparative analysis.

There will always be some unifying link between the three texts; this link will be important, as it will provide the first clue you need for putting together your comparative framework for analysis. These links could include:

- theme
- audience or intended audience

- historical period
- representation or treatment of a particular issue
- mode issues
- purpose
- context.

It is likely that your analysis will always have to take mode issues into consideration whether it is a link or not, since there will always be both writing and speech as part of the unseen material. Similarly, you will probably take into account both audience and purpose, which are two of the key textual determinants we have emphasized during the course. However, the link that connects the three texts should be your first consideration in constructing your analytical framework. Once you have established this, you can start to flesh out the structure of your analysis.

Deciding upon an analytical framework

This isn't as daunting as it first sounds. Throughout the book, we have emphasized the need to answer any question in a structured, logical fashion. It is imperative that you do so throughout the course so that when you reach this point, the construction of your analytical framework is second nature to you as well as an integral part of your planning procedure.

You have to deal with at least three texts here, so it is crucial that you use an analytical framework to help you carry out the analysis. A framework will give you the opportunity to cover the necessary ground in a logical way, while also drawing on the expertise you have developed through answering questions in other units by using such analytical frameworks.

Your first job is to decide upon the nature of your framework by examining the texts closely. You need to view this question as a final examination opportunity to air your personal, informed voice as you respond to the material in front of you; one where you can bring all your analytical experience to bear on the texts. The most effective way to do this is to decide on the parameters of your analysis by constructing an effective framework before you begin.

Areas to consider for your analytical framework

You should consider all the areas you have learned about in your studies and select the appropriate ones to aid your comparison. At the end of this book is a Literary and Linguistic Toolkit (see page 249). To continue the analogy of the toolkit, when a mechanic examines an engine, he or she does not use every tool, but selects only the appropriate tools that will help to do the job effectively and efficiently. The same applies here: select only the relevant terminology and analytical tools and apply them to the appropriate parts of the texts that will help to inform the textual comparison.

Having used the information in the question to establish the unifying link between the texts, you need to consider certain levels of textual discrimination, as outlined in the diagram on the next page. By working through these levels in a systematic way, you will ensure full coverage of the key areas.

First level: textual identification
(first paragraph)

Text type/variety	Mode	Historical period
⇓	⇓	⇓
What kind?	Speech?	When?
Literary?	Writing?	Evidence?
Non-literary?	Mixed modes?	

Second level: key textual determinants
(second paragraph)

Purpose	Audience	Subject matter and representation
⇓	⇓	⇓
What?	Who?	Where?
To do what?	Formality?	How?

Third level: key linguistic determinants
(first section of answer)

⇓

Lexico-semantic   Grammatical   Syntactical   Phonological

Comparison of **meanings** in specific texts and **effects** created, by analysis of specific examples from each text

Fourth level: mode determinants
(second section of answer)

⇓

Identification of specific mode features and **differences** created by them, by **analysis** of specific examples from each text

Fifth level: transmission of values
(third section of answer)

⇓

How each writer/speaker **conveys** his or her values through use of language, by **analysis** of specific examples from each text

Sixth level: evaluation
(final paragraph)

⇓

Cohesion   Authorial detachment   Emotional reaction   Reaction of others

Evaluation of textual **success** through comparative methods you have employed

The main areas you need to work on have all been covered elsewhere in the book. The diagram on the previous page gives an outline from which to design your own analytical framework: it is simply to remind you of the areas that need to be covered in a comparative analysis of this type.

Adopting a particular kind of analytical framework

Your major task is to identify the way in which you will construct your analysis. There are two quite different methods of comparing three texts: the **anchor** method or the **integrated** method, both described below.

Whichever of the methods you choose, you must remember that it would be virtually impossible to cover all the areas that are listed in the analytical framework; you should concentrate on selecting an appropriate focus for your comparative analysis and ensuring that you cover the necessary linguistic and literary points. It would be perfectly possible to amalgamate coverage of the third, fourth and fifth levels, for instance.

The anchor text method

This is where you start by analysing one text, and then compare parts of the other texts to it: this is called *using an anchor text*. What you are doing is using one text as the initial focus of your analysis and then comparing the other two texts to it. The advantage of this method is that you can decide which text to start with, often the one that you think is the most accessible to you, and then decide what other areas of comparison you might make. The disadvantage, of course, is that your initial analysis of your anchor text is not comparative; however, this can sometimes be offset by the close comparative analysis that you provide once you bring the other two texts in to your analysis.

This is an outline of the way you should approach your analysis if you use this method:

- choose which text you are going to start with
- make notes on what you are going to say about it
- use your notes on the first text to help you find comparisons with the other two texts
- write about your anchor text first
- pick out relevant comparisons which help you to show meaningful differences between the texts
- use key comparative words to help you, e.g. *however, but, in comparison to, though, similarly*, etc.
- remember to use the three-point critical sentence throughout
- try to integrate comments about feelings as you make each comparative point.

The integrated method

The difference between this method and the anchor text method is that you compare your texts *from the outset*. This means that you can choose the types of focus that you feel will benefit your answer most. It is, however, still necessary to use a structure to build your answer around. Here is one way of approaching your integrated comparison:

- decide upon the ways you can compare the texts
- use a logical order
- compare audience, purpose and mode

- pick out examples of lexical comparisons, grammatical comparisons, style features, cohesive issues, graphological features
- use key comparative words to help you, e.g. *however, but, in comparison to, though, similarly*, etc.
- remember to use the three-point critical sentence throughout
- try to integrate comments about feelings as you make each comparative point.

Some issues of mode comparison

When we looked at the differences between modes in Chapter 5, Analysing Speech and Speech Representation, we looked at the features of each mode and then looked at some of the ways that speech and the representation of speech could be compared. Because there will always be speech as one of the three unseen texts, it is necessary to look at the differences between speech and writing and point up the ways that you can compare them.

Activity

Read the following three texts. Text A is a poem; Text B is a piece of non-fiction writing; Text C is an extract from a conversation. All three texts are about particular places. Make notes on important points of comparison between the three texts.

Text A

Upon Westminster Bridge

Sept. 3, 1802

Earth has not anything to show more fair:
Dull would he be of soul who could pass by
A sight so touching in its majesty:
This City now doth, like a garment, wear
The beauty of the morning: silent, bare,
Ships, towers, domes, theatres, and temples lie
Open unto the fields, and to the sky;
All bright and glittering in the smokeless air.
Never did sun more beautifully steep
In his first splendour, valley, rock or hill;
Ne'er saw I, never felt, a calm so deep!
The river glideth at his own sweet will:
Dear God! the very houses seem asleep;
And all that mighty heart is lying still!

William Wordsworth

Text B

The Iron Coast

A great black tooth, the ruined abbey of St Hilda, stands high on the cliff above Whitby, facing every wind that is flung against it. The Saxon abbey St Hilda founded, and then this towering Norman one, have stood above the Bay of the Watchtower by the side of the Roman signal station for 1,300 years. It is a place so holy that kings and queens chose to be buried there for centuries, and birds have always been said to be afraid to fly over it because Hilda's magnetism causes them to drop dead to the ground.

Hilda was a Northumbrian princess who spent her childhood hiding from her father's enemies in the Kingdom of Elmet to the west. When at last her father was killed, poisoned by a neighbouring king, she became a nun and then the abbess of Hartlepool on the northern bank of the Tees. The wharves where her ships were tied can still be seen embedded in the harbour wall. She was waiting in East Anglia for a boat to take her to join her sister in a French convent, when St Aidan sent her to Whitby. She was given a piece of land to found what became a great centre of the Church, a monastery and convent of monks and nuns over which she ruled. She became a mighty personality. At the Synod of Whitby in 664 the great decision was taken (reluctantly at first by her) to turn the English Church's face towards Rome. She died after seven years of fever praying for a Church at peace. Caedmon, the 'first English poet', was one of her farm labourers on the abbey lands. His lovely *Hymn to Creation* is the 'first written poem'. Hilda had him made a monk. Often on the cliff-top he must have seen the dawn, the sun coming up out of the icy sea like the first day of the world.

Twenty-five miles north of Whitby, on the Yorkshire bank of the mouth of the Tees, spreads the twentieth-century hell's kitchen of one of the great chemical works of the world, with the nineteenth-century graveyard of the steelworks in front of it and the remains of the streets of poor industrial towns tangled in its entrails. Out of the tops of refinery chimneys flames like lurid petals bend in the wind. The wind takes the fumes and smoke across the coastal plain, deep down into lungs, withering up gardens and struggling attempts at trees, and across to Scandinavia which it coats with bitter, orange dust.

In between is a stretch of coast not well known, a plain so low and bare that it is invisible from the sea and a church spire rises from the water like a needle. The coast appears to begin with the long lines of the Cleveland Hills several miles inland and the broken cone of Roseberry Topping, like a midget volcano. Along the hills is one black dot, the memorial to Captain Cook who was born in a cottage on the marshy fields. Salts and ores have been worked between Roseberry and the sea since medieval times and probably since the Romans, but it was the discovery of massive deposits of iron in the hills during the nineteenth century that brought the poor and homeless and workless swarming here from all over England and starving Ireland. Within one generation the estuary began to seethe with people like the mud flats of Bangladesh. Middlesbrough and 'Teesside' were born.

Jane Gardam

Text C

Speaker A: yer realize the food's rather (1.0) <u>bland</u> I feel (.) actually it's often <u>lukewarm</u> (.) an' a lot of it's the <u>bloody</u> same (.) y'know it's burgers an' chicken 'n' fries 'n' pizzas (.) an' that's it really (2.0) 'n' after a while all I longed for was good ol' English food (.) some Yorkshire puddin' and roast beef (1.0) or even something as simple as beans on toast

Speaker B: dead right (.) I know exactly what yer mean (0.5) I mean I'm a veggie (.) so::: there's very little for me there

Speaker A: aw yeah (.) it's crap for veggies in <u>America</u> as a whole (.) everything's geared to eatin' meat

    [

Speaker B: uhuh (.) yep

        [

Speaker A: an' yer an' yer (.) yer can't get anything other than (1.0) <u>the</u> (.) <u>salad</u> (.) <u>bar</u> (1.0) typical of the place isn't it

Speaker B: it is it is (.) all that type of stuff is the kinda thing y'expect there (1.0) it's a bit like this one here (.) that I've just been reading about (.) or that place where me an' me missus went last week (.) American bar (.) <u>absolute</u> rubbish (.) overpriced (.) an' overrated (1.0)

Speaker A: an' over here (*both laugh*)

Lexical issues

You will have found that there are very obvious differences between the types of linguistic units used in written and spoken texts. This is mainly due to the fact that when we speak we tend to use many more **grammatical** (or **function**) words than **lexical** (or **content**) words. This means that speech has low lexical density; that is, when we calculate the proportion of grammatical words in relation to lexical words, we see that the latter are not as heavily represented. Writing, especially literary writing, has high lexical density.

Look at these extracts from Texts B and C. First, the written text (function words in italics):

A great black tooth, *the* ruined abbey *of* St Hilda, stands high *on the* cliff *above* Whitby, facing *every* wind *that* is flung *against it*.

Secondly, the spoken text (function words in italics):

dead right (.) *I* know exactly *what yer* mean (0.5) *I mean I'm a* veggie (.) *so:::* *there's very* little *for me there*

When we speak we tend to use lexical words from a simple stock of core content words which we use day in, day out. Often these words are fairly concrete and simple in nature. The use of abstract terms can be fairly limited in speech, because the mode is more suited to concrete terminology. When abstracts are used, they are often formulated into verbs. For example, we could convert the abstract noun *hatred* into the form of a pronoun and verb such as 'I hate…' These words are in contrast to the more literary lexis used in written prose.

The two extracts above show this in detail – the written prose passage has twice as many content words as the extract from the piece of speech. You can explore this issue by completing the next task.

Activity

Re-read the openings of the two texts printed below, which we examined in Chapter 5.

1 Highlight the grammatical (function) words in each text and calculate which is the more lexically dense from your results.

2 Identify the content words in each text and compare the use of content words in Extract 1 with Extract 2. What word classes do they fall into? What conclusions can you reach, even from this small sample?

Extract 1

I have very pale skin, very red lips. The lips are a fleshy cushion of pink, but I colour them dark scarlet. The skin is naturally pale, that prized magnolia of lovers, the skin of fairy tales and calves, and it is dusted with Shiseido, a white powder. The journalists have always talked about my skin.

Extract 2

My name's Joanne (0.5) I'm eighteen years old (1.0) an' I live in a small village (0.5) called Castleton (0.5) near Whitby (.) on in the middle o'the North Yorkshire Moors (0.5) with m'mum 'n dad (1.0) an' ma brother Simon (0.5) who's twenty-three a:::nd (0.5) erm (0.5) ma sister Emma.

Other lexical comparisons

Another lexical point of comparison is that of **high-frequency** and **low-frequency** lexis. High-frequency lexis is the occurrence of common or familiar and well-used words. Predictably, this happens frequently in speech. In Text C on page 202, for example, there are many words which you hear often in speech: 'realize', 'simple', 'know' and 'other'. In writing, however, especially poetry, low-frequency lexis is much more prevalent, with less common words and a higher rate of synonyms, simply because poetry is a highly planned form of literature; in Text A, for instance, we see synonyms such as 'majesty', 'splendour', 'glittering' and 'bright.'

Similarly, in speech, as exemplified in this case by Text C, there is a tendency for:

- less abstract vocabulary, e.g. 'it's burgers an' chicken 'n' fries'
- more generalized, simpler vocabulary, e.g. 'all that type of stuff is the kinda thing y'expect there'
- the use of fillers, e.g. 'I mean' and 'y'know.'

In writing, however, as shown in this instance by Text B, there is a leaning towards:

- more abstract vocabulary, e.g. 'She became a mighty personality'
- greater variety of vocabulary and lower levels of repetition: 'it was the discovery of massive deposits of iron in the hills during the nineteenth century that brought the poor and homeless and workless swarming here'
- the use of overt stylistic devices such as metaphors, e.g. 'the twentieth-century hell's kitchen of one of the great chemical works of the world'.

One final area of lexical comparison is that of **deixis**, which is a kind of linguistic pointing, in that it is word usage that relies totally on context. Deictic expression falls into two broad categories. **Proximal** terms are those expressions that refer to things near to the speaker, such as 'this', 'here' or 'now'. **Distal** terms relate to things that are away from the speaker, such as 'that' or 'then'.

The use of **reference** in both speech and writing can often be quite marked. Reference allows us to identify things, people, places and so on. The three major areas are **anaphoric**, **exophoric** and **cataphoric** reference.

Anaphoric reference is by far the most common. It allows us to refer back to something that was mentioned earlier in the conversation.

An example of this from Text C is as follows:

the food's rather (1.0) <u>bland</u> I feel (.) actually it's often <u>lukewarm</u> (.) an' a lot of it's the <u>bloody</u> same

The third-person singular pronoun 'it' is an example of anaphoric reference here, where the last noun mentioned was 'food'; the use of 'it' obviously refers back to that word. We use anaphora all the time in speech, since it allows us to be speedier in communicating what we want to say, as well as making speech less repetitive. When anaphoric reference is used in writing, it is done more thoughtfully, as in this example from Text B:

Hilda was a Northumbrian princess who spent her childhood hiding from her father's enemies in the Kingdom of Elmet to the west. When at last her father was killed, poisoned by a neighbouring king, she became a nun and then the abbess of Hartlepool on the northern bank of the Tees.

This passage uses a number of anaphoric references to the original proper noun 'Hilda', including 'her', 'she', 'nun' and 'abbess'. The writer has been able to vary the use of anaphora in this case as well as introducing extra information.

Exophoric reference means referring to something that only the context or situation can identify, a kind of linguistic pointing or reference. In Text C one of the speakers says 'it's a bit like this one here' and we, as outsiders to the conversation, have no idea what it is that is being referred to, except that the context indicates it is some kind of reading material; the linguistic pointer of 'here' gives us no clue.

Cataphoric reference is much less frequent in speech and much more of a stylistic device used in writing; it is often used to withhold information, since it refers forward to something mentioned later on in the writing. In Text C, Gardam starts her passage with the image '*A great black tooth*, the ruined abbey of St Hilda, stands high on the cliff above Whitby', where the foregrounding of the image highlights the nature of the ruin by using cataphoric reference to draw attention to it.

Grammatical issues

One of the key issues that you will be able to discuss when comparing the use of different modes is that a wide range of grammatical features are unique to speech, and can thus form an interesting and rich comparison to the grammatical complexities of writing.

Elliptical forms are very common in speech, such as 'typical of the place' for '*it is* typical of the place.' In a construction such as this, the subject, in the form of the third-person pronoun, is missed out, as is the verb 'is'. In contrast, writing uses complete sentences with no elliptical constructions, such as in Text B: 'It is a place so holy that kings and queens chose to be buried there for centuries, and birds have always been said to be afraid to fly over it'; the verb and noun are complete.

This also highlights another comparative feature: the high occurrence of contracted forms, such as 'it's' for 'it is' or 'there's' for 'there is'. In Text B Gardam uses the full form 'It is' to start her sentence.

Wordsworth writes in his poem: 'Ne'er saw I, never felt, a calm so deep!' Here we see another unusual yet pertinent feature of planned writing – verb and subject inversion: 'Ne'er saw I' instead of 'I never saw'.

We can go on to examine the clause structure of spontaneous speech. Often, there is a high incidence of subject–verb construction, followed by a postmodifying object, complement or adverbial. These simple clauses are often connected by a variety of co-ordinating features such as fillers, relative pronouns, adverbs, determiners and elliptical forms.

Look at the following section taken from Text C, where the two people are agreeing about the lack of options for vegetarians in America.

Speaker B: dead right (.) I know exactly what yer mean (0.5) I mean I'm a veggie (.) so::: there's very little for me there

Speaker A: aw yeah (.) it's crap for veggies in <u>America</u> as a whole (.) everything's geared to eatin' meat

⎡

Speaker B: uhuh (.) yep

- -

If we break down just a small part of the conversation, we can see that there is a high incidence of simple clause structures, often starting with the pronoun 'I' and followed by a verb then an adverbial, object or complement.

Subject: I

Contracted verb: 'm

Complement: a veggie

Here it is easy to see where each clause ends and the next begins, but as a speaker becomes more animated or excited you will find that clauses become more complex in their construction, or there is a high incidence of co-ordination between the clauses, or the clauses become pared-down phrases – quite often noun phrases – which take the place of a full clause. It is fairly common in unscripted speech for the co-ordinating conjunction *and* to be used as an indication of continuation by the speaker, and as in the example given below, for a speaker to give quite long lists initially before using the co-ordinating conjunction as a signal that he has more to say:

> y'know it's burgers <u>an'</u> chicken '<u>n</u>' fries '<u>n</u>' pizzas (.) <u>an'</u> that's it really (2.0) '<u>n</u>' after a while all I longed for was good ol' English food

This is also why so many children repeatedly use the word *and* in stories when they first learn to write; they are simply replicating a pattern they have heard and use in speech. The continuation markers in writing are so much more varied, however:

> Out of the tops of refinery chimneys flames like lurid petals bend in the wind. The wind takes the fumes and smoke across the coastal plain, deep down into lungs, withering up gardens and struggling attempts at trees, and across to Scandinavia which it coats with bitter, orange dust.

In this passage, the writer uses a range of methods to link her sentences together, including subordinating clauses and other prepositions.

Issues of transmission of values

In speech, attitudes are often indicated by use of the following.

- **Prosody** (the way we utter words, including pitch, pace, rhythm and volume). In Text C, the speakers use emphasis for certain words or phrases to give them precedence in the utterance. For example, Speaker B says: '<u>absolute</u> rubbish' where the stress on the adjective helps to convey his feelings about the subject he is talking about. In Text B, however, the writer conveys her values by use of carefully chosen adjectives: '*lurid* petals' and '*bitter, orange* dust.'

- **Standard and non-standard forms** (whether we conform to the accepted norms in our speech, or deviate and use non-standard words and constructions). In Text C the speakers use some non-standard forms, e.g. 'dead right' meaning 'completely correct', and they also use slang when they say 'crap' and mild swearing when they say 'bloody'. This is in complete contrast to the poem, where highly formalized language is used with interesting syntax: 'This City now doth, like a garment, wear/ The beauty of the morning: silent, bare'.

- **Lexical choice** and use of **modifiers** (certain words are chosen for emphasis or contrast).

In speech, the use of modification can greatly influence the meaning of what is said. Consider what Speaker A says in his first utterance: 'yer realize the food's rather (1.0) <u>bland</u> I feel (.) actually it's often <u>lukewarm</u> (.) an' a lot of it's the <u>bloody</u> same'.

The first modifier he uses is the postmodifying adjective 'bland' followed by 'lukewarm' before descending into mild demotic language with the adjective 'bloody'. The mixture of fairly low-frequency lexis with the first two adjectives, followed by the high-frequency swear word, adds contrast and contributes to the overall meaning, perhaps communicating his exasperation. In writing, however, the contrast can come through stylistic choices such as rhyme, as in Text A: 'This City now doth, like a garment, <u>wear</u>/ The beauty of the morning: silent, <u>bare</u>' or in the form of a simile in Text B: 'Out of the tops of refinery chimneys flames like lurid petals bend in the wind'.

Putting it into practice

Now that you have spent time looking at mode differences in texts, it would be useful to put your ideas into practice and complete a practice question using the activities below.

Activity

Read the three texts that follow. These texts all contain speech representations of some kind. Text A is an article from a football fanzine; Text B is from a contemporary thriller; Text C is a transcript of two old ladies being interviewed on the BBC.

Compare all three texts, commenting in detail on the ways language is used to target purpose, audience and context. Your analysis should include consideration of:

- the writer/speaker's choice of vocabulary, grammar and mode features
- the ways in which the writers/speakers convey their attitudes and values to their intended audience
- any other areas which you consider are important in your reading, analysis and comparison of these texts.

Text A: The Lowdown… Paul 'Ga-Ga' Gascoigne from The Onion Bag (Issue 12)

(This text appeared in a football fanzine when Paul Gascoigne, affectionately known as Gazza, was playing for Glasgow Rangers. The text appeared shortly after England had beaten Scotland in the European Championships, where Gascoigne had scored a wonder goal.)

Full name: Paul Gascoigne the Amazing Giant Baby.

Mental age: 3¼

Team: I'm one of the Powah-Rangers, me. Vroom-vroom! Thakka-thakka-thakka! Ker-POWWWWW!

Previous clubs: Chad Valley, Fisher Price.

International honours: Throwing temper-tantrums, crying, blowing raspberries, being naughty, saying poo an' wee-wee to referees for ma country, Thelma pet.

Biggest influence on career: Having to play in Pampers.

With which historical figure do you most associate yourself? People say I look like Baby-Face Finlayson out of the Beano, and he's a canny lad, like. But one blurk I really look up to is Michael Jackson – he's mad, bad and reet dangerous on the swings.

What did you think when you first saw Sheryl's new breasts? Lunch.

Favourite cartoon: Scrappy-Doo. Or 'Paul Ince' as we call him oot in the playgroond, like.

Food/drink: Gerber doner kekab an' chilli sauce is me favourite flavah jar; and as for a bevvie I like Newcastle Broon mixed with rurse-hip syrup in me bottle.

Hobby: Inapprurpriate surcial behaviah. Ye can call us a sentimental simpleton, but givin' them 'You Bet!' contestants fifty quid for the bairns was straight from the bottom of me gret big Geordie heart. And as for me heartbreakin' revelations on the Danny Baker show…

PG Skill-Tip: Divven't sell a defendah a dummy 'til you're burped an' settled in yer cot, like.

PG Training Tip: Fifteen bottles o' Broon doon me neck followed up with half an hoor o' keep-fit in the doorframe, workin' off the calories in me Giant Baby-Booncer, like.

Most likely to say: 'Haway, Five-Bellies, man! Bleeeeeeurch! Fooled the jocko bastards! Broon and birianis aal roond – an' divven't forget the comedy breasts!'

Least likely to say: Nothing.

If you weren't a footballer, what do you think you'd be? A village idiot.

Text B: from Quite Ugly One Morning

(At this point in this thriller, Jack Parlabane, a journalist nicknamed 'Scotland' by his American friend Larry Freeman, seeks help in researching a particularly interesting but potentially dangerous story.)

A strange scent in the nostrils, stronger all the time. The feeling of being on to something big but not knowing what it was. A lot of corpses and the broken traces of a connection; like discovering short stretches of an overgrown path through a dense forest, but not yet able to see where those stretches came from or were leading to.

Lieutenant Larry Freeman had been nervous. Larry was about seven feet tall with shoulders 'the size of a Kansas prairie', as his wife put it, a frightening sight in black shades and a black, bald head. And Larry was never nervous.

'Something in the air then, big man?'

'Uh-huh,' he had said slowly in that rumbling burr you could feel in your own diaphragm. 'Remember man, cops like the sound of openin' a fresh can of beer when the case is closed. The sound of openin' a fresh can of worms don't fill their heart with joy, know what I'm sayin'? Now I ain't sayin' there's dirty cops in my precinct, but cops gotta talk to snitches and there's gotta be some give and take. And no news travels faster than a secret.

'You gotta be careful what yo askin' and who yo askin', Scotland. Somebody starts playin' join-the-dots with a bunch of random stiffs and a whole lotta people get trigger-happy. Maybe you ain't even connectin' anythin' to them or to stiffs they got anythin' to do with, but they don't know that and they ain't gonna stop to ask if they get you in their sights.'

'You're saying I should back off? Forget it all?'

'That's up to you, man. Maybe it's too late to back off. But you better be watchin' your back. I was you, I'd get me a gun.'

Parlabane shook his head.

'You know how I feel about guns. I couldn't carry one of those things around with me, forget about it.'

'Yeah, but I'd have one all the same. Keep it where I could get to it in a hurry. I got a spare one in the john. In a plastic bag taped under the cistern lid. Someone catches me off-guard at home, I got a chance if he lets me take a leak or I can just make it to the bathroom. Mitch Cacy keeps one in his ice box.'

'What, so he's got a chance if the bad guy asks for a beer? You're all fucking crazy.'

'You ain't from L.A., Jack.'

Christopher Brookmyre

Text C: from Century Road, BBC 1999

(Two women [A and B] recall a time when they were potato pickers, when they were much younger and lived in the railway town of Retford. They are being interviewed by a man [I].)

Key:

(.) Micropause
(1.0) Pause in seconds
] Overlap

A: well this was the field with potatoes in
B: this one here
A: yeah (1.0) we used to have stints didn't we
B: yeah we had stint (.) you know that how that goes up there (.) erm it (.) that's how it was (0.5) an' yer had a stint as long as that (.) and yer had to pick all yer potatoes
A: an' we used to be together didn't we
B: yeah
 I: you used to work together did you
A: yeah
   ]
B: yeah (.) one at one end (.) with yer apron like this *(simulates her apron gathered up and picking off the ground and putting into the apron)*
A: yeah you used to pick 'ard at it as well
 I: that what you used to do (0.5) pick 'em into your apron
B: we used to have (.) a khaki apron
A: wrapped round
   ]
B: sack tied right round yer
A: then yer had to pick it (.) an' pull (.) an' pick yer potatoes into it (.) an' empty it into hampers when you'd got a load on

The next practice activity is followed by a sample student response.

Activity

Read the three texts on the following pages. These texts are linked through their common theme of football. Text A is a poem written by Ted Hughes. Text B is part of a live commentary of a football match on a local BBC radio station. Text C is a report from the Sports section of the *Sunday Times*.

Compare all three texts, commenting in detail on the ways language is used to suit purpose, audience and context. Your analysis should include consideration of:

- the writer/speaker's choice of vocabulary, grammar and style features
- the ways in which the writers/speakers convey their attitudes and values to their intended audience
- any other areas which you consider are important in your reading, analysis and comparison of these texts.

Text A: Football at Slack

Between plunging valleys, on a bareback of hill
Men in bunting colours
Bounced, and their blown ball bounced.

The blown ball jumped, and the merry-coloured men
Spouted like water to head it.
The ball blew away downwind –

The rubbery men bounced after it.
The ball jumped up and out and hung on the wind
Over a gulf of treetops.
Then they all shouted together, and the ball blew back.

Winds from fiery holes in heaven
Piled the hills darkening around them
To awe them. The glare light
Mixed its mad oils and threw glooms.
Then the rain lowered a steel press.

Hair plastered, they all just trod water
To puddle glitter. And their shouts bobbed up
Coming fine and thin, washed and happy

While the humped world sank foundering
And the valleys blued unthinkable
Under depth of Atlantic depression –

But the wingers leapt, they bicycled in air
And the goalie flew horizontal

And once again a golden holocaust
Lifted the cloud's edge, to watch them.

Ted Hughes

Text B

Key:

(.) Micropause
(1.0) Pause in seconds
:: elongation of sound
.h intake of breath
[overlap

(There are two commentators; one is called Ray Simpson (R), the other is called Kevin Smith (K). They are commentating on a Third Round FA Cup match between two soccer clubs, Darlington and Wolverhampton Wanderers.)

The numbers on the left are line numbers for easy reference.

1 **R:** good save by Preece .h he's dropped a a backheader (.) backpass from Andy Crosbie (0.5)
2   .h and Platalainen po:unces on the gift (2.0) and (0.5) my:: wo:rd (2.0) it's Third Division
3   against First Division and Kevin tonight (0.5) we've seen Third Division defendin' (1.5)
4 **K:** we::ll I think there you've seen a bit of park play (1.0) absolutely stunned the crowd here
5   (1.0) even the Wolves er supporters couldn't believe what they were er witnessin there
6   (1.0) absolutely gobsmacked (1.0) again (.) we've seen an individual mistake (1.0) again (.)
7   we've seen Darlington makin' it (0.5) and again (.) we've seen them score from it (3.0)
8 **R:** so Mixu Platalainen makes it two nil (1.0) to (0.5) Wolverhampton Wanderers a gift (0.5)
9   from (.) David Preece (.) fumbled the backpass from Andy Crosbie (.) an' all Platalainen had
10   to do (.) was just pick it up (.) an' knock it (.) into an empty net .h an' should Darlington
11   lose this one (1.0) they will look back on it (.) on the night (.) that they made two mistakes
12   an' went out (.) of the FA Cup (.) the fans in front of us Kevin they're shakin their heads
13   an'
    [
14 **K:** well ah I er er yeh I mean yer er (.) sometimes I feel sorry for keepers with it bein' the last
15   line of defence (.) if they make a mistake they get punished but (1.0) god yer you just do
16   not expect to see that fer from from er (.) a professional footballer (.) between the sticks
17   (2.0)
18 **R:** you
    [
19 **K:** well how Darlington pick theirselves up from this is is is er now (.) a test of character (0.5)
20   give what they've got (.) an' go down fightin'

Text C: No Reward for Gallant Gazza

by Michael Hodges

Middlesbrough 0
Leicester City 0

This was a blurred impression of a football game. The attendance may have matched the number of people to queue for Monet this week, but this game did not deserve public display.

Luckily this was in primary colours. Such was the early to and fro that a clear demarcation between red and blue was needed to maintain perspective.

There were neat strokes; both Paul Gascoigne and Hamilton Ricard showed that Middlesbrough do possess some finesse, even though Brian Deane went out of his way to show how limited it is.

Leicester, playing again with the little and large combination of Tony Cottee and Matt Elliott up front, had little to do with the game until Gerry Taggart was offered an open header at Middlesbrough's goal. Content with missing that, they settled back into the uneasy compromise between the panic and flail their defence produces whenever Elliott plays forward.

Perhaps they were thrown by the blur of Gascoigne's arms; contriving as ever to make the simple look Herculean.

The artist formerly known as Gazza daubed his full palette of passes on the game, but also pumped his limbs madly, grabbed his breath painfully and, in short, generally made the game watchable.

In so doing he was helped by Robbie Mustoe, as good in midfield as he is unsung and a possessor of the rare ability of knowing when to pass.

But the more Middlesbrough got the ball to Deane and Ricard, the less likely they seemed to be able to score – if anything they were more cackhanded than their markers. Colin Cooper did loop a header through the throng, but it was cleared off the line. Then, after Mark Schwarzer had saved an Elliott free-kick with his chin, Ricard slipped Leicester's zig-zagging back line.

Though Kasey Keller's save was good, Ricard should have scored – but on the accumulative evidence of the game, it was perhaps appropriate that he did not.

The shapes, at least were interesting. Martin O'Neill, sensing the bigger picture was a canvas with 0–0 written all over it, brought Elliott back to his usual stamping ground and let captain Steve Walsh wander forward.

Perversely he had more shots in five minutes than Elliott had contrived in 45. Cottee appeared to like the new set-up and was frisky enough to increasingly open up the home defence but it was Gascoigne who continued to be the best user of the ball.

Fit enough now to only need a half-time rest for recovery, he repeatedly cut inside his man and produced excellent passes. Sadly they were usually given away immediately, for if Gascoigne was playing like an artist, his colleagues were the artisans.

Middlesbrough pressed until the end, but to little more than occasional effect. Truly this was stuff to annoy the academy; plenty of content, but little form.

- -

One student responded to this task as follows. Compare this response with your own thoughts about the extracts.

Student response

When first confronted with these texts, my initial reaction was that they shared very little in common other than that they all focus on the topic of football. The texts relate to each other in that they are all pieces *about* football, but the content of the pieces and the approach that they take on football is very much determined by the form they are written in, their context and purpose, and their respective audiences.

Hughes's piece is written in the form of a poem and uses the language of a poem. I believe the content mirrors the form in the way that Hughes writes a poem about the *poetic* side of football. Hughes is, for all intents and purposes, writing about a football match, but does this in a manner that clearly distinguishes his piece as a poem and sets it apart from Text C, where Michael Hodges writes a post-match report. Hughes, however, highlights a side of football that can be seen as 'poetic' and 'romantic'.

This approach is established through the use of images such as men 'spouting' to head the ball, the 'merry-coloured', 'rubbery' men and the wingers 'leaping'. This vocabulary attempts to exaggerate the game, so that the reader sees it not as simply a game of football, but as something fantastic and superhuman. There is evidently a bond between the players and the situation. Images like players 'treading water to puddle glitter' and the location being 'blued unthinkable/ Under depth of Atlantic depression' add mystery and wonder to a poem that is essentially about a common, everyday game. This is not what Hughes would have us believe, though. He portrays it in such a way that someone reading this who had not played football would think that the game was an Earth-moving, perhaps even spiritual, experience. It is this approach which sets it apart from the other pieces. He writes about the romantic, spiritual side of football. Further use of the elements fire and water add to the spiritual angle of the poem. The weather is described as originating from 'fiery holes in heaven', and when it rains it has the quality of cleansing the players in a religious manner: 'their shouts bobbed up… washed and happy'.

But it is the feeling of the superhuman, perhaps even preternatural, feats of the players that permeate this poem, where the players 'bicycled the air' and the goalkeeper 'flew horizontal'. Hughes leaves us with the notion that he is observing men who are sent from the gods and that they have the ability to transcend the weather.

If we then compare the type of language used in Hughes's poem to that used in the BBC radio commentary, we can see clear contrasts. Far from focusing on the romantic side of football, this piece is very much a reflection of its form. It is informative, to the point, and describes only the action that the audience needs to know. Indeed, the audiences of the two are very different. Whereas Hughes's readers are likely to be those who want to broaden their horizons by reading about other experiences, the radio commentary is of parochial interest, probably to the fans of the two clubs.

On the radio, the commentators do not stray from the action to describe how the sun in the sky resembles a 'golden holocaust lifting the cloud's edge', they simply describe what is happening. This is reflected in the use of dynamic verbs: 'dropped' and 'fumbled'. These simple past tense verbs help to convey the action in the commentary. In Hughes's poem we see the romance of the situation and game, a quasi-religious event between players and spectators; in the commentary, the immediate action of the game is conveyed through elliptical utterances, spoken at speed: 'good save by Preece' and 'absolutely stunned the crowd'.

The commentators use football jargon: 'net', 'backpass' and 'two nil'. However, the lexis is even more narrow when the commentators use colloquial terms which reflect their own knowledge of soccer's accepted terminology: 'between the sticks' for 'in goal' and 'park play' for 'lack of professionalism'. These commentators assume the audience understand this terminology simply because they are a specialist audience. In some ways, this linguistic usage is the equivalent of Hughes's metaphors.

The use of non-standard terms underscores the parochial nature of the spoken mode. Such features as the end-clipping of verb forms 'shakin',' 'defendin',' and 'fightin',' the non-standard use of the third-person plural reflexive pronoun form 'theirselves' instead of the standard 'themselves', and the use of slang terms such as 'gobsmacked' all serve to emphasize that this is the spoken mode where the speakers slip into their dialect grammar. The non-fluency features show the speed of the language production, especially in lines 13 and 14 where the adjacency pair is not as clearly delineated as it might be, with Kevin Smith struggling to express his feelings after Simpson has handed over to him: 'well ah I er er yeh I mean yer er'. This contrasts very obviously with the careful alliterative construction in Hughes's poem, used to reflect the basic movement and appearance of the game:

bareback… bunting…
Bounced, and their blown ball bounced

If we then compare the vocabulary we have just analysed in the first two texts to that used in the post-match report, we can see that this text lies somewhere between the poles established by the first two. It differs from the first two pieces in that this text is written with hindsight, with a chance to reflect and ascertain clear views on what has happened. In the case of the poem and the commentary, though in very different styles, the action is described as it happens. The writer and speakers therefore create a certain rhythm and tempo by which we read the pieces, a feature not evident in this final text.

The author in this case has had time to reflect and to insert little anecdotes and analogies that aid the readability and entertainment of the piece, whilst clearly marking it apart from the poem and commentary. We are again presented with another approach to football. Whilst Hughes, Simpson and Smith have all managed to portray the magnificence, action and relentlessness of the game of football, Hodges, through his words and images, strikes these down and reminds us that it is 'just a game'. Perhaps the best example of this point is in the description by Hodges of Paul Gascoigne when in possession of the ball. He describes 'the blur of Gascoigne's arms; contriving as ever to make the simple look Herculean.'

We can see here the difference in approaches of all the texts. Hodges has had time to gather his thoughts, to put all the action into the perspective of the game and the bigger picture, and so what results is a comment that diminishes the magnificence implied by Hughes and causes Simpson and Smith's relentless action to falter slightly. Where Hughes's approach is poetic, and Simpson and Smith's all action, Hodges, whilst admiring and praising certain aspects of the game, creates in the reader a feeling of 'back to reality'. Ironically, he does this by using an extended metaphor of the game being an impressionist painting. Hodges speaks of 'the primary colours' of the two teams in 'red and blue', he speaks of the individual's 'neat strokes', of Gazza 'daub(ing) his full palette of passes on the game' and the 'interesting' shapes created by the teams. This gives the whole text a cohesive quality which the commentary does not have; its cohesiveness arises from its sequential nature, with phrases being linked by simple co-ordinating conjunctions 'and' and 'an' all'. The final concluding and perhaps climactic sentence reiterates the idea that this is just a game by working out the extended metaphor that the game had 'plenty of content, but little form' and that it purports to be more artistic than it actually is, and ends up 'annoy(ing) the academy'.

In all the texts there is the common focus of football. However, they then deviate and differ through their varying approaches to the game. They conspire to both support and condemn each other through their attitudes – Hughes through his exaggeration: 'the humped world sank foundering' and overtly poetic language: 'The glare light/ Mixed its mad oils'; the commentary through its use of prosodic features: 'po:unces' and 'my:: wo:rd' to indicate the speaker's disbelief; and the cohesive quality of the post-match report, through its extended artistic metaphor which is both reductive and belittling of the game of football.

The pieces are, as I mentioned at the beginning of this analysis, reflections of their forms and expected audiences. The poem looks at the poetic side of football. The running commentary looks at the running-action of football. The match report analyses both these features and presents us with an overall picture. Though linked through common focus, the audience, purpose and context of the pieces contrive intriguing and distinguishing contrasts, marking seemingly similar texts clearly apart from one another.

Examiner's comments

This answer shows the variety of approaches that can be adopted when engaging in comparative analysis. The student concentrates on matters of lexis, grammar, purpose, audience and values in his answer. He perhaps plays down quite an important and rich field for comment, that of phonological usage, although he does allude to it in the comments on prosody in the commentary and alliteration in the poem. This does not detract from the fact that this is a first-class answer.

9 Re-casting Non-fiction Texts

As you have already seen, both when you analysed texts and when you constructed texts of your own, audience is a key factor for any text. In the second section of Unit 3, you will once again be writing with a specific audience in mind. However, in this instance you will be given a brief for your writing and it will be based on the study of a non-fiction set text.

One or two extracts from your set text will be provided as the basis for your writing. While knowledge of your set text is vitally important, it is the principles of textual adaptation and re-casting that are paramount to your success in this unit. So practice on unseen texts is just as valuable as practice on extracts from your set text. What is extremely important in your completion of this particular question is:

- your focus on the audience for your new text
- your focus on the task
- your knowledge of how to reshape materials that you are given.

Let us begin by revisiting some of the key definitions which are integral to this particular type of question. First, the definition of audience that we worked with when looking at constructing our own texts in Chapter 2 was as follows:

Audience

Who the text is written for or aimed at; the audience can vary from the very general to the very specific.

Obviously, you will remember that the reaction of the people for whom a text is written (or spoken) is very important; how a writer conveys attitudes, values and concerns is paramount to the success or failure of a text. For instance, in Chapter 2 you looked at how to make your own writing successful by targeting specific effects when producing a diary or a letter, for example. In Chapter 4 you looked at the way dramatists takes into account the audience in the theatre, and you considered the theatricality of texts. In Chapter 6 you looked at the ways in which poets convey their concerns and ideas to the readers of their verse, then compared the ways poems are written. In all of these instances, you have noted the intention and the intended audiences behind the texts, whether these are your own or another writer's.

In Section B of Unit 3, the emphasis switches somewhat as you will need to consider which adaptations and changes you need to bring to bear on specific texts when you construct your new text, based on an original text or texts, for a new audience.

You also need to given an evaluation of the success of your own text in the form of a short and focused commentary.

As a consequence, a key skill that you will need to develop is the ability to plan, write and revise the material for this answer in about 60 minutes. This is a tall order; however, you are given stringent word limits for your textual adaptation, and the commentary is also bound by word limits, so you should be able to practise the skills needed to help you write a successful answer in the time available. In addition, you should be familiar with the text or texts which appear on the examination paper.

The task

In Section B of Unit 3, the specification gives guidance on the nature of the tasks that you will be expected to perform. You will be asked to adapt and re-cast one longer or two shorter printed passages from your set texts for a new audience and purpose; as already mentioned, you will also need to write a short commentary.

The first of these tasks, adapting writing to a particular requirement, could be compared with the job of a theatrical director. As you have seen in Chapter 4, any dramatic text places great value on its audience and the reaction that can be attained; theatrical productions of dramatic texts are given individuality and angled towards particular audience reactions by means of the interpretation that the director imposes on the production. This notion of a play being given an interpretation by an individual director can be applied to this examination task. You are asked to take material you should be familiar with and place your stamp of individuality on it by 'interpreting' it, through textual adaptation and re-casting, so that a new audience can view it.

Textual adaptation

As in all cases where you are expected to produce answers that require a systematic approach, it is a good idea to adopt a framework to help you construct your text and then use a short analytical framework to help you to deconstruct the relevant parts of it that you want to comment on.

It is vital therefore to remind yourself of two parts of the specification that directly feed into this section. You should first re-read Chapter 2 on Introducing Production, to help you focus on how to construct texts. Secondly, it is important to remind yourself of the process you have adopted for textual analysis, initially given in Chapter 1, as you will need to be aware of the stylistic features you are going to target in your comparative analysis. It is best to make these decisions before you re-cast your text, as it will help you to focus on the relevant features and issues.

Having reminded yourself of the relevant processes, you can now look at one way of approaching this section.

Approaching and analysing the task

The examination paper first refers to your source material; you will of course be familiar with it through the work you have done during the course. You should have read and analysed it and had practice in re-casting some of the texts.

The next part describes the task you need to complete. It will describe the new audience that your piece should be aimed at. Underline the key points (task and audience) in the question. This will enable you to focus and you should then be able to target the necessary parts of the texts you are given to adapt, leaving out redundant material. The question will then remind you to use appropriate language when addressing the purpose and audience; you are also reminded that you need to use accurate written English.

The second question will then be given, which describes the commentary. Finally, the material for adaptation is printed.

Since your first job is to look carefully at the task and pick out the key words, let's look at the way in which you might do this.

The framework below shows that there are three levels to task analysis; if you follow this methodology, you should have the main points of the task firmly in your mind before you read the materials for adaptation. The framework functions as follows.

1 **Level 1** questions help you to establish the main criteria and parameters of your adapted piece of writing. You need to identify if there is an intended:

- purpose – are you asked to write for a particular reason?
- audience – are you asked to write for a particular group of people?
- content base – are you given a subject to write about?

2 **Level 2** questions go beyond this, by identifying the nature of the task.

- What is the purpose? What is it that you are actually required to do?
- Who is the audience? Who do you have to write for?
- What is the content? What material are you likely to need?

3 **Level 3** questions are not always needed but it is safer to ask them since it helps you to focus even more closely on the task.

- Purpose: How are you meant to convey your information? Do you need to adopt a particular viewpoint or a particular style?
- Audience: Are there issues of audience that link to the purpose of the task? Is the audience limited in any way that affects what you do and how you do it?
- Subject matter: What limitations are put on your subject matter? Remember the word limit.

Activity

Use the following task to apply the three levels of questions given above.

1 Read the source material which follows and answer **both** parts of the question.

Text A is an extract from a history book on the First World War. Text B is a review of the film *The Trench* which was published in the *Independent* newspaper.

Using information from Texts A and B, write a first-person account that records the experiences and feelings of a soldier during the First World War in the form of a letter home.

You should adapt the source material, using your own words as far as possible. Your letter should be 330–350 words in length.

In your adaptation you should:

- use language appropriately to address purpose and audience
- write accurately and coherently.

2 Write a commentary which explains the choices you made when writing your letter, commenting on:

- how language and form have been used to suit audience and purpose
- how vocabulary and other stylistic features have been used to shape meaning and achieve particular effects.

Text A: Death of a Generation

The volunteers flocked to the recruiting offices at Kitchener's call: 'Your country needs you.' Kitchener had expected to assemble an army of 500,000 volunteers; by the end of 1914 he had nearly 1,000,000, and the machinery for training and equipping them creaked badly.

At the front, the British regulars were sceptical. Kitchener's 'ridiculous and preposterous army of twenty-five corps is the laughing stock of every soldier in Europe', declared one senior general, and '... under no circumstances could these mobs take the field for two years'. The generals expected, anyway, to have broken through the German lines long before then.

The winter of 1914–15 in fact gave the Allied commanders no grounds for this optimism. The invincible sweep of machine-gun fire across No Man's Land was already demonstrating its defensive power, and the enemy's barbed wire entanglements, covered too by machine-guns, were proving a murderous barrier in front of his better-sited trenches.

The wire became the new horror. It 'terrified and obsessed the infantryman. All his daring and courage came to naught when he ran against an incompletely destroyed network. He knew that he would get caught and lacerated in its entangled mass of snares and meshes. His would be a slow and agonising death.' The German wire had to be destroyed if any attack was to succeed, and high explosive shells were the weapon. But these were in desperately short supply. Starting with more in the first place, the Germans had been quicker than the Allies to expand their own supplies of artillery and ammunition. The French, having concentrated on their light 75s designed for offensive action in open country, were seriously short of heavy guns capable of oblique fire; but the British lack of guns and shells was far more critical. The fire-power of the British artillery was quite inadequate even for the defence of its own trenches, let alone for the pulverisation of the enemy's wire. In the factories in Britain, Kitchener's recruiting for the army had resulted in a grave shortage of skilled munition workers, which in turn led to a disastrous shell shortage.

Lacking artillery support, lacking the weapons of trench warfare, the mortar and the hand-grenades, dependent on their own rifle fire to contend with patrols and local attacks, short of trained junior officers and NCOs, the British infantry had to man their trenches in strength, unable to rely on their guns to ease the burden of defence.

The pattern of trench warfare, which was to eat up the years, was now emerging. The German defence, with strong, permanent trenches guarded by the almost unbreakable partnership of barbed wire and machine guns, was building itself a fortified barrier of enormous strength. The Allied generals, with an optimism which was to prove quite unfounded, believed that they could break through with well-prepared offensive actions, supported by a concentration of artillery fire-power which they did not yet possess. Joffre, and his subordinate General Ferdinand Foch, now in command of the French armies in the north of France, though temperamentally different, were united in their amazing optimism, and in their plans for early offensive action and for tying in the British with their schemes.

Haig saw the immediate obstacle clearly, the lack of guns and shells, but thought too readily that artillery would utterly destroy the German defences: his dream of the final cavalry manoeuvre – his own arm – blinded him perhaps to the infantryman's tactical problems. Although some of Haig's instructions in 1914 and early 1915 show that he was aware of the problem of the machine-gun, he was also capable of pronouncing at this time that it was 'a much overrated weapon'. Like most other commanders, French and British, he underestimated the strength of the German positions, summing the matter up for The Times correspondent in January 1915: '... as soon as we were supplied with ample artillery ammunition of high explosive, I thought we could walk through the German lines at several places.'

So the stage was set for the five offensives the British and French were to make against the German lines in 1915 – each of them planned to be the great breakthrough. The men themselves – as well as the generals – were keen; the French to redeem their sacred soil, the British to have another go at the Hun as a change from the wretched winter, crowded in their inadequate, half-flooded trenches.

Alistair Horne

Text B: Oh what a lonely war!

On the morning of 1 July 1916, a continuous line of British soldiers climbed out of their trenches along the Somme and began to walk slowly towards the German lines. There was a general belief that the furious bombardment of the enemy during the previous week had destroyed their positions. That belief proved unfounded, and by the end of the day the British Army had suffered the bloodiest slaughter in its history, with 60,000 casualties, killed or wounded.

The novelist William Boyd has taken on this momentous subject for his directorial debut – momentous in that it marks the point when the twentieth century really began – yet 'The Trench' is no more a 'war movie' than was Terrence Malick's 'The Thin Red Line' earlier this year. While both films concentrate on the psychological torment of men preparing to face their death, Malick treated this in a dreamy, expansive, near-philosophical way. Boyd, in contrast, pulls the focus tight into a tense, airless space.

Set over the 48 hours leading up to the Battle of the Somme, 'The Trench' acquaints us with a squad of young soldiers, the volunteers of Kitchener's Army who joined up in the first flush of patriotic ardour, little suspecting what was awaiting them at the front.

As in R.C. Sherriff's play *Journey's End*, the intention is to undermine the romantic conception of the Great War. But where Sherriff's men were of the educated, well-spoken officer class, 'The Trench' mostly explores the earthier comradeship of soldiers such as 17-year-old Billy Macfarlane (Paul Nicholls), the platoon's tough-nut Sergeant Winter (Daniel Craig) and the nerve-jangled Second Lieutenant Hart (Julian Rhind-Tutt), who keeps himself going on crafty nips of scotch. Navigating the claustrophobic spaces, the camera absorbs not just the dread but the boredom, discomfort, squalor, sleeplessness and dislocation of trench life, these miseries counterpointed by the mirth and energetic profanity of what were essentially young lads together. When a toe-rag corporal named Dell (Danny Dyer) charges his fellows a penny each for a look at his porn photos, you're tempted to snort at such juvenile behaviour – until you remember that most of these soldiers are juveniles.

Boyd has previously covered the horrors of the Western Front in his capacious and brilliant novel *The New Confessions* (1987), from which he occasionally borrows details. When Billy's brother Eddie is shot in the mouth by a sniper, a soldier standing nearby catches one of his teeth in the face, a direct quotation from the moment in the novel when Todd, on his first unprotected view of no-man's land, is hit just above the eye from a flying tooth fragment.

Later on, Billy comes across a ration party that has been blasted by a direct hit, all that remains of them a hideous confusion of flesh and bone. The camera glimpses this briefly before turning back to Billy, yet its impact cannot match Todd's description of a similarly unspeakable sight: 'I saw what looked like a horrifically mangled side of beef, flayed by a maniac butcher with an axe. At the top there was an ear, some hair and part of a cheek.' It seems to me that the novel's description is more unsettling than what we witness in the film, because the suggestiveness of the words 'flayed' and 'maniac butcher' force us towards the perilous uncertainties of our own imagination – far scarier than what we see in plain view.

This is not the place to discuss the superiority of the novel over film, though it must be said that in terms of richness of characterisation, Boyd's soldiers on film pale beside Todd's platoon in the book, whose names I can still recall from the last time I read it.

The young cast of 'The Trench' certainly look the part, from their close-cropped heads to their eager, open faces, yet in general we accumulate little sense of them as individuals. A notable exception is the uneasy relationship between the hard-bitten Sergeant Winter played by Daniel Craig and Julian Rhind-Tutt's ineffectual junior officer; both actors have a presence which they use to tremendous effect in a sequence near the end of the film. The platoon's rum ration – vital Dutch courage for those about to go over the top – has been stolen, and in desperation Winter asks the Second Lieutenant to donate his personal supply of whisky for the sake of his men. The latter refuses, and for the first and last time we feel the repressed hostility crackle between the two; only afterwards did I remember that Winter himself was teetotal, his persistence an act of true selflessness. It's one of the film's great moments. The film's other problems are mainly to do with budget. The interior recreation of the trench never quite allows you to ignore the studio lighting or the slightly artificial atmosphere: there seems a peculiar absence of flies and mosquitoes for a reeking, mud-bound trench in high summer. I also didn't much care for the cymbal crashes on the score whenever a dramatic title – 'The Trench, 1st July 1916' – flashed up on screen. These are minor shortcomings. What Boyd and his team have done, given their means, is remarkable. One emerges from it with a sense of tragic limitation, of young men who barely accustomed themselves to life before they were suddenly forced to confront death. It addresses with profound seriousness and humanity an experience of war that still holds and horrifies, even as it fades from the edges of living memory.

Anthony Quinn, The Independent, 17 September 1999

The type of text you may have to produce

It is likely that the new text you are asked to produce will be of a type that you have seen or read. You will have read all kinds of texts to help you prepare for this section, and you will have some notion of their forms and styles as well as some of the communicative methods used by their writers. The task above requires you to write a distinct type of text – a letter – and you should have acquired an awareness of this form from your own reading, as well as the practice you will have had when writing for Unit 1.

Activity

Look at the following list of forms of writing. Think about what you know about each from your own reading. Note down for each one some of your ideas on form and possible styles of writing:

- an entry for a children's encyclopaedia
- an editorial for a tabloid newspaper
- a letter to a Member of Parliament
- a leaflet on the dangers of smoking for teenagers
- a consumer report on a particular product, e.g. Internet phones
- a quick-start instruction sheet for computers
- an advertisement for high-class wines in a magazine
- a travel piece for a broadsheet newspaper
- a review of a one-off rock concert or festival.

It is always useful to reflect on the knowledge you have about particular texts before you start reading the source material or writing your own text. Note down any ideas you have, as this may help you take a particular stance later in the recasting process.

Reading through the source materials

You will be faced with one or two pieces of source material; these are always non-fiction. You may find that the materials are linked in a particular way. The following list gives some examples of possible links:

- theme or subject matter
- historical era
- genre
- audience
- context.

Have a pen or pencil at the ready so you can identify and mark the relevant information as you read through the source. Since you have already analysed the task in detail, you should be focused on the material you will need. Remember that your word limit is likely to be between 300 and 400 words, which means you have hardly any latitude with the material. Make sure that you select only the necessary content and do not get sidetracked.

You might like to consider the following list of techniques that writers often use to help them get their points across. Examine such techniques carefully, since they may be there only to improve the effectiveness of the writer's message and they will often be redundant aspects of the source material in terms of *content*:

- imagery or use of other literary conventions
- analogy or parallel situations
- use of rhetorical features for effect
- use of exemplar material to illustrate the point
- use of humour.

These methods may give you ideas on how to deal with the content in your own piece of writing, however, so do not ignore the writer's methodologies altogether.

It may be that you are only given one source from which to draw your material. This will probably mean that the original is quite lengthy and that you will have to trawl through it with care.

Activity

Read the source material which follows. It is called *Visiting Hiroshima*, and was written on 9 September 1945 by Marcel Junod.

Using the extract, imagine you have to write a piece for a history textbook for teenagers, describing the effects of the atomic bomb dropped on Hiroshima. You should adapt the source material, using your own words as far as possible.

Select the relevant material and facts from this passage, as you would in your first read-through in an examination situation. Remember, all you are doing here is identifying the material you will use.

Visiting Hiroshima

The bare cone of Fujiyama was just visible on the horizon as we flew over the 'inland sea' which lay beneath us like a lavender-blue carpet picked out in green and yellow with its numerous promontories and wooded islands.

Towards midday a huge white patch appeared on the ground below us. This chalky desert, looking almost like ivory in the sun, surrounded by a crumble of twisted ironwork and ash heaps, was all that remained of Hiroshima.

The journalist described the main official buildings of the town, which were built of reinforced concrete and dominated a sea of low-roofed Japanese houses extending over six miles to the wooded hills I could see in the distance.

'The town was not much damaged,' he explained. 'It had suffered very little from the bombing. There were only two minor raids, one on March 19th last by a squadron of American naval planes, and one on April 30th by a Flying Fortress. On August 6th there wasn't a cloud in the sky above Hiroshima, and a mild, hardly perceptible wind blew from the south. Visibility was almost perfect for ten or twelve miles.

'At nine minutes past seven in the morning an air-raid warning sounded and four American B-29 planes appeared. To the north of the town two of them turned and made off to the south and disappeared in the direction of the Shoho Sea. The other two, after having circled the neighbourhood of Shukai, flew off at high speed southwards in the direction of the Bingo Sea. At 7.31 the all-clear was given. Feeling themselves in safety people came out of their shelters and went about their affairs and the work of the day began.

'Suddenly a glaring whitish pinkish light appeared in the sky accompanied by an unnatural tremor which was followed almost immediately by a wave of suffocating heat and a wind which swept away everything in its path.

'Within a few seconds the thousands of people in the streets and the gardens in the centre of the town were scorched by a wave of searing heat. Many were killed instantly, others lay writhing on the ground screaming in agony from the intolerable pain of their burns. Everything standing upright in the way of the blast, walls, houses, factories and other buildings, was annihilated and the debris spun round in a whirlwind and was carried up into the air. Trams were picked up and tossed aside as though they had neither weight nor solidity. Trains were flung off the rails as though they were toys. Horses, dogs and cattle suffered the same fate as human beings. Every living thing was petrified in an attitude of indescribable suffering. Even the vegetation did not escape. Trees went up in flames, the rice plants lost their greenness, the grass burned on the ground like dry straw.

'Beyond the zone of utter death in which nothing remained alive houses collapsed in a whirl of beams, bricks and girders. Up to about three miles from the centre of the explosion lightly built houses were flattened as though they had been built of cardboard. Those who were inside were either killed or wounded. Those who managed to extricate themselves by some miracle found themselves surrounded by a ring of fire. And the few who succeeded in making their way to safety generally died twenty or thirty days later from the delayed effects of the deadly gamma rays. Some of the reinforced concrete or stone buildings remained standing but their interiors were completely gutted by the blast. About half an hour after the explosion whilst the sky all around Hiroshima was still cloudless a fine rain began to fall on the town and went on for about five minutes. It was caused by the sudden rise of over-heated air to a great height, where it condensed and fell back as rain. Then a violent wind rose and the fires extended with terrible rapidity, because most Japanese houses are built only of timber and straw.

'By the evening the fire began to die down and then it went out. There was nothing left to burn. Hiroshima had ceased to exist.'

The Japanese broke off and then pronounced one word with indescribable but restrained emotion: 'Look.'

We were then rather less than four miles away from the Aioi Bridge, which was immediately beneath the explosion, but already the roofs of the houses around us had lost their tiles and the grass was yellow along the roadside. At three miles from the centre of the devastation the houses were already destroyed, their roofs had fallen in and the beams jutted out from the wreckage of their walls. But so far it was only the usual spectacle presented by towns damaged by ordinary high explosives.

About two and a half miles from the centre of the town all the buildings had been burnt out and destroyed. Only traces of the foundations and piles of debris and rusty charred ironwork were left. This zone was like the devastated areas of Tokyo, Osaka and Kobe after the mass fall of incendiaries.

At three-quarters of a mile from the centre of the explosion nothing at all was left. Everything had disappeared. It was a stony waste littered with debris and twisted girders. The incandescent breath of the fire had swept away every obstacle and all that remained upright were one or two fragments of stone walls and a few stoves which had remained incongruously on their base. We got out of the car and made our way slowly through the ruins into the centre of the dead city. Absolute silence reigned in the whole necropolis.

Marcel Junod

Evaluating the source materials

Having identified the main content to be used in your new text, the final job you need to do before writing is to evaluate the material in terms of its linguistic content so that you can ensure that the changes you make are appropriate for the new target audience and purpose. This allows you to focus on the kinds of changes you will make, and thus reflect on them in your comparative commentary.

Use the following checklist to make a linguistic evaluation of your source material, ensuring that this includes consideration of the particular features you need to focus on in your adaptation.

Evaluate source texts		Consideration of changes for adapted text
Audience:	⇒	Identify:
• who?		• new audience
• how linked to style?		• new style
Mode:	⇒	Identify:
• speech		• new mode?
• writing		• same mode?
• mixed modes		• mixed modes?
Genre:	⇒	Identify:
• what?		• new genre?
		• same genre?
		• mixed genres?
Written style:	⇒	Identify:
• use of lexis		• lexical changes
• use of syntax		• syntactical changes
• use of grammar		• grammatical changes
• phonological features		• phonological changes
• rhetorical features		• rhetorical changes
Structure and cohesion:	⇒	Identify:
• order		• new order
• chronology		• new chronology
Graphological features:	⇒	Identify:
• any presentational device		• new presentational devices (if needed)

Obviously, since there are only about 40 minutes at your disposal for the whole of this exercise, it is essential that this part of the process is undertaken quickly and efficiently; however, by focusing on the way you are to adapt your text at this stage and engaging in a hypothetical comparison, you will save yourself time when planning the comparative commentary, since you will already have identified the major areas for analysis.

The second question asks you to comment on some of the linguistic and stylistic choices you have made in adapting the text for a new audience and purpose. It is usually presented in the following format:

Write a commentary which explains the choices you made when writing your piece, commenting on:

• how language and form have been used to suit audience and purpose
• how vocabulary and other stylistic features have been used to shape meaning and achieve particular effects.

Here you are asked to reflect on the stylistic choices you have made and how they helped you to meet the demands of the new purpose and audience. It is wise to note down some of the key stylistic choices you make when you are planning out your writing, as this means you will be able to deal with the short commentary quickly and effectively. There will be more on the nature of the commentary later in this chapter.

Adopting an approach to or perspective on the source material

It may be that the task you are set does not specify the nature of the writing you have to do beyond its subject matter. In the question we have been examining, a specific genre is given, which has an impact on the style and communicative strategies you might use. You are required to use a first-person pronominative form, but beyond that, you are given a fairly free rein to write the letter in your own style.

If you are not given a particular angle from which to write, there are many methods you could consider. Examine some of the following ideas.

Use of narrators, characters or figures

- first-person pronominative form, adopting a persona through which you can deliver your material
- third-person narrative: construction of a particular character through which the source information can be channelled
- creation of a situation where characters interact, using the source material as a narrative base.

Use of particular forms

- a personal diary or reflective journal
- the epistolary form
- a short story or narrative.

Use of the spoken mode

- dialogue between a number of characters
- a range of different narrators, each with his or her own distinctive speech style, accent, dialect forms, etc.

Use of presentational features

- time-lines or chronological representations
- summaries, précis, abstracts and synopses
- glossaries, word boxes and definitions
- bullet points and subheadings.

Use of graphological devices

- illustrations, images and pictures (where appropriate)
- headlines, titles and captions.

Remember that your choice of strategy for delivering your new text, should you have the opportunity to choose it, is very important and will help to ensure the overall success of your piece.

Structuring selected material to use in your new text

As with any piece of written work you undertake, planning is vital. Because you have been given word limits and parameters within which to write, it is best if you first prepare an outline of your text.

A paragraph plan is usually the best way of doing this. Simply note down the order of the details you wish to use, remembering the overall angle or approach you have chosen. You should consider cohesive details such as plot, story line, sequencing and chronology here, too.

Marrying the outline with the style

Having established the approach you are to take with your material, you can now decide upon the ways in which you are going to write your new text. At this point you need to reflect on the stylistic details that will enhance your new text, giving it the elements that will help it to succeed. Use the following framework to help you.

Lexical and semantic choices

- semantic field
- connotations and denotations of words
- formality
- jargon or specialist terms
- abstract ideas or concrete facts.

Grammatical choices

- pronouns and pronominative form
- noun types: abstract or concrete
- use of modifiers: adjectives (factual, emotive, descriptive, evaluative); adverbials (time, place, direction, situation, quality).

Sentence types

- statements, questions, commands, etc.
- simple, compound or complex
- co-ordination and subordination
- premodification and postmodification.

Verb usage

- tense
- voice.

Use of rhetorical and phonological devices

- repetition and patterning
- imagery and other literary devices.

Writing your new text

It is now time to write. You will have practised the work outlined in the previous sections until you can do it effortlessly, so it should have taken you about 5–10 minutes to do, leaving you about 25 minutes to write your new text. When you write, take the following points into consideration:

- double space your text in case you want to amend or add to it when you re-read your piece
- stick to the word limit – quantity does not necessarily equal quality in this section
- check back to your plan at every opportunity to ensure consistency of style and delivery

- focus on those aspects of the adaptation that will be part of your commentary; underline them in another colour (not red or green) if necessary to remind you to refer to them in the next question

- re-read your text once you have finished; it is surprising how many mistakes you can make when writing under such intense pressure.

Recasting

Here is the recasting methodology in outline.

1 Analyse the task and adopt an approach.

2 Reflect on your own knowledge of the type of text you will produce.

3 Read through the source materials.

4 Evaluate the source materials for content and appropriate stylistic changes.

5 Adopt an approach to or perspective on the source material.

6 Structure the material you have selected to use in your new text.

7 Marry your text outline with your chosen style.

8 Write your new text.

9 Revise text as necessary.

Activity

Here is a sample recasting question for you to attempt.

Read the following source material on the subject of the *Titanic* disaster. All the texts are first-person accounts from survivors of the disaster.

Your task is to write a journalistic report for the *Times* of the details of the disaster, a day after your newspaper has already reported that the ship has sunk. The first story had few factual details. With more details to hand, you can now write your piece.

Your word limit is 300–400 words. You should include a headline to your piece.

Text A: A Fireman's Story

I was in my bunk when I felt a bump. One man said, 'Hello. She has been struck.' I went on deck and saw a great pile of ice on the well deck before the forecastle, but we all thought the ship would last some time, and we went back to our bunks. Then one of the firemen came running down and yelled, 'All muster for the lifeboats.' I ran on deck, and the Captain said, 'All firemen keep down on the well deck. If a man comes up I'll shoot him.'

Then I saw the first lifeboat lowered. Thirteen people were on board, eleven men and two women. Three were millionaires, and one was Ismay [J. Bruce Ismay, Managing Director of the White Star Line; a survivor].

Then I ran up on to the hurricane deck and helped to throw one of the collapsible boats on to the lower deck. I saw an Italian woman holding two babies. I took one of them, and made the woman jump overboard with the baby, while I did the same with the other. When I came to the surface the baby in my arms was dead. I saw the woman strike out in good style, but a boiler burst on the *Titanic* and started a big wave. When the woman saw that wave, she gave up. Then, as the child was dead, I let it sink too. I swam around for about half an hour, and was swimming on my back when the *Titanic* went down. I tried to get aboard a boat, but some chap hit me over the head with an oar. There were too many in her. I got around to the other side of the boat and climbed in.

Text B: The Wireless Operator's Story

From aft came the tunes of the band. It was a ragtime tune. I don't know what. I went to the place I had seen the collapsible boat on the boat deck, and to my surprise I saw the boat, and the men still trying to push it off. I guess there wasn't a sailor in the crowd. They couldn't do it. I went up to them and was just lending a hand when a large wave came awash of the deck. The big wave carried the boat off. I had hold of an oarlock and I went with it. The next I knew I was in the boat. But that was not all. I was in the boat, and the boat was upside-down, and I was under it. And I remember realizing I was wet through and that whatever happened I must not breathe, for I was under water. I knew I had to fight for it, and I did. How I got out from under the boat I do not know but I felt a breath of air at last. There were men all around me – hundreds of them. The sea was dotted with them, all depending on their lifebelts. I felt I simply had to get away from the ship. She was a beautiful sight then. Smoke and sparks were rushing out of her funnel. There must have been an explosion, but we heard none. We only saw the big stream of sparks. The ship was turning gradually on her nose – just like a duck that goes for a dive. I had only one thing on my mind – to get away from the suction. The band was still playing. I guess all of them went down. I swam with all my might. I suppose I was 150 feet away when the *Titanic*, on her nose, with her after-quarter sticking straight up in the air, began to settle – slowly.

When at last the waves washed over her rudder there wasn't the least bit of suction I could feel. She must have kept going just so slowly as she had been... I felt after a little while like sinking. I was very cold. I saw a boat of some kind near me, and put all my strength into an effort to swim to it. It was hard work. I was all done when a hand reached out from the boat and pulled me aboard. It was our same collapsible. The same crowd was on it. There was just room for me to roll on the edge. I lay there not caring what happened. Somebody sat on my legs. They were wedged in between slats and were being wrenched. I had not the heart left to ask the man to move. It was a terrible sight all around – men swimming and sinking.

I lay where I was, letting the man wrench my feet out of shape. Others came near. Nobody gave them a hand. The bottom-up boat already had more men than it would hold, and it was sinking. At first the larger waves splashed over my clothing. Then they began to splash over my head, and I had to breathe when I could. As we floated around on our capsized boat and I kept straining my eyes for a ship's lights, somebody said, 'Don't the rest of you think we ought to pray?' The man who made the suggestion asked what the religion of the others was. Each man called out his religion. One was a Catholic, one a Methodist, one a Presbyterian. It was decided the most appropriate prayer for all was the Lord's Prayer. We spoke it over in chorus with the man who first suggested that we pray as the leader. Some splendid people saved us. They had a right-side-up boat and it was full to capacity. Yet they came to us and loaded us all into it. I saw some lights off in the distance and knew a steamship was coming to our aid.

Text C: From a Lifeboat

We did not begin to understand the situation till we were perhaps a mile or more away from the *Titanic*. Then we could see the rows of lights along the decks begin to slant gradually upward from the bow. Very slowly the lines of light began to point downward at a greater and greater angle. The sinking was so slow that you could not perceive the lights of the deck changing their position. The slant seemed to be greater about every quarter of an hour. That was the only difference.

In a couple of hours, though, she began to go down more rapidly. Then the fearful sight began. The people in the ship were just beginning to realize how great their danger was. When the forward part of the ship dropped suddenly at a faster rate, so that the upward slope became marked, there was a sudden rush of passengers on all the decks towards the stern. It was like a wave. We could see the great black mass of people in the steerage sweeping to the rear part of the boat and breaking through into the upper decks. At the distance of about a mile we could distinguish everything through the night, which was perfectly clear. We could make out the increasing excitement on board the boat as the people, rushing to and fro, caused the deck lights to disappear and reappear as they passed in front of them.

This panic went on, it seemed, for an hour. Then suddenly the ship seemed to shoot up out of the water and stand there perpendicularly. It seemed to us that it stood upright in the water for four full minutes.

Then it began to slide gently downwards. Its speed increased as it went down head first, so that the stern shot down with a rush.

The lights continued to burn till it sank. We could see the people packed densely in the stern till it was gone.

As the ship sank we could hear the screaming a mile away. Gradually it became fainter and fainter and died away.

Evaluating your writing and writing your commentary

Once you have written your own text, the final part of the section requires you to reflect on the ways in which you have constructed it and the stylistic choices you have made.

Since this is advanced level and the production task here is more demanding than those at AS level, it is imperative that you leave yourself enough time to do justice to this section of the paper. You are only given a relatively short amount of time to write your commentary, so you will need to have a number of strategies to hand to help you.

Analysing the demands of the task

Your first step is to analyse the task so that you can build your own analytical framework which highlights the choices you made when writing your new text.

If you have done your planning and writing in a systematic way in the previous section, you should be able to tackle this as an extension of the recasting process. Remind yourself of the section where you evaluated the source material and decided on the nature of the changes that were necessary.

At the beginning of the recasting process, you will have examined the nature of the task and you should have noted:

- the purpose of the task – what it is you are required to do
- the intended audience of the piece – who you are addressing
- the content from the source texts that you can usefully adapt.

Your next step was to identify the methods you needed to consider for effective textual transmission. You should have noted:

- how you are meant to convey your information – careful consideration of viewpoint and style

- how issues of audience link to the purpose of the task – a reflection on any audience limitation
- how to use your subject matter – judgement of limitations and word limit, which texts have the relevant material, and textual length.

If these parts of the process have been addressed, the final question should be very straightforward, since your framework for analysis will already be established in your mind.

Firming up your analytical framework

When you evaluated the source material in the previous section you used a particular process; this process allowed you to be systematic in your textual construction. For your evaluation of your own writing, simply follow the same process, reflecting on whether any consideration of each particular point was needed before progressing on to the next:

- audience
- mode
- genre
- written style:
    – use of lexis
    – use of syntax
    – use of grammar
    – phonological features
    – rhetorical features
- structure and cohesion of the material
- graphological features.

Once you have reminded yourself of the outline of how you constructed your text in the light of the source texts, you can start to consider some of the details which characterize your own writing. You need to pick out some salient examples and explain them fully.

Fleshing out your analytical comparison

One way of putting flesh on the bones of your analysis is to consider the outline above in terms of a table, as below. This is an easy way of selecting the material you are to discuss.

Source texts		Adapted text	
Issues	**Intended effect and illustrative example**	**Issues**	**Intended effect and illustrative example**
Audience: – who? – how it is linked to style		**Audience:** – new – new style	
Mode		**Mode**	
Genre		**New genre**	

Written style		New style	
– use of lexis – use of syntax – use of grammar – phonological features – rhetorical features		– lexical changes – syntactical changes – grammatical changes – phonological changes – rhetorical changes	
Structure and cohesion		New order or chronology	
Presentational devices		New presentational devices	

You may find the above table useful in the practice stages of writing your evaluative commentary, and you may be able to come up with a shorthand version for use in the timed situation of the examination. The advantage of using a table such as this is that it allows you to reflect on your processes of initial textual consideration and appraisal of the source texts, and follow them up by selecting the most important changes you made in your adaptation. Obviously some of these areas will require little or no attention in your commentary; others may need only one example, while there will be some you want to emphasize by giving a couple of examples. Remember your very strict time limitations and that your word limit is around 250 words.

Writing your commentary

When you begin your analysis, remember the analytical model you were given at the start of this book, which will help to keep your comparison focused on explanation and interpretation. You can chain your points together by using the three-point critical sentence:

1 Identify the point you want to discuss from your own text in order to highlight the linguistic or stylistic point you wish to make.

2 Give a clear example from your text: quotation is necessary.

3 Explain and interpret how it works within your text in terms of purpose, audience and subject matter.

This will help you build up an effective commentary that will be systematic, since it uses the outline above and also an analytical model that covers identification, description and explanation of linguistic issues.

It is vital that you cover the range of methods you have drawn on to help you make your adaptation. This is where your knowledge of other, similar texts you have read might help you. You should draw on your knowledge of the variety of literary and non-literary texts you have read and make reference to them wherever necessary. Try to relate this to your understanding of audience and purpose also, by showing how language is used in targeting audience and helping to underpin the purpose of the text.

Be brief and focused in your analysis so that you are not spending unnecessary time on one area when you could be discussing other issues. Remember, if your adaptation has been successful, there should be a range of areas to choose from and discuss; you can select the appropriate ones. However, don't make obvious points: use examples that highlight your own writing skills and remember to use concrete examples.

The following activity is the follow-up task to the adaptation question given earlier, on the *Titanic* extracts.

> **Activity**
>
> Write a commentary which explains the choices you made when writing your article, commenting on:
>
> - how language and form have been used to suit audience and purpose
> - how vocabulary and other stylistic features have been used to shape meaning and achieve particular effects.
>
> You should aim to write 150–250 words in this commentary.

Examination-style questions

> **Activity**
>
> 1 Read the source material which follows and answer both parts of the question.
>
>   Text A is from an article entitled 'Into the Heart of Borneo' by Redmond O'Hanlon.
>
>   You have just returned for an expedition to a tropical country as part of an award scheme. You have been asked to give an introductory talk to a group of students who are interested in making a similar trip next year. Your talk should give advice on equipment, coping strategies and the type of conditions you might expect.
>
>   Using the source material, write the text for your talk.
>
>   Your audience will be 18-year-old students.
>
>   You should adapt the source material, using your own words as far as possible. Your talk should be 350–400 words in length.
>
>   In your adaptation you should:
>
>   - use language appropriately to address purpose and audience
>   - write accurately and coherently.
>
> 2 Write a commentary which explains the choices you made when writing your speech, commenting on:
>
>   - how language and form have been used to suit audience and purpose
>   - how vocabulary and other stylistic features have been used to shape meaning and achieve particular effects.

Text A: Into the Heart of Borneo

(In this extract O'Hanlon enlists the help of the SAS to give training in jungle survival.)

We drew up by a fearsome assault-course and made our way into the local SAS jungle. Apart from the high-wire perimeter fence, the frequency with which Landrovers drove past beyond it, the number of helicopters overhead and the speed with which persons unknown were discharging revolvers from a place whose exact position it was impossible to ascertain, it might have been a wood in England.

'What a pity,' said Malcolm, our SAS instructor and guide, 'that you can't come to Brunei with us for a week. We could really sort you out and set you up over there.'

'What a pity,' I agreed, moistening with sweat at the very thought.

'Now,' said Malcolm, taking a small green package out of the newly-designed Bergen back-pack, 'it's all very simple. You find two trees eight feet apart where there's no evidence of any silt on the ground – the rivers can rise eighteen feet overnight and you don't want to drown in a wet dream, do you? Check the tree trunks for termites. Termites mean dead branches and dead branches, sooner or later, mean dead men. We lost a lot of men like that, in storms at night. Tie these cords round the trees, put these metal stiffeners across each end like this, and there's your hammock. Now – here's your mossie net, and you just tie it over your hammock and peg it out by these strings to the surrounding bushes until it forms a good tight box like that – and you really want to watch it, because malaria pills only give you thirty per cent protection. Here's your top cover and that's it. There's your genuine basha.'

A long green tube had materialized above the brambles in front of us, seemingly in a minute or two.

'Stop around three or four in the afternoon,' said Malcolm, 'give yourself plenty of time. Light one of these blocks that makes no smoke and boil up a cup of tea. And just sit by your tree until dark if the enemy are about.'

Back at the quartermaster's stores we signed for our new kit. One silver and one prismatic compass (black and tight and heavy as a little bomb in its canvas belt-case); two *parangs* – thick knives eighteen inches long which had chopped and slashed their way through the Indonesian confrontation from 1962 to 1966; torches, belts, pouches, powders, insect repellents, parachute cord, water bottles, water purifying tablets, stoves, fuel blocks, mess tins, the complete basha equipment and rations enough (Menu C) for three patrols moving in groups of four for three weeks.

We were in the company of a soft-spoken major. A veteran of Special Forces campaigns in Occupied Europe in the Second World War, of the war in Malaya, of Jebel Akhdar, Aden, Borneo and Dhofar, he was huge. It was vastly reassuring to think that so much muscle could actually squeeze itself into a jungle and come out again undiminished. And his office, hung with battle honours, SAS shields emblazoned with the regiment's motto, *Qui ose gagne*; with a mass of wall charts documenting the progress of his latest candidates; with cartoons of all the wrong ways to resist interrogation; and libraried with strictly practical works of natural history – on edible fungi, on traps and tracking and poaching, on different recipes for the cooking of rats and instructions on the peeling of cockroaches – was an impressive place.

'You'll find the high spot of your day,' said the major, 'is cleaning your teeth. The only bit of you you can keep clean. Don't shave in the jungle, because the slightest nick turns septic at once. And don't take more than one change of clothes, because you must keep your Bergen weight well down below sixty pounds. And don't expect your Iban trackers to carry it for you, either, because they have enough to do transporting their own food. So keep one set of dry kit in a sealed bag in your pack. Get into that each night after you've eaten. Powder yourself all over, too, with zinc talc – don't feel sissy about it – you'll halve the rashes and the rot and the skin fungus. Then sleep. Then get up at 5.30 and into your wet kit. It's uncomfortable at first, but don't weaken – ever; if you do, there'll be two sets of wet kit in no time, you'll lose sleep and lose strength and then there'll be a disaster. But take as many dry socks as you can. Stuff them into all the crannies in your pack. And, in the morning, soak the pairs you are going to wear in autan insect repellent, to keep the leeches out of your boots. Stick it on your arms and round your waist and neck and in your hair, too, while you're about it, but not on your forehead because the sweat carries it into your eyes and it stings. Cover yourself at night, too, against the mosquitoes. Take them seriously, because malaria is a terrible thing and it's easy to get, pills or no.

'Get some jungle boots, good thick trousers and strong shirts. You won't want to nancy about in shorts once the first leech has had a go at you, believe me. Acclimatize slowly. The tropics takes people in different ways. Fit young men here just collapse in Brunei. You'll think it's the end of the world. You can't breathe. You can't move. And then after two weeks you'll be used to it. And once in the jungle proper you'll never want to come out.

'It's a beautiful country and the Iban are a fine people. I was on the River Baram myself, but to go up the Rajang and the Baleh will be better for your purposes. That's a good plan. The Baleh is very seldom visited, if at all, up-river, and the Tiban mountains should be very wild indeed. They look small on a map, those mountains, but they're tough going. One steep hill after another. And you have to be good with a compass. Any questions? No. Good. Well done, lads, goodbye and good luck.'

Redmond O'Hanlon

10 Revising Set Texts and Handling Unseen Texts

Set texts

You will need to revise set texts for the following units:

- Unit 1: Integrated Analysis and Text Production
- Unit 2: Section B, Analysing the Representation of Speech
- Unit 3: Section B, Adaptation of Texts for an Audience.

Analytical questions linked to set texts

In Unit 1 you will have two set texts to study; you will need to prepare both so that you are able to answer both the analytical question and the production-type question. More on the latter is outlined below.

It is vital that you carry out a couple of key tasks before your Unit 1 examination. You need first to re-read or skim read your text simply to remind yourself of what happens. You will have your text with you in the examination, but you must use it as a point of reference (for quotations and so on) rather than some kind of crutch to help you through the exam. It is worth revising all your set texts as if you weren't taking them into the examination room; indeed, in units 2 and 3 you won't be able to take them.

Here are a few ideas to help you revise your set texts for units 1 and 2.

- Make a summary or time line of what happens in the novel or play so that you are absolutely certain of the intricacies of the plot.
- List all the important characters and their characteristics.
- Write down appropriate quotations which help to illustrate the disposition or personality of the characters you have listed.
- Know where these quotations are in the book so that you can find them easily: remember, your copy of the texts that you take into the examination room must be completely clean and free from any marks whatsoever.
- List all the relevant themes which are explored and link them to characters and key events in the books.
- List all the different stylistic techniques that the writers or dramatists use with an example of each to help you remember how they work.
- Integrate these with linguistic terminology too, so that you remember to use this terminology in your answers.

Some students find it useful to put their notes on small cards rather than on paper; some like to have an exercise book dedicated to the revision of each set text; some students like to use technology and put notes on their computer, laptop or PDA. Use whatever method works best for you: the important thing is that you complete some form of revision notes which are easily accessible and are useful to you.

When revising the set text for Unit 2, the key difference is that you will have to revise it in a much more structured way, since you will not have access to it in the examination room. So you should take note of all the above points but also do the following.

- Know and learn the plot structure.
- Learn key quotations from the texts, which your teachers should help you to identify, for each of the characters and themes.
- Remind yourself of the key features of speech and then learn them so that you can use them to help analyse the passage from the text that is printed on the exam paper. See Chapter 5 for speech features.

The use of the set text in Unit 3 is slightly different. Because the passage that is being used will be printed on the exam paper and will be the focus of your question, it is hardly necessary to go through each and every article in your set text; however, it is vital that you have read and re-read all the articles in the book and have had some practice in re-casting texts. Chapter 9 deals with this topic.

Once you have made the appropriate notes, you should revise them by reading them, learning them and testing yourself as appropriate. You should also keep practising the writing skills that you need: use past papers and the exercises in this book to help you.

Language production questions linked to set texts

Remind yourself of the outline frameworks associated with units 1 and 3 and the areas of production that you might encounter. These frameworks allow you to manage the construction of your texts, but there are some other points you need to be aware of, when you are about to start planning and then writing your responses.

- Always double check that you have identified the key words of the question and that you know what its focus is.
- Think about your knowledge of the kinds of text you have seen in your own reading which have similarities to what you have been asked to produce; it is likely you will be able to draw on this to help you.
- Plan out your framework for production (as you have already learned to do).
- Ensure that your text is interesting and takes due note of purpose, audience, form and context; if you find it unappealing, it is likely that the examiner will feel the same way. On Unit 1 it is vitally important to remember that your production task will also be rooted in your knowledge of the text: about plot, character, theme and other issues.

Do not go over the top in your production or try to write something that is outside your capabilities; you would probably write a wholly unconvincing text. It is much better to play safe and write a text that works and is intrinsically interesting, rather than something that might totally flop! See chapters 2 and 9 for further information on language production.

Remember that the language production task in Unit 3 has an analytical part in the form of a commentary. This can largely be your own construction in terms of its focus, since you are the person who has written the text to be analysed, and you will (it is hoped) know why you have written it in the way you have!

Unseen texts

Unseen texts are vital elements of many examination papers and you need to prepare for them just as comprehensively as for those papers that deal with set texts.

The units of AQA Specification A where there are unseen elements are as follows:

- Unit 2: Comparing speech
- Unit 3: Section A, Analytical Comparison.

If necessary, remind yourself of the details of each of these by re-reading the relevant sections from this book. A good deal of specialist knowledge is linked to each of the units, and you must be thoroughly familiar with that before anything else. However, there are certain points that you can take into consideration with any unseen examination paper; in this chapter we will look briefly at some strategies that can help you through these unseen questions and allow you to write your answers effectively.

The unseen elements in units 2 and 3 both ask you to respond in a comparative fashion.

Unseen textual analysis

Students often find unseen textual analysis very demanding and often adopt an 'ad hoc' approach to it; if you do this, it is likely that your marks will be lower than those you could have achieved.

The first aspect of critical analysis that needs to be put into place is your literary and linguistic toolkit; as we have mentioned before, you need the correct tools for the job and to know how to use them. Re-read the sections in this book that underpin your understanding of each unit; this will give you the background you need to approach the questions.

Your background reading should have formed the foundation of your critical responses, as you will be familiar with the kinds of text you are likely to find in unseen analysis questions. If you do not read widely, your analysis is likely to be somewhat stilted and mechanical, since you will not be able to take account of such important matters as context, authorial values and form.

When you analyse an unseen piece, you need to consider the whole of the text; it will have been chosen not because parts of it are interesting, but because the whole of the text has intrinsic appeal, allowing a variety of approaches and possible comments to be made. It is vital that you read for meaning and that you consider how the writer (or speaker) conveys his or her thoughts, ideas and concerns as well as what those issues are. The relationship between the two is vital, since each one informs the other, and they cannot be considered as separate entities.

Reading for meaning should lead you into the main analytical areas: considering style, language use and overall form. These should open up rich critical seams for you to mine, comparing usage to other texts if necessary. Once you have opened up these seams, you need to organize your analysis logically; always use a framework and remember to pattern your analysis by using the three-part critical sentence outlined elsewhere in this book:

- identify the point you want to discuss
- give a working example from the text or texts
- comment on how it works within the text, referring to your critical framework where necessary.

The major points you need to cover in any unseen critical analysis are as follows:

- Construct a logical framework for analysis.
- Read for meaning.
- Always consider your *how* and *what* questions together in any textual analysis.
- Always think about what the writer (or speaker) wants to convey to his or her audience, and how language use achieves this.
- Ensure that you make comparisons between texts, either using an integrated comparison or an anchor text approach. See Chapter 8 for further details on this.

The key to effective performance in unseen analysis is to be confident in what you are doing, consistent in how you apply your analytical frameworks, and cogent in your written response.

11 Handling Coursework

As we discussed in Chapter 7, for Unit 4 of your course you will need to complete a piece of coursework based on the comparison of two texts.

What are the benefits of coursework?

The benefits that the coursework element can bring to your course and the breadth that it can give to your studies are well acknowledged, and that is the reason that it is used extensively as a means of assessment in English.

In particular coursework can:

- offer you some freedom in terms of choice of texts and more of a say in the nature of the assignment you undertake
- provide you with opportunities to set your own tasks and goals and pursue particular literary interests, so developing more independence in your learning
- allow you to produce work free of the constraints of exam conditions so that you can present more carefully planned and considered responses and employ the drafting process
- develop skills which will help you perform more effectively in the exams
- help you to gain experience in undertaking research and wider reading in preparation for studying English at degree level.

Coursework requirements and assessment

For a detailed explanation of what you need to do for your coursework unit, see Chapter 7.

Coursework tasks

The type of coursework task that you face will depend on a number of factors. If your whole group is studying particular coursework texts, it is likely that you will have little input into the questions that you are set. You will probably be supplied with several appropriate titles and asked to choose one as the basis of your assignment. On the other hand, if you have chosen the texts you are writing on, you will probably negotiate an essay title with your teacher. If so, you will need to identify aspects of the texts about which you would like to write. Your teacher will discuss these ideas with you and will help you to formulate an essay title that is both suitable and phrased in the right way.

An essential difference between an exam essay and a coursework essay is reflected in the kinds of task set. Examination questions are specifically designed to be answered within strict time limits under exam conditions, whereas you might work on a coursework task for several weeks, using various research skills, reference to other writers, and critical works. This needs to be kept in mind if you have some input into creating your coursework question.

The title

Devising a suitable title is essential. Here are some points to bear in mind when constructing your title.

- Keep it simple and straightforward – overly complex titles should be avoided.
- Make sure that the title involves you comparing texts.
- Make sure that your title involves analysing the language of the texts.
- If you have chosen to focus on mixed genres, make sure that you are quite clear about the focus of your comparison so that it is not too broad. For example, a title such as 'Compare *The Wife of Bath's Tale* by Chaucer with *The Handmaid's Tale* by Atwood' is far too broad. A better title might be 'Compare Chaucer's presentation of women in *The Wife of Bath's Tale* with Atwood's presentation of women in *The Handmaid's Tale*'.
- Avoid being over-verbose in the wording of your title. For example, 'Compare the ways in which linguistic variations as used by Blake and Heaney in their poetry reflect the intellectual frameworks they focus on' would be better expressed as 'Compare the ways in which Blake and Heaney use language in their poetry to express their ideas'.
- Avoid titles that involve only description, or plot or character summary. For example, 'Write about the stories presented in the poetry of Wordsworth and the short stories of Joyce' would be better expressed as 'Compare the narrative techniques used by Wordsworth in his poetry and Joyce in his short stories'.

Potential weaknesses

Overall, examiners report that a high standard of work is produced by students through coursework. However, here are some points that they have highlighted as weaknesses or problem areas in some of the work they have assessed:

- inappropriately framed or worded assignments
- tasks that centre on a general discussion of themes or 'character studies'; these tend to lack interest and focus
- titles that do not require close attention to texts and critical judgement
- work that is limited to a personal response only and lacks analysis
- including too much biographical or historical background
- too much narrative retelling of the plot or events.

The use of secondary sources

In producing coursework it is important that, if you use secondary sources, you learn how to use and acknowledge them correctly. Clearly, the primary source for the essay is the texts that you are studying. The secondary sources are any other materials that help you in your work, such as study aids, critical works, or articles about the texts. It can also be useful to 'read around' the texts.

Certainly use secondary sources if you wish. They can help to broaden your view of the texts and show you other ways of looking at them. It does not matter whether you agree or disagree with the views and interpretations you read, because they will all help you to arrive at what you think. Remember that there are rarely right answers as far as literature is concerned – all texts are open to a variety of interpretations. Your view can be 'informed' by other sources but never let other views substitute for your own. Have confidence in your view, develop your own voice, and avoid plagiarism (even accidental) at all costs. This means that if you use secondary source material you must make sure that you acknowledge every text you have used in the bibliography at the end of your assignment.

The bibliography

In order to acknowledge appropriately the books and other materials that you have read or consulted while writing your coursework essay, it is important to understand the conventions of bibliography writing.

Even if you have read only a part of a particular book or article it should be included in your bibliography. If you have used only the texts themselves, you should still include a bibliography simply consisting of relevant details about the editions used. This will clearly show the examiner that you have used nothing other than the texts and it will also give information about the particular editions that you have used.

Your bibliography should be arranged in the following format.

- The surname of the author (authors listed alphabetically).
- The initials of the author.
- The title of the book (underlined or in italics) or article (in inverted commas) and source.
- The publisher's name.
- The date of publication (usually the date when first published).

Here is the bibliography from a student's essay on *The Wife of Bath* and *Hamlet*.

Bibliography

The Wife of Bath's Prologue and Tale

Anderson, J.J. (editor), *The Canterbury Tales: A Selection of Critical Essays*. Macmillan Casebook Series, 1974

Lisowska, P.S., *The Wife of Bath's Tale*. Hodder and Stoughton, 2000

Marsh, N., *The Wife of Bath's Tale*. Macmillan Master Guides, 1987

Martin, P., *Chaucer's Women: Nuns, Wives and Amazons*. Macmillan, 1990

Tasioulas, J.A., *The Wife of Bath's Prologue and Tale*. York Notes Advanced, 1998

Hamlet

Baker, S., 'Hamlet's Bloody Thoughts and the Illusion of Inwardness' in *Comparative Drama* (Vol. 21. No. 4) Winter, 1987–88

Bradley, A.C., *Shakespearean Tragedy*. Macmillan, 1904

Brooks, J., *Hamlet*. Macmillan Master Guides, 1986

Dover Wilson, J., *What Happens in Hamlet*. Cambridge University Press, 1935

Holderness, G., *Hamlet: Open Guides to Literature*. The Open University Press, 1987

Jump, J. (ed.), *Shakespeare: Hamlet*. Macmillan Casebook Series, 1968

Rossiter, A.C., *Angel With Horns*. Longman, 1961

12 The Chief Examiner's Perspective: Helping You to Succeed

Reflecting carefully on the aims of English Language and Literature study at AS and A level will serve to highlight what you should be achieving in your integrated studies. All the specifications aim to encourage you to study language and literature as interconnecting disciplines in particular ways that will help deepen your understanding and enjoyment. More specific aims are detailed below.

The specification encourages you to:

- select and apply relevant concepts and approaches from integrated linguistic and literary study, using appropriate terminology and accurate, coherent written expression
- demonstrate detailed critical understanding in analysing the ways in which structure, form and language shape meanings in a range of spoken and written texts
- use integrated approaches to explore relationships between texts, analysing and evaluating the significance of contextual factors in their production and reception
- demonstrate expertise and creativity in using language appropriately for a variety of purposes and audiences, drawing on insights from linguistic and literary studies.

Having studied all the units, you are now in a position to reflect upon these aims and contextualize them, observing how the course has enabled you to fulfil each one. The objective of this chapter is to give you some practical advice on how you can build these aims into your everyday studies and how you can use them as hints to ensure your success in exam situations.

Recommended reading

The simple maxim that can enable you to target these aims is: read widely and discriminatingly!

Students often limit their reading to the texts on which they will answer questions in the examination and those that their teachers introduce them to in the classroom. But other students are in a better position. It is becoming increasingly obvious to examiners that the most successful students are those who take responsibility for their reading and can show a breadth of reading when analysing texts. If you want to succeed you have to do the same – otherwise you put yourself at an immediate disadvantage. The following list shows a range of the types of text with which it is useful to become familiar. Keep a reading journal and make notes on the key textual discriminators: genre, purpose, audience, form, and context.

- A range of contemporary and classical literature covering all the genres, using your set texts as a good starting point, especially in contemporary writing.
- A range of non-literary materials including:
  - journalistic writing, to include 'quality' and popular daily newspapers
  - magazines (e.g. female issues, male issues, vocational, scientific, sporting, musical, consumer, media-related, specialist hobbies or interests, household, new technology)
  - periodicals (e.g. historical, economic, scientific, political, literary, linguistic, medical)
  - comics (adult and children's)
  - advertisements
  - reports
  - manuals and instruction sheets
  - catalogues
  - forms and applications
  - legal and governmental literature
  - essays
  - diary forms
  - travel writing
  - encyclopaedias, reference and text books
  - children's books and literature.

- A range of speech events, to include:
  - spontaneous speech
  - scripted speech and rhetoric
  - dramatized speech
  - representations of speech in literature
  - screenplays
  - teletext subtitles
  - interviews.

- Use of new technologies, to include:
  - the Internet
  - e-mails
  - on-line discussions
  - chatrooms
  - messaging services
  - corpora.

It would be admirable to familiarize yourself with examples of all of these, but there is a limit to your time and resources, so dip into the list. You will begin to recognize common forms and styles, which can then be replicated or analysed in your responses. If you read widely, you are more likely to develop confidence and accuracy of written expression in all your answers, and your language will become more cohesive and organized.

In the examination

When you are in the examination room and under pressure, there are various pointers that you can always count on to help you.

- Always use the prompts in the questions to guide you, especially if you are in any doubt as to what is required in terms of frameworks.
- Highlight key words when planning out your answer.

- Plan your response, and never use pre-prepared answers: they rarely hit the pass mark and they stand out like sore thumbs!
- Use the terminology you have learned accurately and naturally, as an aid to enhance your critical responses.
- When answering questions on set texts, familiarize yourself with the assessment objectives at the beginning of the paper to ensure you know what the focus of your answer needs to be; you will probably need to have an understanding of the interplay between plot, character and textual issues and their representation in terms of language use, form and structure. You must then communicate this in your analysis.
- Write about authorial (or speaker's) intention, methods, values and attitudes, and how they are communicated.
- Ensure that your responses are informed (by background reading), logical (through the use of frameworks), critical (by the use of the literary and linguistic toolkit), realistic (within the bounds of the question), and represent your personal voice.

Reflect on your present level of performance by looking at the mark schemes for past papers, especially those you have used as trial papers or practice in class. These can often help inform you about those areas you have missed or misunderstood.

Pitfalls to avoid

There are certain things that you should avoid at all costs; examiners complain regularly about these and they usually show that a student suffers from lack of awareness about the subject and insecurity about writing examination responses.

Never:

- simply retell the story in the hope that it will do you some good: it won't!
- start writing immediately; always take five minutes to formulate and plan out your response
- panic: take a minute, brainstorm your ideas if necessary, then crystallize them and finally plan your answer
- quote at length; be economical with textual reference and quotation, and always show why you have used a quotation by interpreting it
- ignore the question and write an answer to a question that was set last year, or by your teacher: you will fail!

It is perhaps appropriate to finish off this section with a mnemonic which spells out those aspects of integrated literary and linguistic study you need to concentrate on to ensure you are as well prepared as anyone else:

D	evelop your ability to produce interesting, informative and fluent examples of your writing
E	xpand your critical vocabulary so that your answers are informed, logical and represent your own personal voice
P	ractise timed essays including planning, drafting and evaluating
E	xplore different approaches to answering questions until you have mastered the technique and found your preferred model(s)
N	ever go into an examination situation unprepared: it is essential you are familiar with all aspects of each unit, including texts and frameworks
D	o read widely! Read for meaning and always consider the text as a whole.

Literary and Linguistic Toolkit

Accent: A distinctive manner of pronunciation that marks a regional or social identity.

Adjacency pairs: A term relating to the structure of spoken language, indicating a sequence of utterances that form a recognizable structure. Adjacency pairs follow each other, are produced by different speakers, have a logical connection, and conform to a pattern. Questions and answers, commands and responses, greetings and responses form adjacency pairs, e.g. **A:** Hurry up. **B:** I'll be out in a minute. **A:** Are you well? **B:** Very well, thank you.

Adjective: A word that describes a noun – e.g. the *wooden* table; the *red* balloon. They can also indicate degree, e.g. the *tallest* girl was the *slowest*. Adjectives are also sometimes known as **modifiers**.

Adverb: A word that describes the action of a verb – e.g. the cat jumped *swiftly*; the boy ate *hungrily*. Adverbs are also sometimes known as **modifiers**. Adverbs can also act as **intensifiers** – e.g. the man became *very* angry.

Allegory: A story or a narrative, often told at some length, which has a deeper meaning below the surface. *The Pilgrim's Progress* by John Bunyan is a well-known allegory. A more modern example is George Orwell's *Animal Farm*, which on a surface level is about a group of animals who take over their farm, but on a deeper level is an allegory of the Russian Revolution and the shortcomings of Communism.

Alliteration: The repetition of the same consonant sound, especially at the beginning of words. For example, 'Five miles meandering with a mazy motion' (*Kubla Khan* by S.T. Coleridge).

Allusion: A reference to another event, person, place or work of literature. The allusion is usually implied rather than explicit, and often provides another layer of meaning to what is being said.

Ambiguity: Use of language where the meaning is unclear or has two or more possible interpretations. It could be created through a weakness in the writer's expression, but often it is deliberately used by writers to create layers of meaning in the mind of the reader.

Ambivalence: The situation where more than one possible attitude is being displayed by the writer towards a character, theme, or idea, etc.

Anachronism: Something that is historically inaccurate – for example, the reference to a clock chiming in Shakespeare's *Julius Caesar*. The Romans did not have chiming clocks, of course.

Anapaest: A unit of poetic metre made up of two unstressed syllables followed by a stressed syllable – e.g. there are four anapaests in:

˘ ˘ / ˘ ˘ / ˘ ˘ / ˘ ˘ /
The Assyrian came down like the wolf on the fold
(*The Destruction of Sennacherib* by Lord Byron)

Anaphoric: A form of **referencing** in which a pronoun or noun phrase points back to something mentioned earlier – e.g. the party was a great success and *it* was enjoyed by everyone.

Antithesis: Contrasting ideas or words that are balanced against each other, e.g. 'To be, or not to be' (*Hamlet* by William Shakespeare).

Antonyms: Words that are opposite in meaning (*dark/light, fast/slow*).

Archaism: Use of language that is old-fashioned – words or phrases that are not completely obsolete, but no longer in current usage.

Assonance: The repetition of similar vowel sounds. For example, 'There must be Gods thrown down and trumpets blown' (*Hyperion* by John Keats). This shows the paired assonance of *must, trum* and *thrown, blown*.

Attitude: A particular stance or viewpoint adopted by a writer or speaker.

Audience: The people addressed by a piece of writing, speech, etc. This is closely associated with the idea of **purpose**. Language (either written or spoken) is used in various kinds of ways depending on the audience that it is aimed at and the purpose that it is designed to achieve.

Ballad: A narrative poem that tells a story (traditional ballads were songs) usually in a straightforward way. The theme is often tragic or contains a whimsical, supernatural or fantastical element.

Bias: Language used in such a way as to express a prejudice against someone or something, or which favours a particular point of view.

Blank verse: Unrhymed poetry that adheres to a strict pattern in that each line is an iambic pentameter (a ten-syllable line with five stresses). It is close to the natural rhythm of English speech or prose and is used a great deal by many writers, including Shakespeare and Milton.

Caesura: A conscious break in a line of poetry, e.g. 'Fix'd were their habits; they arose betimes,/ Then pray'd their hour, and sang their party rhymes' (Thomas Crabbe).

Caricature: A character described through the exaggeration of the features that he or she possesses.

Cataphoric: See **referencing**.

Catharsis: A purging of emotions such as takes place at the end of a tragedy.

Chaining: The linking together of adjacency pairs to form a conversation.

Clause: A group of words, usually with a finite verb, which is structurally larger than a **phrase**. Clauses are made up of elements, each of which expresses a particular kind of meaning. There are five types of clause element:

- the *subject* – identifies the theme or topic of the clause
- the *verb* – expresses a range of meanings, such as actions, sensations or states of being
- the *object* – identifies who or what has been directly affected by the action of the verb
- the *complement* – gives further information about another clause element
- the *adverbial* – adds information about the situation, such as the time of an action or its frequency.

All five elements appear in the above order in the sentence: *The teacher/had told/me/to listen/three times.*

Cliché: A phrase, idea, or image that has been over-used so that it has lost much of its original meaning, impact and freshness.

Cohesion: Links and connections that unite the elements of discourse or text.

Coinage: The creation and addition of new words to the existing word stock.

Collective noun: See **noun**.

Collocation: Two or more words that frequently appear together as part of a set phrase. They are often well known and predictable, so many could also be described as **idioms** or **clichés**, e.g. *safe and sound, loud and clear, here and there*.

Colloquial: An everyday or non-formal quality in speech or writing, often characterized by the use of slang or non-standard features.

Comedy: Originally, simply a play or other work that ended happily. Now we use the term to describe something that is funny and makes us laugh. In literature, comedy is not necessarily a lightweight form. Shakespeare's *Measure for Measure*, for example, is for the most part a serious and dark play, but as it ends happily it is described as a comedy.

Command: The type of sentence in which someone is told to do something – e.g. *Stand up immediately!*

Common noun: See **noun**.

Complement: A clause element that adds extra information about the subject or object of the clause after the copular verb – e.g. The student was *tired*.

Complex sentence: See **sentence**.

Compound: A word made up of at least two free morphemes – e.g. *babysitter, skateboard, mother-in-law*.

Compound sentence: See **sentence**.

Conceit: An elaborate, extended, and sometimes surprising comparison between things that, at first sight, do not have much in common – e.g. in John Donne's poem *A Valediction: Forbidding Mourning* he compares the souls of himself and his lover with the legs of a draughtsman's compasses.

Conjunction: A word that connects words or other constructions. There are two kinds of conjunctions – co-ordinating and subordinating.

- *Co-ordinating* conjunctions – *and, but* and *or* – are the most common. These can join single words as in fish *and* chips or they can join phrases: Loved by the poor *but* hated by the rich. They can also join sentences by replacing full stops: He agreed to come. He did not speak. He agreed to come *but* he did not speak.

- *Subordinating* conjunctions also join but they use a different process. Co-ordinating conjunctions join two equal parts and they remain equals. Subordinating conjunctions join statements by making one less important than the other. One statement becomes the main statement and the other a subordinate supporting one, as in this example, where *although* becomes the subordinating conjunction: *Although* John was clever, he did not do enough work to pass his exams. Other subordinating conjunctions include *because, unless, whenever, if, that, while, where, as*.

Connotation: The associations attached to a word in addition to its dictionary definition.

Context: The social circumstances in which speech or writing takes place.

Contextual framework: The application of a particular socio/historical standpoint used to analyse a text.

Contraction: A shortened word, e.g. *isn't, don't*

Convergence: A process of linguistic change in which accents or dialects become more alike.

Conversation analysis: A study of the key features of informal spoken interaction.

Couplet: Two consecutive lines of verse that rhyme, e.g. 'Had we but World enough and time,/ This coyness, lady, were no crime.' (Andrew Marvell)

Dactyl: A unit of poetic metre consisting of a stressed syllable followed by two unstressed ones – e.g. there are three dactyls in:

/ ˘ ˘ / ˘ ˘
Half a league, half a league,
/ ˘ ˘ / ˘
Half a league, onward.
(*The Charge of the Light Brigade* by Alfred Lord Tennyson)

Declarative: A grammatical mood that expresses a statement – e.g. *I am a hard-working student.*

Degree: Comparison of adjectives or adverbs. Most adjectives or adverbs can be compared in one of three ways. The thing they express can be related to a higher degree, to the same degree or to a lower degree. For example, John is *tall* (*absolute* form). Kate is *taller* (*comparative* form). David is *tallest* (*superlative* form). Some examples adopt an irregular form such as *good/better/best, bad/worse/worst.*

Deixis: Words that can be interpreted only with reference to the speaker's position in space or time. These are known as *deictic forms* and fall into three main types. *Personal deixis* includes the use of such pronouns as *you* or *I* that identify who is taking part in the discourse. *Spatial deixis* shows the speaker's position in relation to other people or objects, e.g. *this, that, here, there. Temporal deixis* relates the speaker to time using words such as *tomorrow, now, yesterday.*

Demonstrative: A term used to describe determiners or pronouns that distinguish one item from other similar ones – e.g. *this, that, these, those.*

Denotation: The dictionary definition of a word (see **connotation**).

Denouement: The ending of a play, novel or short story where 'all is revealed' and the plot is unravelled.

Determiner: Words that 'determine' the number and definiteness of the noun. There are three kinds of determiners: *central determiners, predeterminers* and *postdeterminers.*

- *Central determiners* consist of the definite article (*the*) and several other words that can take its place – *this, that, each, every, some* and *any.* Words like this are called determiners only when used before the noun. If they are used alone instead of the noun they are being used as a pronoun – e.g. I need *some* paper (determiner). I need *some* (pronoun).
- *Predeterminers* can be used before the central determiners. They can include words such as *all, both, half, double* – e.g. *all* this money.
- *Postdeterminers* follow the central determiners but come before any adjectives. Cardinal numbers (*one, two, three*), ordinals (*first, second, third*), and quantifiers (*much, many, several*) can be used in this way.

Diachronic: A term used to describe language change that occurs over a period of time.

Diacritics: Marks added to text, or phonetic symbols, to specify various sound qualities such as syllabus stress, length, tone, etc. Often used in literature to indicate poetic metre.

Dialect: A language variety marked by a distinctive grammar and vocabulary, used by people with a common regional or social background.

Dialogue: Language interaction between two or more people.

Diction: The choice of words that a writer makes – another term for **vocabulary** or **lexis**, although less used these days.

Didactic: A term describing a work that is intended to preach or teach, often containing a particular moral or political point.

Direct speech: The actual words spoken by a person, recorded in written form using speech marks or quotation marks.

Discourse: Any spoken or written language that is longer than a sentence.

Divergence: A process in which accents or dialects move further apart and the differences between them increase.

Double negative: A part of speech or writing in which more than one negative is used in one verb phrase, frequently used in certain dialects – e.g. *I haven't done nothing*. In Standard English it has the effect of creating an opposite meaning to that intended.

Dynamic verb: A verb that expresses an action rather than a state, and can be used in the progressive form – e.g. *jump/jumping*; *clap/clapping*.

Elegy: A meditative poem, usually sad and reflective in nature. Sometimes, but not always, it is concerned with the theme of death.

Elision: The omission of an unstressed syllable so that the line conforms to a particular metrical pattern – e.g. *o'er* (over) and *e'en* (even).

Ellipsis: The omission of a part of a sentence, which can be understood from the context – e.g. I'd like to go to the concert but I can't (*go to the concert* omitted because the repetition is not necessary).

End-stopped: A verse line with a pause or stop at the end of it.

Enjambment: A line of verse that flows on into the next line without pause.

Etymology: The study of the history and origins of words.

Euphemism: A word that replaces a word or term that is unpleasant, could offend or is a taboo word – e.g. *to pass away* meaning to die.

Exophoric: See **referencing**.

Fabliau: A short comic tale with a bawdy element, akin to the 'dirty story'. Chaucer's *The Miller's Tale* contains strong elements of the fabliau.

Farce: A play that aims to entertain the audience through absurd and ridiculous characters and actions.

Feedback: The reaction speakers receive from their listeners or the information speakers gain from monitoring their own speech.

Field: An area of meaning (for example, education) which is characterized by common lexical items (*teacher*, *classroom*, *headteacher*, *caretaker*, *examination*, etc.)

Figurative language: Language that is symbolic or metaphorical and not meant to be taken literally.

Foot: A group of syllables forming a unit of verse – the basic unit of metre (see Chapter 6, Studying Poetry).

Formality: A scale of language use relating to the formality of the social context within which it is used. Language can be used formally or informally depending on the context.

Formulaic: A term to denote language that is patterned and always appears in the same form – e.g. *Yours faithfully*, *Bye for now*.

Framework: A critical skeleton that could be applied to analyse texts in various ways to suit the purpose of the analysis. A literary framework could be applied, or a linguistic framework, a contextual framework, etc.

Free verse: Verse written without any fixed structure (either in metre, rhythm or form).

Genre: A particular type of writing, e.g. prose, poetry, drama.

Heptameter: A verse line containing seven feet.

Hexameter: A verse line containing six feet.

Homograph: A word with the same spelling but different meanings – e.g. *fair*: The girl had *fair* hair. The children went to the *fair*. The result was not *fair*.

Homonym: A word with the same sound or the same spelling as another but with a different meaning – e.g. *maid* and *made*; *May* (the month) and *may* (is allowed to). Note: *Homograph* can be used for words with the same spelling, *homophone* for words with the same sound, but *homonym* covers both.

Homophone: A word that sounds the same as another but has a different meaning – e.g. *rode*, *road* and *rowed*.

Hyperbole: A deliberate and extravagant exaggeration.

Hyponymy: The relationship between specific and general words where the meaning of one form is included in the meaning of another. For example, *dog* is an hyponym of *animal*. *Yew*, *oak*, *sycamore* are hyponyms of *tree*.

Iamb: The most common metrical foot in English poetry, consisting of an unstressed syllable followed by a stressed syllable.

Idiom: A sequence of words that is a unit of meaning – e.g. *kick the bucket*, *put your foot in it*.

Imagery: The use of words to create a picture or 'image' in the mind of the reader. Images can relate to any of the senses – not just sight, but also hearing, taste, touch and smell. The term is often used to refer to the use of descriptive language, particularly to the use of **metaphors** and **similes**.

Imperative: A grammatical mood expressing a directive (command, warning, request, etc.).

Incompatibility: A linguistic feature that defines one item and thereby excludes others. For example, it would not be possible to say *I am writing in one colour of ink and it is red and blue*. As it has to be either red or blue, one term excludes the other.

Indirect speech: The words of a speaker that are reported rather than being quoted directly – e.g. *David said that he was going out*. **Direct speech** would be *'I am going out,' said David*. (See Chapter 3, Analysing Prose.)

Infinitive: A non-finite verb in the base form – e.g. they might *see*. Often the verb is preceded by the preposition *to* – e.g. *to see*. A split infinitive, which is often considered grammatically incorrect, is where another word is placed between the preposition and the base form of the verb. Perhaps the most famous example is Star Trek's *To boldly go...*

Insertion sequence: A feature occurring in spoken discourse where the original conversation is suspended because of an interruption caused by a speech sequence from another source. When the interruption has been dealt with, the original speech sequence resumes.

Intensifier: A word or phrase that adds emphasis – e.g. *very*, *unbelievably*, *awfully*, *terribly*.

Internal rhyme: Rhyming words within a line rather than at the ends of lines.

Interrogative: A grammatical mood expressing a question.

Inter-textual: Having clear links with other texts through the themes, ideas or issues explored.

Intonation: The tone of voice in speech.

Inversion: Reversing the order of clause elements, so that subject and verb appear in the reverse of their normal order – e.g. *Here is the milkman*, instead of *The milkman is here.*

Irony: At its simplest level, irony means saying one thing while meaning another. It occurs where a word or phrase has one surface meaning but another, contradictory and possibly opposite meaning is implied. Irony is frequently confused with sarcasm. Sarcasm is spoken, often relying on tone of voice, and is much more blunt than irony.

Lament: A poem expressing intense grief.

Language acquisition: The process of learning a first language as a child.

Language change: The process of change in a language over a period of time.

Language of speech: Spoken language of any kind.

Lexis: The vocabulary of a language or particular use of language.

Loan word: A word borrowed from another language.

Lyric: Originally a lyric was a song performed to the accompaniment of a lyre (a stringed harp-like instrument) but now it can mean a song-like poem or a short poem expressing personal feeling.

Main clause: A clause that is not dependent and makes sense on its own. See **clause**.

Malapropism: A mixing up of words that sound similar. Made famous by Mrs Malaprop, a character in Sheridan's *The Rivals*, who said 'He is the very *pineapple* of politeness' (for *pinnacle*) and 'She is as headstrong as an *allegory* on the banks of the Nile' (for *alligator*).

Manner: An adverbial answering the question 'How?', e.g. *slowly*.

Metalanguage: The language used to talk about language.

Metaphor: A comparison of one thing to another in order to make description more vivid. Unlike a **simile**, a metaphor states that one thing *is* the other. For example, a simile could be *The wind went through me like a knife*, whereas the metaphor might state *The wind cut through me*. (See **simile** and **personification**).

Metonymy: A feature where an attribute of the thing being described stands for the whole thing. For example, the term *crown* could be used to mean the king or the queen; *the turf* could stand for horse racing; and *Fleet Street* could mean the Press.

Metre: The regular use of stressed and unstressed syllables in poetry (see Chapter 6, Studying Poetry).

Modal: An auxiliary verb which cannot be used as a main verb – e.g. *can, may, will, shall, must, could, might, would, should.*

Mode: A particular medium of communication – e.g. speech, writing, etc.

Modification: The use of one linguistic item to specify the nature of another. Adjectives act as modifiers – e.g. the *blue* sky – as do adverbs: He ducked *quickly* to avoid being seen.

Modifier: A word that specifies the nature of another word or tells us more about it. **Adverbs** and **adjectives** act as modifiers.

Monologue: Speech or writing produced, and often performed, by one person.

Monometer: A line of verse containing only one foot.

Monosyllabic: Having only one syllable.

Mood: Main clauses can have one of three moods: the *declarative* mood is used to make statements; the *imperative* mood is used to issue orders, commands or make requests; and the *interrogative* mood is used to ask questions.

Narrative: A piece of writing or speech that tells a story.

Neologism: Sometimes called a nonce-word or **coinage** – a new or invented word or expression. Usually they are made up of adaptations of existing words, although the term nonce-word was originally applied to words that had a 'one-off' use such as the combination of *fair* and *joyous* to give *frabjous*, used by Lewis Carroll. Examples of more modern neologisms are *zeroized*, *shopaholic*, *computerate*. Of course, when a word has been in use for a while it ceases to be new and is no longer considered a neologism.

Non-standard English: Any variety of language use that does not conform to the standard, prestige form of English accepted as the norm by society. See **Standard English** and **received pronunciation**.

Noun: A word class with a naming function, which can be used as a subject or an object in a clause. They can be grouped in several ways. Here are the main kinds.

- *Proper nouns*: the names of specific people, places, times, occasions, events, publications and so on – e.g. *London, Lulu, The English Magazine, July, Christmas Day*. They are usually written with an initial capital letter.
- *Common nouns*: general objects or ideas – e.g. *table, window, book, pen*.
- *Abstract nouns*: qualities or states that exist only in our minds – e.g. *cleverness, courage, justice, loyalty, mercy*.
- *Collective nouns*: groups of people, or collections of things as a whole – e.g. *crowd, flock, regiment, convoy, forest, crew*.

Octave: The first eight lines of a sonnet.

Octometer: A verse line consisting of eight feet.

Ode: A verse form similar to a lyric but often more lengthy and containing more serious and elevated thoughts.

Onomatopoeia: The use of words whose sounds copy the sounds of the thing or process they describe. On a simple level, words like *bang, hiss* and *splash* are onomatopoeic, but it also has more subtle uses.

Oxymoron: A figure of speech that joins together words of opposite meanings – e.g. *the living dead, bitter sweet*.

Paradox: A statement that appears contradictory, but when considered more closely is seen to contain a good deal of truth.

Parallelism: The patterning of pairs of sounds, words or structures to create a sense of balance in spoken or written discourse – e.g. 'I am the way, the life and the truth.'

Parody: A work that is written in imitation of another work, very often with the intention of making fun of the original.

Participle: The non-finite form of verbs that can occur after an auxiliary verb – e.g. was *running* (present participle); had *run* (past participle). Can also occur before a head noun – e.g. the *running* man, or the *completed* task.

Particle: A grammatical function word that never changes its form – e.g. *up, down, in, after*.

Pastoral: Generally, literature concerning rural life with idealized settings and rustic characters. Often pastorals are concerned with the lives of shepherds and shepherdesses, presented in idyllic and unrealistic ways.

Pathos: The effect in literature that makes the reader feel sadness or pity.

Patterning: Language used in such a way as to create discernible patterns, perhaps through **imagery**, or a repeated symbol or motif, or use of **parallelism**, etc.

Pentameter: A line of verse containing five feet.

Periphrasis: A round-about or long-winded way of saying something.

Personification: The attribution of human feelings, emotions, sensations or physical attributes to an inanimate object. Personification is a kind of **metaphor**, where human qualities are given to things or abstract ideas.

Phatic: A term describing language used to make social contact, which is intended more to convey general sociability than to communicate meaning – e.g. *Nice morning, isn't it?*

Phonetic alphabet: Symbols and **diacritics** designed to represent exactly the sound of spoken language.

Phonetic transcription: A detailed transcription, using phonetic symbols, concentrating on the details of pronunciation.

Phonetics: The study of spoken sounds and the way in which they are produced.

Phrase: A group of words smaller than a **clause** which forms a grammatical unit, but does not contain a finite verb and therefore does not make complete sense on its own.

Pitch: The auditory level of sound.

Pleonasm: The unnecessary use of words – e.g. *here and now, this present day and age*. Also called **tautology**.

Plot: The sequence of events in a poem, play, novel or short story that makes up the main story line.

Polysyllabic: Having more than one syllable.

Preposition: A word expressing a relationship of meaning between two parts of a sentence, most often showing how the two parts are related in space or time – e.g. We had a meal *in* a restaurant. I'll take you *to* the cinema.

Pronoun: A word that stands for a noun – e.g. Kate went to the cinema and *she* bought an ice cream. My car is red but my friend has a maroon *one*. Pronouns include *he, she, they, we, her, him, all, both, each*.

Prose: Any kind of writing that is not verse – usually divided into fiction and non-fiction.

Protagonist: The main character or speaker in a poem, monologue, play or story.

Pun: A play on words that have similar sounds but quite different meanings. For example, in Shakespeare's *Romeo and Juliet*, after he has been mortally wounded by Tybalt and is dying, Mercutio says 'Ask for me tomorrow, and you will find me a grave man.'

Purpose: The reason why a piece of writing has been written or a speech made – e.g. to entertain, to explain, to persuade, to argue.

Quatrain: A stanza of four lines, which can have various rhyme schemes.

Received pronunciation: Sometimes know as RP, the prestige British accent that has a high social status and is not related to a specific region or influenced by regional variation.

Recursive: Said of a grammatical rule that is capable of repeated application.

Referencing: References point to something else in the discourse. Pronouns are often used to make these references, although comparative structures that express certain similarities or differences can also be used. In this sentence a pronoun is used: The student worked hard, so *she* had little spare time. In this sentence a comparative structure is used: The second team was good but *the first one* was better.

There are three main kinds of reference:

- *Anaphoric* references point *backwards* in a text. The reader or listener must refer to a previous reference to make sense of the pronoun or comparative structure. Both examples given above are of this kind of reference.

- *Cataphoric* references point *forwards* in a text. In other words the reader or listener must refer to a future reference in order to understand the structure used, e.g. *Those* were *the days* my friend.

- *Exophoric* references point *beyond* the text. The reader or the listener has to make a connection with something outside the text, e.g. The fish was *this* big. Some kind of context or sign is needed here so that the statement makes sense.

Refrain: Repetition throughout a poem of a phrase, line or series of lines as in the 'chorus' of a song.

Repetition: A device that emphasizes an idea through repetition.

Representational features: Language use where one thing is used to represent another, as in **symbolic language** or the use of **imagery**.

Rhetoric: Originally, the art of speaking and writing in such a way as to persuade an audience to a particular point of view. Now it is often used to imply grand words that have no substance in them. There are a variety of rhetorical devices such as the rhetorical question – a question that does not require an answer, as the answer is obvious or implied in the question itself.

Rhyme: Corresponding sounds in words, usually at the end of each line of verse, but not always.

Rhyme scheme: The pattern of the rhymes in a poem.

Rhythm: The 'movement' of a poem as created through the metre and the way that language is stressed within the poem.

Satire: The highlighting or exposing of human failings or foolishness within a society, by ridiculing them. Satire can range from gentle and light to extremely biting and bitter in tone, e.g. Swift's *Gulliver's Travels* or *A Modest Proposal*, or George Orwell's *Animal Farm*.

Scansion: The analysis of metrical patterns in poetry.

Semantic features: Features that provide speech or writing with a linguistic meaning.

Semantic field: Areas of meaning identified by a set of mutually defining words. For example, *red, blue, green, yellow* are all words identified with colour. *Regiment, soldier, battalion, barracks, parade* are identified as describing military things.

Semantics: The study of the meaning of language.

Sentence: A grammatical structure made up of one or more clauses. Usually in written language it begins with a capital letter and ends with a full stop or a feature that performs the function of a full stop, such as a question mark. In analysing spoken language, **utterances** are often referred to rather than sentences.

In terms of purpose, there are four kinds of sentences.

- Command – *Get up, now!*
- Question – *How are you?*
- Statement – *I am going out tonight.*
- Exclamation – *Stop that immediately!*

There are also three kinds of sentences in terms of their structure.

- *Simple sentence* – all the above examples are of simple sentences. A simple sentence has just one finite verb (a finite verb is a verb that has a subject).

- *Compound sentence* – consists of two or more simple sentences joined together by a co-ordinating conjunction – e.g. *I hope to pass my exams and then go on to university.*

- *Complex sentence* – has one main clause and any number of subordinate clauses joined to it by subordinating conjunctions – e.g. *The strikers will continue to hold their demonstrations because their concerns have not been addressed.*

Septet: A seven-line stanza.

Sequencing: The rules governing the succession of utterances in discourse.

Sestet: The last six lines of a sonnet.

Side-sequence: In spoken discourse, an explanation of something that has already been uttered.

Simile: A comparison of one thing with another in order to make description more vivid. Similes use the words *like* or *as* to make the comparison.

Slang: Distinctive words and phrases associated with informal speech. Very often it is used within certain social groups or age groups.

Soliloquy: A speech in which a dramatic character, alone on stage, expresses his or her thoughts and feelings aloud for the benefit of the audience, often in a revealing way.

Sonnet: A 14-line poem, usually with ten syllables in each line. There are several ways in which the lines can be organized, but they often consist of an **octave** and a **sestet**.

Spondee: A unit of poetic metre containing two stressed syllables.

Standard English: The form of English considered to be and accepted as the norm in society, and used as the medium of government, education, law, etc. Language that differs from this standard is known as **non-standard**.

Stanza: The blocks of lines into which a poem is divided. Sometimes these are referred to less precisely as verses, which can lead to confusion as poetry is sometimes called 'verse' too.

Stream of consciousness: A technique in which the writer puts down thoughts and emotions in a 'stream' as they come to mind, without imposing order or structure.

Structure: The way that a poem, play or other piece of writing has been put together. This can include the metre pattern, stanza arrangement, the ways the ideas are developed, etc.

Style: The individual way in which a writer has used language to express his or her ideas.

Stylistics: The study of lexical and structural variations in language according to use, audience and purpose.

Sub-plot: A secondary story line in a novel or play. Often, as in some plays by Shakespeare, the sub-plot can provide some comic relief from the main action, but sub-plots can also relate to the main plot in quite complex ways.

Sub-text: Ideas, themes, or issues that are not dealt with overtly by a text but exist below the surface meaning.

Syllable: A word or part of a word that can be uttered in a single effort of the voice. Patterns of stressed and unstressed syllables make up the rhythm pattern of the language.

Symbolic language: The use of words or phrases to represent something else.

Synecdoche: A device in which a part is used to represent the whole – e.g. There were several new *faces* at the meeting.

Synonyms: Different words with the same or nearly the same meanings – e.g. *shut* and *close* or *ship* and *vessel*.

Syntax: The study of the structure of sentences.

Tag question: An interrogative structure added to the end of a sentence which requires a reply – e.g. *Terrible weather, isn't it?*

Tautology: Saying the same thing twice over in different words – e.g. *The visitors arrived one after the other in succession.*

Tetrameter: A verse line of four feet.

Text: A piece of spoken or written language with a definable communicative function.

Theme: The central idea or ideas that a writer explores through his or her text.

Tone: The tone of a text is created through the combined effects of a number of features, such as **diction**, **syntax**, **rhythm**, etc. The tone can be a major factor in establishing the overall impression of a piece of writing.

Topicality: The topic of a spoken encounter is directly related to its **manner** and its participants. The topic can determine the level of **formality**, and topic shifts can occur when speakers move from one topic to another. These mark key points in the discourse.

Transcription: A written record of spoken language, which may use symbols to represent the distinctive features of speech.

Trimeter: A unit of poetic metre containing three feet.

Trochee: A unit of poetic metre containing a stressed followed by an unstressed syllable.

Turn-taking: Organization of speakers' contributions in a conversation. Turns may be fairly equal, or one of the participants may dominate.

Utterance: A piece of spoken language. Also used to describe a spoken 'sentence', since it can be difficult to apply the normal rules of a written sentence to speech.

Verb: A word that expresses actions, states of being or processes. There are three types of verb that can occur within a verb phrase.

- *Full* (or *lexical*) verbs have a clearly stateable meaning. These act as main verbs, such as *run, jump, go, look*.
- *Modal auxiliary verbs* express a range of judgements about the likelihood of events. These function only as auxiliary verbs – *will, shall, may, might, can*.
- *Primary* verbs can function either as main verbs or auxiliary verbs. There are three of them: *be, have* and *do*.

Vernacular: The native language a community uses for speech.

Vocabulary: The words of a language – the same as **lexis**.

Zeugma: A device that joins together two apparently incongruous things by applying a verb or adjective to both of them which really applies to only one of them – e.g. 'Kill the boys and the luggage' (Shakespeare's *Henry V*).

Index

Headings in *italics* refer to prose, drama and poetry titles. Page numbers in **bold** type refer to definitions; those in *italics* to extracts or direct quotations.

abbreviations 119
　in conversation 115
About the Ouse (Swift) *193–5*
Achebe, Chinua, *Things Fall Apart 29*
adjacency pairs 111–13
Advent (Rossetti) *150*, 151
advertisements *9*, 10, *11*
alliteration 127, 173
Anaesthetist, The (Armitage) *169*
analytical comparisons 183–4, 197–215, 232–3
analytical frameworks **1**, 2, 183–4, 197–201, 219
analytical questions, set texts 237
anapaestic stress 160
anaphoric references 204–5
anchor text method 200
Anderson-Dargatz, Gail, *The Cure for Death by Lightning 5*
antithesis
　in drama 84
　in poetry 175–6
anyone lived in a pretty how town (Cummings) *166*
apostrophe 170
Armitage, Simon
　Anaesthetist, The 169
　I Say I Say I Say 150
　On an Owd Piktcha 161
As You like It (Shakespeare) 58
assonance 127, 174
asyndetic listing 126
At a Potato Digging (Heaney) *156–8*
atmosphere, creating 50–1
audience 2, 3, 7, 8, **9**, **217**

ballad 154
Banks, Iain, *The Business 132–3*
Beckett, Samuel 59
Beloved (Morrison) *41*

bibliographies 243
Blake, William, *A Poison Tree 5*
Bleak House (Dickens) *41*
Briscoe, Joanna, *Skin 98*
Brontë, Charlotte, *Jane Eyre 31–3*
Brontë, Emily, *Wuthering Heights 15–16*, *39–40*
Brookmayne, Christopher, *Quite Ugly One Morning 208–9*
Brown, Gordon, speeches *121–2*, 122–7
Bryson, Bill, *Notes from a Small Island 48–9*
Business, The (Banks) *132–3*
Byron, Lord, *So We'll Go No More A-Roving 163*, 164

caesura 156–8
Canterbury Tales (Chaucer)
　General Prologue 176–7
　Wife of Bath 189–92
Captain Corelli's Mandolin (de Bernieres) *8*
Caretaker, The (Pinter) *134–5*
cataphoric references 204–5
chaining 113
characters, creation of 49–50, 176–7
Chaucer, Geoffrey, *Canterbury Tales*
　General Prologue 176–7
　Wife of Bath 189–92
Clockwork (Pullman) *8*
closing sequences, conversation 115
cognitive development 107
cohesion 47–50
collocations 47
Color Purple, The (Walker) *52*
Combe, The (E. Thomas) *178*
comic strips, speech representation in 137–9
commentaries 233
commissive utterances 104
comparative analysis
　devising questions 182
　frameworks for 183–4, 197–201
conflicts, in drama 58
connotation, lexical choice 161

consonance 127
constative utterances 103
context 2, 3, 7, 9, **10**
    speech 102, **102**
contextual variation, drama 87–91
contractions 119
    in conversation 115
conversation *see also* speech
    adjacency pairs 111–13
    closing sequences 115
    constative utterances 103
    contractions 115
    directives 103
    elisions 115
    ellipsis 115–16
    expressive utterances 103
    false starts 117
    hedging 118
    insertions 114
    interactional nature of 103
    juncture 116
    liaison 116
    non-standard language 116,
        133–4, 206–7
    non-verbal aspects 117–18
    overlaps 117
    pauses 117
    phatic utterances 103
    side sequences 114–15
    slang 116–17
    spontaneous 109–13
    turn-taking 113–14
Cope, Wendy, *Strugnell in Liverpool*
    179–80
couplet 173
coursework
    bibliographies 243
    preparing 182–3
    tasks 241
    titles for 242
    use of sources 242–3
cultural transmission 107
Cummings, E.E. 164–8
    anyone lived in a pretty how town
        166
Cure for Death by Lightning, The
    (Anderson-Dargatz) *5*

dactylic stress 160
Darkling Thrush, The (Hardy) *173*
de Bernieres, Louis, *Captain Corelli's*
    Mandolin 8
Death of a Generation (Horne) *220–1*

deixis 119, 204
denotation 161
dialogue
    in drama 61–4
    in prose 39
Dickens, Charles
    Bleak House 41
    Great Expectations 37–8, 49–50,
        55–6, 132
    Hard Times 46–7, 51
diction *see* lexical choices; lexis
dictionaries 107
direct speech 39
    free 40–2
directives 103
Discord in Childhood (Lawrence) *178*
distal terms 204
Do not go gentle into that good night
    (D. Thomas) *162–3*
drama
    antithesis 84
    asides 71–2
    character presentation 64–9
    conflict in 58
    contextual variation 87–91
    dialogue in 61–4
    hyperbole 85
    irony 86–7
    listing 84
    metaphorical techniques in 79–81
    nature of 57–8
    opening scenes 74–7
    performances 57
    plot 59–60
    puns 85
    realism in 58–9
    repetition 83–4
    rhetorical techniques in 83–5
    soliloquies 69–71
    speech representation in 134–6
    stage directions 135
    structure 60
    and theatre 59
    themes 77–9
dramatic irony 86–7
Drayton, Michael, *An Evil Spirit 153*
Duffy, Carol Ann
    Havisham 188–9
    Welltread 188

e-mails 140
Eden Close (Shreve) *130*, 131
education 107

egocentric speech 105
elisions 115
ellipsis, in conversation 115–16, 205–6
emoticons 140
emphatic stress 158
end stop 156
enjambment 156
entertainment, speech in 104–5
ethical propositions 104
Evil Spirit, An (Drayton) *153*
examination-style questions
    Unit 1 23–4, 53–5, 91
    Unit 2 55–6, 92–3
    Unit 3 207–12, 234–6
examinations
    set texts 237–8
    strategies for 246–7
    unseen texts 239–40
exclamations, in speeches 123
exophoric references 204–5
experimental language *see* non-standard
    language
expressive utterances 103
eye/sight rhymes 172

false starts, in speech 117
feedback, spoken **112**
field **35**
    semantic 47
figurative language 46–7
figures of speech 168
First Sight (Larkin) *153, 185,* 186–7
first-person narration 26–7
Football at Slack (Hughes) *210*
form 10–11, **11**
frameworks **1**, 2
    comparative analysis 183–4, 197–201
    language production 12–13
    non-fiction textual adaptation 219
    speech comparison 142–3
free direct speech 40–2
free indirect speech 42–3
free verse 155–6
Friel, Brian, *Translations* 78–9
Futility (Owen) *170*

Gardam, Jane
    Iron Coast, The 201–2
    Stone Trees 43–4
Gervais, Ricky and Stephen Merchant,
    The Office 135–6
Goldsmith, Oliver, *The Village*
    Schoolmaster 177

grammar
    features of 44
    issues in 205–6
    non-standard uses of 164–8
    parts of speech 164
    in poetry 163–8
graphology 100
Great Expectations (Dickens) *37–8,*
    49–50, 55–6, 132

half/slant/para-rhymes 172
Hamlet (Shakespeare) 59, *74–5,* 77, *85,*
    86–7
    review of *17–18*
Hard Times (Dickens) *46–7,* 51
Hardy, Thomas, *The Darkling*
    Thrush 173
Hare, David, *Murmuring Judges* 58, *71,*
    76, 77
Havisham (Duffy) *188–9*
Heaney, Seamus, *At a Potato*
    Digging 156–8
Heart of It, The (Hines) *133–4*
hedging, in conversation 118
Hey There Now! (Nichols) *149*
high-frequency lexical choices 204
Hill, Susan, *In the Conservatory* 42
Hines, Barry, *The Heart of It 133–4*
Hopkins, Gerard Manley,
    Inversnaid 175–6
Horne, Alistair, *Death of a*
    Generation 220–1
Hosseini, Khaled, *The Kite Runner 28–9*
Hughes, Ted, *Football at Slack 210*
hyperbole, drama 85

I Say I Say I Say (Armitage) *150*
iambic pentameter 159, 173
imaginative narrative writing 14–16
Importance of Being Earnest,
    The (Wilde) *23–4*
In the Conservatory (Hill) *42*
indirect speech 39–40
    free 42–3
information-based writing 19–22
insertions, conversation 114
instructional writing 21–3
integrated method, analytical
    framework 200–1
internal rhymes 172
interviews, media 129–30, 136–7, *209*
Into the Heart of Borneo (O'Hanlon)
    234–6

intonation 127
Inversnaid (Hopkins) *175–6*
Iron Coast, The (Gardam) *201–2*
irony
   dramatic 86–7
   verbal 87
Irving, John, *Prayer for Owen Meany,
   A 134*

Jane Eyre (C. Brontë) *31–3*
juncture, in conversation 116
Junger, Sebastian, *The Perfect Storm 4*
Junod, Marcel, *Visiting Hiroshima 224–5*

Keats, John
   To Autumn 170–1
   When I Have Fears 159, *160*
Kennedy, John F., speeches *128–9*
kennings 168–9
kinesics 100
kitchen sink dramas 59
Kite Runner, The (Hosseini) *28–9*

language production 7–24
   framework for 12–13
   purposes for 13
language production questions,
   set texts 238
Larkin, Philip, *First Sight 153*, *185*,
   186–7
Lawrence, D.H.
   Discord in Childhood 178
   *To Women, As Far As I'm Concerned
   155–6*
legal documentation 107, 119
letter writing
   formal 18–19
   informal 19
lexical choice 160–3, 203–5
   connotation 161
   deixis 119, 204
   denotation 161
   high-frequency 204
   low-frequency 204
   and modifiers 207
   neologisms 161
lexis (lexicon, diction) 35–6
liaisons, in conversation 116
listing
   asyndetic 126
   in drama 84
   in speeches 126
   syndetic 126

Look Back in Anger (Osborne) 58
low-frequency lexical choices 204

magazines, interviews in 136–7
manner **35**
Martin, Valerie, *Property 20–1*
Measure for Measure (Shakespeare) *83–4*
media
   interviews 129–30
   scripts 135–6
   speech in 104–5
*Merchant of Venice,
   The* (Shakespeare) *84*
metaphorical devices
   apostrophes 170
   in drama 79–81
   figures of speech 168
   kennings 168–9
   literal images 169
   metonymy 170
   personification 170
   representational language 168
   similes 46, 169
   symbolism 46, 170
   synecdoche 170
metaphors 46
   in poetry 169
   in speeches 126–7
metonymy 170
metre, poetic 159–60
modes **35**, **97**
   comparison of 201–7
modifiers **36**
   and lexical choices 207
monologue 39
moods
   creating 50–1
   poetic 149, 178
Morning Song (Plath) *185*, 186–7
Morrison, Toni, *Beloved 41*
Murmuring Judges (Hare) 58, *71*, *76*, 77

narration
   first-person 26–7
   restricted/unrestricted 27
   stream of consciousness 28
   third-person 27
narrative voice 29
narrative writing, imaginative 14–16
narrators, omniscient 27
neologisms 161
Nichols, Grace, *Hey There Now! 149*

non-fiction
    analytical comparisons 232–3
    analytical frameworks 231–3
    audiences 217–18
    re-casting 217–23, 228–9
    source materials 223–8
    speech representation in 136–7
non-standard language
    in conversation 116, 133–4, 206–7
    neologisms 161
    in poetry 164–8, 179–80
    purposes 51–2
non-verbal aspects of conversation
    false starts 117
    overlaps 117
    pauses 117
    stuttering 117
    sympathetic circularity 118
Notes from a Small Island (Bryson) *48–9*
nouns, types of **36**

octave 173
Ode to Duty (Wordsworth) *154–5*
ode 154–5
Office, The (Gervais & Merchant) *135–6*
Oh what a lonely war! (Quinn) *221–2*
O'Hanlon, Redmond, *Into the Heart of Borneo 234–6*
On an Owd Piktcha (Armitage) *161*
on-line messaging 141–2
onomatopoeia 174
opinions, in speeches 123
Osborne, John, *Look Back in Anger* 58
Othello (Shakespeare) 58, *62*, 64, 65–7, *70–3*, 73–4, 79, *80–1*, 81–2, 84
overlaps, in conversation 117
Owen, Wilfred, *Futility 170*

paralinguistic features 99
    kinesics 100
parallelism 174–5
Parker, Dorothy, *Resume 175*
patterning, in speeches 125
pauses, in conversation 117
pedagogic talk 103–4
Perfect Storm, The (Junger) *4*
performances, drama 57
performative utterances 104
personal guarantees, in speeches 123–4
personification 170
persuasive/argumentative writing 16–18
phatic utterances 103
phonemic transcription 101

phonetic transcription 101
phonological features 172
phonological techniques
    alliteration 127, 173
    assonance 127, 174
    consonance 127
    intonation 127
    onomatopoeia 174
    rhyme 127, 172–3
    stress 127
    volume and speed of delivery 128
Pinter, Harold, *The Caretaker 134–5*
planned speech 121–2
Plath, Sylvia, *Morning Song 185*, 186–7
plays *see* drama
plot 59–60
poetic devices
    caesura 156–8
    end stop 156
    enjambment 156
poetry
    ballad 154
    characterization in 176–7
    features of 147–8
    form and structure of 152–3
    formality levels in 148
    free verse 155–6
    grammar in 163–8
    lexical choice 160–3
    metaphorical devices 168–71
    metre 159–60
    moods in 149, 178
    nature of 147
    non-standard language in 164–8, 179–80
    ode 154–5
    purposes of 148
    rhetorical techniques 171–6
    rhyme 172–3
    rhythm 158–9
    scene setting 178
    sonnet 152–3
    stanzas 152
    stichic 152
    strophic 152
    structural features of 174–6
    tone 148–9
point of view, prose fiction 26–8
Poison Tree, A (Blake) *5*
Prayer for Owen Meany, A (Irving) *134*
pronouns, uses of 48
Property (Martin) *20–1*

prose forms 107
prose fiction
    features of 26, 53
    nature of 25–6
    point of view in 26–8
    speech representation in 130–4
prosody 206
proximal terms 204
Pullman, Philip, *Clockwork 8*
punctuation, and rhythm 159
puns, in drama 85
purpose 2, 3, 7, 8, **9**, 148

quatrain 173
questions, devising for coursework 182
Quinn, Anthony, *Oh what a lonely war!*
    221–2
Quite Ugly One Morning (Brookmayne)
    208–9

radio commentaries, sport *9*, 10, 211–15
reading, recommended background
    245–6
realism, in drama 58–9
re-casting non-fiction 218–23, 228–9
references
    anaphoric 204–5
    cataphoric 205
    exophoric 205
    written 107
referential utterances 104
register 35
repetition
    in drama 83–4
    in conversation 117
    in poetry 174–5
    in speeches 125–6
representation of speech 130–42
representational language 168
Resolution and Independence
    (Wordsworth) *192–3*
Resume (Parker) *175*
review writing 17–18
revision, for set texts 237–8
rhetoric, in speech 105, 121–4, **121**
rhetorical questions, in speeches 126
rhetorical techniques 47
    in drama 83–5
    in poetry 171–6
rhyme 127, 172–3
    eye/sight 172
    half/slant/para- 172

internal 172
    patterns 173
    schemes 172
Rhys, Jean, *Wide Sargasso Sea 30–1*
rhythm 158–60
    emphatic stress 158
    punctuation 159
    syllable stress 158
Rivals, The (Sheridan) 57, *61–2*, 63–4,
    88–90
Rossetti, Christina, *Advent 150*, 151

scenes
    describing 50
    setting 178
secondary source materials 242–3
semantic field 47
sentences
    functions of 45–6
    structure 44–5
    types of 45
sestet 173
set texts
    analytical questions 237
    language production questions 238
    revision for 237–8
Shakespeare, William
    As You like It 58
    Hamlet 59, *74–5*, 77, 85, *86–7*
    Measure for Measure 83–4
    Merchant of Venice, The 84
    Othello 58, *62*, 64, *65–7*, *70–3*, *73–4*,
    79, *80–1*, 81–2, 84
    Tempest, The 6, 59
Sheridan, Richard, *The Rivals* 57, *61–2*,
    63–4, *88–90*
Shreve, Anita, *Eden Close 130*, 131
side sequences, conversation 114–15
similes 46, 169
Skin (Briscoe) *98*
slang 116–17
SMS (text messages) 140
So We'll Go No More A-Roving (Byron)
    163, 164
soliloquies 69–71
sonnet 152–3
source materials for re-casting
    evaluating 225–7
    reading through 223–4
    types of 227
    using 227–8
speech *see also* conversation; speech

representation; speeches
adjacency pairs 111–13
commissive utterances 104
context 102, **102**
dialogue 39
direct 39
egocentric 105
in entertainment 104–5
ethical propositions 104
feedback **112**
free direct 40–2
free indirect 42–3
functions of 108
indirect 39–40
mode **97**, 201–7
monologue 39
paralinguistic features 99–100
pedagogic talk 103–4
performative utterances 104
phonological techniques 127–8
planned 121–2
prosody 206
referential utterances 104
representation of 130–42
rhetoric 105, 121–4, **121**
spontaneous 109–13
topic shifts 110–11
transcriptions 101–2, **101**
and writing 97–101, 108, 119–20
speech comparison, framework for
    142–3
speech representation
comic strips 137–9
in drama 134–6
electronic media 140–2
in non-fiction 136–7
in prose fiction 130–4
speeches
exclamations in 123
lists in 126
metaphors in 126–7
opinions in 123
patterning in 125
personal guarantees in 123–4
repetition in 125–6
rhetorical questions in 126
speeches (Brown) *121–2, 122–7*
speeches (Kennedy) *128–9*
spondaic stress 160
spontaneous speech 109–13
sport, radio commentaries *9*, 10, 211–15
stage directions 135

stanzas 152
stichic poetry 152
Stone Trees (Gardam) *43–4*
stream of consciousness 28, 43
Streetcar Named Desire, A (Williams)
    62–3, 64
stress 127
strophic poetry 152
Strugnell in Liverpool (Cope) *179–80*
style 11, **11**
Swift, Graham, *About the Ouse 193–5*
syllable stress, rhythm 158
symbolism 46, 170
sympathetic circularity 118
synecdoche 170
syndetic listing 126
syntax 44–6

Tempest, The (Shakespeare) *6*, 59
text messages (SMS) 140
    emoticons 140
texts **1**
textual adaptation, non-fiction 218–23,
    228–9
    framework 219
textual analysis, methods 1–4
theatres 59
themes, drama 77–9
third-person narration 27
Thomas, Dylan, *Do not go gentle into
    that good night 162–3*
Thomas, Edward, *The Combe 178*
thoughts
    presentation of 43–4
    stream of consciousness 43
Tintern Abbey (Wordsworth) *192*
Titanic disaster, accounts of 229–31
To Autumn (Keats) *170–1*
To Women, As Far As I'm Concerned
    (Lawrence) *155–6*
tone, poetry 148–9
topic shifts, speech 110–11
topic **10**
transcriptions
    phonemic 101
    phonetic 101
    speech 101–2, **101**
Translations (Friel) *78–9*
trochaic stress 159
turn-taking, conversation 113–14

unseen texts 239–40

Upon Westminster Bridge (Wordsworth)
201
utterances 103–4, 109

verbal ironies 87
verbs, types of **36**
Village Schoolmaster, The (Goldsmith)
177
Visiting Hiroshima (Junod) *224–5*
voice-filled pauses 117
volume and speed of delivery, speech
128

Walker, Alice, *The Color Purple 52*
Welltread (Duffy) *188*
When I Have Fears (Keats) 159, *160*
Wide Sargasso Sea (Rhys) *30–1*
Wilde, Oscar, *The Importance of Being
Earnest 23–4*
Williams, Tennessee, *A Streetcar Named
Desire 62–3*, 64
Wordsworth, William

Ode to Duty 154–5
Resolution and Independence 192–3
Tintern Abbey 192
Upon Westminster Bridge 201
World is too much with us, The 152–3
World is too much with us, The
(Wordsworth) *152–3*
writing
cohesion in 47–50
figurative language 46–7
functions of 106–8
graphology 100
information-based 19–22
instructional 21–3
letters 18–19
mode **97**, 201–7
narrative 14–16
persuasive/argumentative 16–18
and speech 97–101, 108, 119–20
Wuthering Heights (E. Brontë) *15–16,
39–40*